PRINT AND BROADCAST MEDIA

PRINT AND BROADCAST MEDIA

Rajiv Saxena

CENTRUM PRESS
NEW DELHI-110002 (INDIA)

CENTRUM PRESS
H.O.: 4360/4, Ansari Road, Daryaganj,
New Delhi-110002 (India)
Tel: 23278000, 23261597, 23255577, 23286875
B.O.: No. 1015, Ist Main Road, BSK IIIrd Stage,
IIIrd Phase, IIIrd Block, Bangalore-560085 (INDIA)
Tel: 080-41723429
Email: centrumpress@gmail.com
Visit us at: www.centrumpress.com

Print and Broadcast Media

First Edition, 2010

ISBN 978-93-80540-57-3

PRINTED IN INDIA

Printed at Mehra Offset Press, Delhi

Contents

Preface

Print and Broadcast Media encompasses details with respect to contemporary elements and trends as far as modern day's mass development planning and management are concerned. This book provides and Introductory overview of interrelationship. Besides this an elaborate social Systems perspective on print media development is provided while discussing the whole process of development of print media and broadcast journalism.

The Indian media in particular is discussed in detail. How the phenomenal spread and evolution of computer software and hardware is impacting upon the Indian media is upon briefly. Also the connection between multi lingualism and mass media of mass communication such as press radio television have their respective roles to bring betterment for the welfare of people.

Each of them has specific role in this process and no single medium can be replaced any other. Broadcasting functions to bring consumers entertainment informative and educational bring consumers entertainment informative and educational material and advertising. This book contains valuable informative on print and broadcast journalism news reporting broadcasting etc. It be highly informative to both the media persons and general public.

Chapter 1

Introduction

Mass media is a term used to denote a section of the media specifically envisioned and designed to reach a very large audience such as the population of a nation state. It was coined in the 1920s with the advent of nationwide radio networks, mass-circulation newspapers and magazines, although mass media (like books and manuscripts) were present centuries before the term became common.

The term public media has a similar meaning: it is the sum of the public mass distributors of news and entertainment across media such as newspapers, television, radio, broadcasting, which may require union membership in some large markets such as Newspaper Guild, AFTRA, & text publishers.

The concept of mass media is now complicated by Internet media (like blogs, message boards, podcasts, and video sharing) because individuals now have a means to exposure that is comparable in scale to that previously restricted to a select group of mass media producers. The communications audience has been viewed by some commentators as forming a mass society with special characteristics, notably atomization or lack of social connections, which render it especially susceptible to the influence of modern mass-media techniques such as advertising and propaganda. The term "MSM" or "mainstream media" has been widely used in the blogosphere in discussion of the mass media and media bias.

Types of drama in numerous cultures were probably the first mass-media, going back into the Ancient World. The first dated printed book known is the "Diamond Sutra", printed in China in 868 AD, although it is clear that books were printed earlier. Movable clay type was invented in 1041 in China. However, due to the slow spread of literacy to the masses in China, and the relatively high cost of paper there, the earliest printed mass-medium was probably European popular prints from about 1400. Although these were produced in huge numbers, very few early examples survive, and even most known to be printed before about 1600 have not survived. Johannes Gutenberg printed the first book on a printing press with movable type in 1453. This invention transformed the way the world received printed materials, although books remained too expensive really to be called a mass-medium for at least a century after that.

Newspapers developed around from 1612, with the first example in English in 1620; but they took until the nineteenth century to reach a mass-audience directly. During the 20th century, the growth of mass media was driven by technology that allowed the massive duplication of material. Physical duplication technologies such as printing, record pressing and film duplication allowed the duplication of books, newspapers and movies at low prices to huge audiences. Radio and television allowed the electronic duplication of information for the first time.

Mass media had the economics of linear replication: a single work could make money proportional to the number of copies sold, and as volumes went up, units costs went down, increasing profit margins further. Vast fortunes were to be made in mass media. In a democratic society, independent media serve /electorate about issues regarding government and corporate entities. Some consider the concentration of media ownership to be a grave threat to democracy.

PURPOSES

Mass media can be used for various purposes:

- Advocacy, both for business and social concerns. This can include advertising, marketing, propaganda, public relations, and political communication.
- Entertainment, traditionally through performances of

acting, music, and sports, along with light reading; since the late 20th century also through video and computer games.
- Public service announcements.

NEGATIVE CHARACTERISTICS OF MASS MEDIA

Another description of Mass Media is central media which implies:

- An inability to transmit tacit knowledge (or perhaps it can only transfer bad tacit).
- The manipulation of large groups of people through media outlets, for the benefit of a particular political party and/or group of people.
- Marshall McLuhan, one of the biggest critics in media's history, brought up the idea that "the medium is the message."
- Bias, political or otherwise, towards favoring a certain individual, outcome or resolution of an event.
- "The corporate media is not a watchdog protecting us from the powerful, it is a lapdog begging for scraps."

This view of central media can be contrasted with lateral media, such as email networks, where messages are all slightly different and spread by a process of lateral diffusion.

JOURNALISM

Journalism is the discipline of collecting, analyzing, verifying and presenting information regarding current events, trends, issues and people.

Those who practice journalism are known as journalists. News-oriented journalism is sometimes described as the "first rough draft of history" (attributed to Phil Graham), because journalists often record important events, producing news articles on short deadlines.

While under pressure to be first with their stories, news media organizations usually edit and proofread their reports prior to publication, adhering to each organization's standards of accuracy, quality and style. Many news organizations claim proud traditions of holding government officials and institutions accountable to the public, while media critics have raised questions about holding the press itself accountable.

PUBLIC RELATIONS

Public relations is the art and science of managing communication between an organization and its key publics to build, manage and sustain its positive image. Examples include:

- Corporations use marketing public relations (MPR) to convey information about the products they manufacture or services they provide to potential customers to support their direct sales efforts. Typically, they support sales in the short and long term, establishing and burnishing the corporation's branding for a strong, ongoing market.
- Corporations also use public-relations as a vehicle to reach legislators and other politicians, seeking favorable tax, regulatory, and other treatment, and they may use public relations to portray themselves as enlightened employers, in support of human-resources recruiting programs.
- Non-profit organizations, including schools and universities, hospitals, and human and social service agencies, use public relations in support of awareness programs, fund-raising programs, staff recruiting, and to increase patronage of their services.
- Politicians use public relations to attract votes and raise money, and, when successful at the ballot box, to promote and defend their service in office, with an eye to the next election or, at career's end, to their legacy.

FORMS

Electronic media and print media include:

- Broadcasting, in the narrow sense, for radio and television.
- Various types of discs or tapes. In the 20th century,

these were mainly used for music. Video and computer uses followed.
- Film, most often used for entertainment, but also for documentaries.
- Internet, which has many uses and presents both opportunities and challenges. Blogs and podcasts (such as news, music, pre-recorded speech, and video)
- Mobile phones, often called the 7th Mass Media, used for rapid breaking news, short clips of entertainment like jokes, horoscopes, alerts, games, music, and advertising
- Video games, which have developed into a mass form of media since cutting-edge devices such as the PlayStation 3, XBox 360, and Wii broadened their use.

AUDIO RECORDING AND REPRODUCTION

Sound recording and reproduction is the electrical or mechanical re-creation and/or amplification of sound, often as music. This involves the use of audio equipment such as microphones, recording devices and loudspeakers. From early beginnings with the invention of the phonograph using purely mechanical techniques, the field has advanced with the invention of electrical recording, the mass production of the 78 record, the magnetic wire recorder followed by the tape recorder, the vinyl LP record. The invention of the compact cassette in the 1960s, followed by Sony's Walkman, gave a major boost to the mass distribution of music recordings, and the invention of digital recording and the compact disc in 1983 brought massive improvements in ruggedness and quality. The most recent developments have been in digital audio players.

An album is a collection of related audio recordings, released together to the public, usually commercially. The term record album originated from the fact that 78 RPM Phonograph disc records were kept together in a book resembling a photo album. The first collection of records to be called an "album" was Tchaikovsky's *Nutcracker Suite,* release in April 1909 as a four-disc set by Odeon records. It retailed for 16 shillings – about £15 in modern currency.

A music video (also promo) is a short film or video that accompanies a complete piece of music, most commonly a song. Modern music videos were primarily made and used as a marketing device intended to promote the sale of music recordings. Although the origins of music videos go back much further, they came into their own in the 1980s, when Music Television's format was based around them. In the 1980s, the term "rock video" was often used to describe this form of entertainment, although the term has fallen into disuse. Music videos can accommodate all styles of filmmaking, including animation, live action films, documentaries, and non-narrative, abstract film. The sequencing of content in a broadcast is called a schedule.

With all technological endeavours a number of technical terms and slang are developed please see the list of broadcasting terms for a glossary of terms used. This format was invented, designed, and engineered by a Massachusetts company called General Voice. It can only be created with their patented software known as The MVL File Creator. This software allows people to create a file which incorporates the use of text, pictures and audio and builds them into one unique file. The new type of file created which has a unique format can then be viewed in one of three ways. It can be opened and viewed by the MVL File Creator programme. In which case the viewer must also have a version of the MVL File Creator on their system or the MVL can be converted to an executable file or a shockwave flash file either is viewable by anybody with a computer.

Television and radio programs are distributed through radio broadcasting over frequency bands that are highly regulated by the Federal Communications Commission. Such regulation includes determination of the width of the bands, range, licencing, types of receivers and transmitters used, and acceptable content. Cable programs are often broadcast simultaneously with radio and television programs, but have a more limited audience. By coding signals and having decoding equipment in homes, cable also enables subscription-based channels and pay-per-view services.

A broadcasting organisation may broadcast several programs at the same time, through several channels (frequencies), for example BBC One and Two. On the other hand, two or more organisations may share a channel and each use it during a fixed part of the day. Digital radio and digital television may also transmit multiplexed programming, with several channels compressed into one ensemble. When broadcasting is done via the Internet the term webcasting is often used. In 2004 a new phenomenon occurred when a number of technologies combined to produce podcasting. Podcasting is an asynchronous broadcast/narrowcast medium, with one of the main proponents being Adam Curry and his associates the Podshow.

FILM

Film is a term that encompasses motion pictures as individual projects, as well as the field in general. The origin of the name comes from the fact that photographic film (also called filmstock) has historically been the primary medium for recording and displaying motion pictures. Many other terms exist — *motion pictures* (or just *pictures* and "picture"), *the silver screen, photoplays, the cinema, picture shows, flicks* — and commonly *movies*. Films are produced by recording people and objects with cameras, or by creating them using animation techniques and/or special effects.

They comprise a series of individual frames, but when these images are shown rapidly in succession, the illusion of motion is given to the viewer. Flickering between frames is not seen due to an effect known as persistence of vision — whereby the eye retains a visual image for a fraction of a second after the source has been removed. Also of relevance is what causes the perception of motion; a psychological effect identified as beta movement. Film is considered by many to be an important art form; films entertain, educate, enlighten and inspire audiences. Any film can become a worldwide attraction, especially with the addition of dubbing or subtitles that translate the film message. Films are also artifacts created by specific cultures, which reflect those cultures, and, in turn, affect them.

INTERNET

The Internet (also known simply as "the Net" or "the Web") can be briefly understood as "a network of networks". Specifically, it is the worldwide, publicly accessible network of interconnected computer networks that transmit data by packet switching using the standard Internet Protocol (IP). It consists of millions of smaller domestic, academic, business, and governmental networks, which together carry various information and services, such as electronic mail, online chat, file transfer, and the interlinked Web pages and other documents of the World Wide Web.

Contrary to some common usage, the Internet and the World Wide Web are not synonymous: the Internet is the system of interconnected *computer networks*, linked by copper wires, fibre-optic cables, wireless connections etc.; the Web is the contents, or the interconnected *documents*, linked by hyperlinks and URLs. The World Wide Web is accessible through the Internet, along with many other services including e-mail, file sharing and others described below.

Toward the end of the 20th century, the advent of the World Wide Web marked the first era in which any individual could have a means of exposure on a scale comparable to that of mass media. For the first time, anyone with a web site can address a global audience, although serving to high levels of web traffic is still relatively expensive. It is possible that the rise of peer-to-peer technologies may have begun the process of making the cost of bandwidth manageable. Although a vast amount of information, imagery, and commentary (i.e. "content") has been made available, it is often difficult to determine the authenticity and reliability of information contained in web pages (in many cases, self-published).

The invention of the Internet has also allowed breaking news stories to reach around the globe within minutes. This rapid growth of instantaneous, decentralized communication is often deemed likely to change mass media and its relationship to society. "Cross-media" means the idea of distributing the same message through different media channels. A similar idea is expressed in the news industry as "convergence". Many authors understand cross-media publishing to be the ability to publish in both print and on the web without manual conversion effort. An increasing number of wireless devices with mutually incompatible data and screen formats make it even more difficult to achieve the objective "create once, publish many".

The internet is quickly becoming the centre of mass media. Everything is becoming accessible via the internet. Instead of picking up a newspaper, or watching the 10 o'clock news, people will log onto the internet to get the news they want, when they want it. Many workers listen to the radio through the internet while sitting at their desk. Games are played through the internet. The Internet and Education: Findings of the Pew Internet & American Life Project Even the education system relies on the internet. Teachers can contact the entire class by sending one e-mail. They have web pages where students can get another copy of the class outline or assignments. Some classes even have class blogs where students must post weekly, and are graded on their contributions. The internet thus far has become an extremely dominant form of media.

BLOGS (WEB LOGS)

Blogging has become a huge form of media, popular through the internet. A blog is a website, usually maintained by an individual, with regular entries of commentary, descriptions of events, or other material such as graphics or video. Entries are commonly displayed in reverse chronological order. Many blogs provide commentary or news on a particular subject; others function as more personal online diaries.

A typical blog combines text, images, and links to other blogs, web pages, and other media related to its topic. The ability for readers to leave comments in an interactive format is an important part of many blogs. Most blogs are primarily textual, although some focus on art (artlog), photographs (photoblog), sketchblog, videos (vlog), music (MP3 blog), audio (podcasting) are part of a wider network of social media. Micro-blogging is another type of blogging which consists of blogs with very short posts.

RSS FEEDS

RSS is a format for syndicating news and the content of news-like sites, including major news sites like Wired, news-oriented community sites like Slashdot, and personal blogs. It is a family of Web feed formats used to publish frequently updated content such as blog entries, news headlines, and podcasts. An RSS document (which is called a "feed" or "web feed" or "channel") contains either a summary of content from an associated web site or the full text. RSS makes it possible for people to keep up with web sites in an automated manner that can be piped into special programs or filtered displays.

PODCAST

A podcast is a series of digital-media files which are distributed over the Internet using syndication feeds for playback on portable media players and computers. The term podcast, like broadcast, can refer either to the series of content itself or to the method by which it is syndicated; the latter is also called podcasting. The host or author of a podcast is often called a podcaster.

MOBILE

Mobile phones were introduced in Japan in 1997 but became a mass media only in 1998 when the first downloadable ringing tones were introduced in Finland. Soon most forms of media content were introduced on mobile phones, and today the total value of media consumed on mobile towers over that of internet content, and was worth over 31 billion dollars in 2007 (source Informa).

The mobile media content includes over 8 billion dollars worth of mobile music (ringing tones, ringback tones, truetones, MP3 files, karaoke, music videos, music streaming services etc); over 5 billion dollars worth of mobile gaming; and various news, entertainment and advertising services. In Japan mobile phone books are so popular that five of the ten best-selling printed books were originally released as mobile phone books. Similar to the internet, mobile is also an interactive media, but has far wider reach, with 3.3 billion mobile phone users at the end of 2007 to 1.3 billion internet users (source ITU). Like email on the internet, the top application on mobile is also a personal messaging service, but SMS text messaging is used by over 2.4 billion people.

Practically all internet services and applications exist or have similar cousins on mobile, from search to multiplayer games to virtual worlds to blogs. Mobile has several unique benefits which many mobile media pundits claim make mobile a more powerful media than either TV or the internet, starting with mobile being permanently carried and always connected. Mobile has the best audience accuracy and is the only mass media with a built-in payment channel available to every user without any credit cards or paypal accounts or even an age limit. Mobile is often called the 7th Mass Medium and either the fourth screen (if counting cinema, TV and PC screens) or the third screen (counting only TV and PC).

PUBLISHING

Publishing is the industry concerned with the production of literature or information – the activity of making information available for public view. In some cases, authors may be their own publishers. Traditionally, the term refers to the distribution of printed works such as books and newspapers. With the advent of digital information systems and the Internet, the scope of publishing has expanded to include websites, blogs, and the like.

As a business, publishing includes the development, marketing, production, and distribution of newspapers, magazines, books, literary works, musical works, software, other works dealing with information. Publication is also important as a legal concept; (1) as the process of giving formal notice to the world of a significant intention, for example, to marry or enter bankruptcy, and; (2) as the essential precondition of being able to claim defamation; that is, the alleged libel must have been published.

BOOK

A book is a collection of sheets of paper, parchment or other material with a piece of text written on them, bound together along one edge within covers. A book is also a literary work or a main division of such a work. A book produced in electronic format is known as an e-book. In library and information science, a book is called a monograph to distinguish it from serial publications such as magazines, journals or newspapers.

Publishers may produce low-cost, pre-proof editions known as galleys or 'bound proofs' for promotional purposes, such as generating reviews in advance of publication. Galleys are usually made as cheaply as possible, since they are not intended for sale.

MAGAZINE

A magazine is a periodical publication containing a variety of articles, generally financed by advertising and/or purchase by readers. Magazines are typically published weekly, biweekly, monthly, bimonthly or quarterly, with a date on the cover that is in advance of the date it is actually published. They are often printed in colour on coated paper, and are bound with a soft cover.

Magazines fall into two broad categories: consumer magazines and business magazines. In practice, magazines are a subset of periodicals, distinct from those periodicals produced by scientific, artistic, academic or special interest publishers which are subscription-only, more expensive, narrowly limited in circulation, and often have little or no advertising.

Magazines can be classified as:

- General interest magazines (e.g. Frontline, India Today, The Week, etc)

- Special interest magazines (women's, sports, business, scuba diving, etc)

NEWSPAPER

A newspaper is a publication containing news and information and advertising, usually printed on low-cost paper called newsprint. It may be general or special interest, most often published daily or weekly. The first printed newspaper was published in 1605, and the form has thrived even in the face of competition from technologies such as radio and television. Recent developments on the Internet are posing major threats to its business model, however. Paid circulation is declining in most countries, and advertising revenue, which makes up the bulk of a newspaper's income, is shifting from print to online; some commentators, nevertheless, point out that historically new media such as radio and television did not entirely supplant existing.

SOFTWARE PUBLISHING

A software publisher is a publishing company in the software industry between the developer and the distributor. In some companies, two or all three of these roles may be combined (and indeed, may reside in a single person, especially in the case of shareware). Software publishers often license software from developers with specific limitations, such as a time limit or geographical region. The terms of licensing vary enormously, and are typically secret. Developers may use publishers to reach larger or foreign markets, or to avoid focussing on marketing. Or publishers may use developers to create software to meet a market need that the publisher has identified.

MASS WIRE MEDIA

Mass wire media is a new frontier of news reporting in the high-tech age. A few decades ago news reporting was through newspapers and radio and television. The radio broadcasts that were made famous by Franklin D. Roosevelt during World War II changed the way radio was looked at.

These fireside chats made the radio news and news radio. Things are different now as we are witnessing a revolution of people-oriented reporting in real time and other times. This element of intimate knowledge of the event or story being reported has dramatically changed the way we all view news stories. This is called by some the Social Media Revolution. This revolution has intrinsically altered the way news is reported almost the way it happens. The trend of people-oriented reporting is only on the rise as reporting news becomes more personal and more accurate - although also more subjective.

VIDEO GAMES

A video game is a computer-controlled game where a video display such as a monitor or television is the primary feedback device. The term "computer game" also includes games which display only text (and which can therefore theoretically be played on a teletypewriter) or which use other methods, such as sound or vibration, as their primary feedback device, but there are very few new games in these categories. There always must also be some sort of input device, usually in the form of button/joystick combinations (on arcade games), a keyboard & mouse/trackball combination (computer games), or a controller (console games), or a combination of any of the above. Also, more esoteric devices have been used for input.

Usually there are rules and goals, but in more open-ended games the player may be free to do whatever they like within the confines of the virtual universe. In common usage, a "computer game" or a "PC game" refers to a game that is played on a personal computer. "Console game" refers to one that is played on a device specifically designed for the use of such, while interfacing with a standard television set. "Arcade game" refers to a game designed to be played in an establishment in which patrons pay to play on a per-use basis. "Video game" (or "videogame") has evolved into a catchall phrase that encompasses the aforementioned along with any game made for any other device, including, but not limited to, mobile phones, PDAs, advanced calculators, etc.

Chapter 2

The Marketing/Media Ecology

Media ecology is an interdisciplinary field of media theory involving the study of media environments. According to the Media Ecology Association, media ecology can be defined as "the study of media environments, the idea that technology and techniques, modes of information and codes of communication play a leading role in human affairs."

In 1977, Marshall McLuhan said that media ecology:

...means arranging various media to help each other so they won't cancel each other out, to buttress one medium with another. You might say, for example, that radio is a bigger help to literacy than television, but television might be a very wonderful aid to teaching languages. And so you can do some things on some media that you cannot do on others. And, therefore, if you watch the whole field, you can prevent this waste that comes by one canceling the other out.

Inspired by McLuhan, Neil Postman founded the Programme in Media Ecology at New York University in 1971. He described it as:

Media ecology looks into the matter of how media of communication affect human perception, understanding, feeling, and value; and how our interaction with media facilitates or impedes our chances of survival. The word ecology implies the study of environments: their structure, content, and impact on people.

Along with McLuhan and Postman, media ecology draws from many authors, including the work of Harold Innis, Walter Ong, Lewis Mumford, Jacques Ellul, Eric Havelock, Susanne Langer, Erving Goffman, Edward T. Hall, George Herbert

Mead, Margaret Mead, Claude Lévi-Strauss, Benjamin Lee Whorf, and Gregory Bateson.

Nearly four decades ago, Neil Postman, NYU professor, media theorist, and cultural critic, (as well as a member of my very own Doctoral Dissertation Committee) predicted the coming of what he termed a "media ecology." Postman noted, "Media ecology is how the media of communication affect human perception, understanding, feeling and value," an observation which astoundingly reflects the problem modern marketers are faced with daily. Especially when it comes to strategic planning, branding, advertising, promotion, co-branding, media planning, engagement and, well, pretty much modern marketing.

Ten years later, Marshall McLuhan observed that a "media ecology means arranging various media to help each other buttress one medium with another," which even more astoundingly sounds like the current challenge marketers and planners face regarding cross-media consumption and the effect it has on engagement, brand development, and sales. (McLuhan also said, "most of our assumptions have outlived their usefulness," and that was 40 years ago before things got so complicated.

And he was an optimist!) Anyway, one can argue about the precise date this media ecology finally arrived in its full-blown complexity – usually without an appointment – in the reception areas of major corporations like P&G and General Motors and Coca Cola and at advertising agencies like Omnicom, Interpublic, and JWT. Or you can debate upon which convoluted continuum the old media environment migrated.

While you're doing that, keep in mind the absolutely incontrovertible truth, which is a real, 21st century media ecology – an environment where consumers are virtually cocooned by/have access to media of one sort or another on a literal 24:7 basis – has arrived.

Oh, yes, and one other thing, that media planning for successfully winning the battle for consumers' hearts, minds, and wallets in this multi-media ecology is more complex than ever before. Particularly when it comes to "cross-media consumption." And it's not just the media. The need for a real measure of cróss-media consumption has been further amplified by the rapidly evolving ways in which consumers use, juggle, adopt, and "gate keep" old and new media. Also, in light of the reality that burgeoning "new" media technologies have become more and more accepted – and used - as "media platforms."

Many prescient companies like ABC TV and Rainbow Media have been researching media engagement "models." They're not the only ones, of course, but typically most of the less-useful forays into cross-media consumption relate only to "awareness," "brand favorability," and "purchase intent." Now that may sound impressive, but marketers should be wary when they hear those words.

It's prudent to remember that the brands that are actually doing enough marketing to warrant some curiosity and concern regarding cross-media consumption have already attained high levels of awareness, brand favorability, and purchase intention. These days, those kinds of excellent answers to meaningless questions are worth about 10¢ a ton.

Content providers, like Disney's ESPN, who have been developing digital media – including Internet, mobile, digital audio and video (with an emphasis on supporting digital media growth, ad sales, branding and content development) – have recently brought in specialists to help advance cross-media research.

That's because they realise that you can't keep arguing that more is better, even if it is a "sports" venue that you're talking about! Yes, some media formats are more practicable than others. Others more "cost-effective." But that has always been the case, even in simpler times. Each touch point's sales force argues that they incorporate a unique set and subset of values and nuances and capabilities to engage, communicate, inform, and persuade.

And – based upon our predictive Brand-to-Media Engagement (B2ME) metrics – some are actually more efficacious for certain categories and brands than others –

especially when one considers that more and more content providers are looking to support digital media growth.

It is equally true, for that very reason, that more and more marketers are utilizing a variety of touch points to communicate their existence and differentiation, and their messages and values to their intended target audiences, with, one hopes, the ultimate goal – beyond awareness, favorability, and purchase intent – of getting target audiences to actually reach into their wallets and buy their products.

Embracing more and different media touch points theoretically optimizes the opportunity the brand has to engage the target consumer, since any one consumer uses different forms of media at different times, some even simultaneously.

And that being the case, reasonable men might ask that if each medium has its strengths, and *if* a combination of media might have greater potency, won't the brand with the most touch points win?

Good question. In fact, we've conducted research that answers that by demonstrating that cross-media consumption can be predicted as to whether it has positive or neutral or negative effects to brand engagement levels and, therefore, actual sales. And no matter what the medium promises, without real and meaningful metrics you won't know if you've won or lost until after you've made the buy, which seems – from both a planning and budget-management perspective – too little too late!

Anyway, Brand Keys will be presenting this new cross-media engagement research later this month. The current version of our cross-media metrics measures 26 individual media touch points that marketers might use to win over the consumer to the brand's particular point-of-view.

We identified 11 discrete cross-media consumption segments. In this particular study we surveyed Unilever's Dove brand bar soap users and the engagement-based findings prove that relying upon cross-media consumption on a "time spent" basis produces dramatically misleading "insights" in terms of in-market consequences. This is also true if you rely on some assessment based on identifying media touch points that consumers "love," "trust," or even think, "inspiring."

And don't get me started on metrics that are based on the assumption that being engaged with the entertainment or the editorial environment is the same thing as being engaged with the advertising!

So, once again, loyalty and engagement metrics win the day. Build those into your planning system and media can be allocated on a more synergistic and efficient basis. In a more complex marketplace, that's what you need if you want your brand to be the big winner in its category. Winning may not be everything, but in the current media ecology, losing has little to recommend it.

Media studies is an academic discipline that deals with the content, history and effects of various media, in particular mass media.

Media scholars vary in the theoretical and methodological focus they bring to mass media topics, including the media's political, social, economic and cultural roles and impact. Media studies draw on traditions from both the social sciences and the humanities, and overlap in interests with related disciplines like mass communication, communication, communication sciences and communication studies.

Researchers develop and employ theories and methods from disciplines including cultural studies, rhetoric, philosophy, literary theory, psychology, political science, political economy, economics, sociology, social theory, art history and criticism, film theory, and information theory.

KEY THEMES

In addition to the interdisciplinary nature of the academic field, popular understandings of media studies encompass:

- Journalism
- Mass communication
- Media influence
- Creative industries
- Political economy
- Cultural sociology

Most production and journalism courses incorporate media studies content, but academic institutions often establish separate departments. Media studies students may see themselves as observers of media, not creators or practitioners. These distinctions vary across national boundaries.

Separate strands exist within media studies, such as television studies. Film studies is often considered a separate discipline, though television and video games studies grew out of it, as made evident by the application of basic critical theories such as psychoanalysis, feminism and Marxism. Critical media theory looks at how the corporate ownership of media production and distribution affects society, and provides a common ground to social conservatives (concerned by the effects of media on the traditional family) and liberals and socialists (concerned by the corporatization of social discourse). The study of the effects and techniques of advertising forms a cornerstone of media studies.

Contemporary media studies includes the analysis of new media with emphasis on the internet, video games, mobile devices, interactive television, and other forms of mass media which developed from the 1990s. Because these new technologies allow instant communication across the world (chat rooms and instant messaging, online video games, video conferencing), interpersonal communication is an important element in new media studies. It has been argued that media studies has not fully acknowledged the changes which the internet and digital interactive media have brought about, seeing these as an 'add-on'. David Gauntlett has argued for a 'Media Studies 2.0' which fully recognises the ways in which media has changed, and that traditional boundaries between 'audiences' and 'producers' has collapsed.

POLITICAL COMMUNICATION AND POLITICAL ECONOMY

From the beginning, media studies are closely related to politics and wars such as campaign research and war propaganda. Political communication mainly studies the connections among politicians, voters and media. It focused on the media effects. There are four main media influence theories: hypodermic needle model (1930s behaviorism), two-step flow model (Lazarsfeld, 1948), limited effects (Lang & Lang, 1953), and the spiral of silence (Noelle-Neumann, 1984). Also, many scholars studied the technique of political communication such as rhetoric, symbolism and etc. Much of this research has been developed in journals of mass communication and public opinion scholarship.

In the last quarter century, political economy has played a major part in media studies literature. The theory gained notoriety in media studies particularly with the publication of Edward S. Herman and Noam Chomsky's *Manufacturing Consent*, published in 1988. In the book, the authors discuss a theory of how the United States' media industry operates, which they term a "propaganda model." The model describes a "decentralized and non-conspiratorial market system of control and processing, although at times the government or one or more private actors may take initiatives and mobilize co-ordinated elite handling of an issue."

MEDIA STUDIES AND MEDIA PSYCHOLOGY

An EdD concentration in Media Studies, grounded in Media Psychology and a PhD programme in Media Psychology were launched at Fielding Graduate University in 2002 by Bernard Luskin. These programs advanced Media Studies in acknowledging the importance of human behaviour. The PhD programme in Media Psychology is the first in any university.

Though not yet named as such, media studies' roots are in the Chicago School and thinkers such as John Dewey, Charles Cooley and George Mead. These authors saw American society on the cusp of positive social change toward pure democracy. Mead argued that for an ideal society to exist, a form of communication must be developed to allow the unique individual to appreciate the attitudes, viewpoints and positions of others unlike herself, and allow her to be understood by others as well. Mead believed that this "new media" would allow humans to empathize with others, and therefore moves toward an "ideal of human society." Where Mead sees an ideal society, Dewey names it the "Great Community," and further asserts the assumption that humans are intelligent enough for self government, and that that knowledge is "a function of association and communication." Similarly, Cooley asserts that political communication makes public opinion possible, which in turn promotes democracy. Each of these authors represent the Chicago School's attention to electronic communication as a facilitator of democracy, its faith in the informed electorate, and its focus on the individual as opposed to the mass.

PROPAGANDA STUDIES

Between the First and Second World Wars, the Institute for Propaganda Analysis briefly rose to importance. Their definition of propaganda was "expression of opinion or action by individuals or groups deliberately designed to influence opinion or actions of other individuals or groups with reference to predetermined ends."

Harold Lasswell, who worked in the paradigm of the Chicago School of sociology wrote Propaganda Technique in the World War, which included this definition of propaganda:

"Propaganda in the broadest sense is the technique of influencing human action by the manipulation of representations. These representations may take spoken, written, pictorial or musical form."

These definitions of propaganda clearly show that this was a school of thought that focused on media effects, as it highlighted the influence that media could have over its audiences attitudes and actions. Epitomizing this early school of media effects studies are experiments done by The Experimental Section of the Research Branch of the U.S. War Department's Information and Education Division. In the experiments, the effects of various U.S. wartime propaganda films on soldiers were observed.

Current Propaganda studies are applied into many fields besides politics. Herman described a propaganda model as "a model of media behaviour and performance, not of media effects." He argued: "They are profit-seeking business, owned by very wealthy people (or other companies); and they are funded largely by advertisers who are also profit-seeking entities, and who want their advertisements to appear in a supportive selling environment."

He also presented "five factors: owner ship, advertising, sourcing, flak and anti-communist ideology-work as filters through which information must pass, and that individually and often in cumulative fashion they greatly influence media choices." Until now, there is no conclusion of propaganda, debate still continues.

FRANKFURT SCHOOL AND CRITICAL THEORY

Typified by the philosophical and theoretical orientations of Max Horkheimer, Theodor Adorno, Walter Benjamin, Leo Lowenthal, and Herbert Marcuse, the Frankfurt school contributed greatly to the development and application of critical theory in media studies.

Their Marxist critique of market-driven media was critical of its atomizing and leveling effects. The Frankfurt school also lamented the effects of the "culture industry" on the production and appreciation of art. For example, in *A Social Critique of Radio Music,* Adorno asserts:

"...music has ceased to be a human force and is consumed like other consumers' goods. This produces 'commodity listening'...The listener suspends all intellectual activity."

As the Frankfurt school lamented on the effects of the "culture industry" they also began to identify mass culture and high culture as two distinct entities. Scholars like Benjamin (1936) and Adorno (1945) can be credited with what would eventually become known as popular culture and high culture. Their finite distinction of equating original production with ritualistic behaviour as compared with mass culture that finds its identifying symbols in reproductions. These reproductions are souless and lacking in definition and originality.

MEDIA EFFECTS

The less paradigm in media studies since the Second

World War has been associated with the ideas, methods and findings of Paul F. Lazarsfeld and his school: media effect studies. Their studies focused on measurable, short-term behavioral 'effects' of media and concluded that the media played a limited role in influencing public opinion. The "Limited-Effects" Model developed by Lazarfeld and his colleges from Columbia was highly influential in the development of media studies.

The model claims the mass media has "limited-effects" on voting patterns. Voters are influenced, rather, through the 'two-step flow' model, the idea that media messages are disseminated through personal interaction with 'opinion leaders'. The model of limited- effects was so influential that the question of media "effects" on politics was left largely unaddressed until the late 1960s. Eventually Mass Communication scholars began to study political behaviour again and the limited-effects model was called into question.

USES AND GRATIFICATION MODEL

As a response to the previous emphasis upon media effects, from the 1970s researchers became interested in how audiences make sense of media texts. The "uses and gratifications" model, associated with Jay Blumler and Elihu Katz, reflected this growing interest in the 'active audience'. One such example of this type of research was conducted by Hodge and Tripp, and separately Palmer, about how school-children make sense of the Australian soap opera *Prisoner*. They found that pupils could identify with the prisoners: they were "shut in", separated from their friends and wouldn't be there had they not been made to be, etc.

Also, the children could compare the wardens to their teachers: "the hard-bitten old [one], the soft new one, the one you could take advantage of..." John Fiske summarises:

The children inserted meanings of the programme into their social experience of school in a way that informed both — the meanings of school and the meanings of *Prisoner* were each influenced by the other, and the fit between them validated the other.

MEDIA STUDIES THROUGHOUT THE WORLD

AUSTRALIA

Media is studied as a broad subject in most states in Australia, with Victoria being a world leader in curriculum development. Media Studies was first developed as a study area in the early 1960s in Victorian universities. Film studies began in secondary schools in the mid 1960s and by the early 1970s Media Studies was being taught in secondary schools. Most notable in curriculum development at secondary level were Peter Greenaway, Peter Dodds, and Trevor Barr - who developed one of the first media text books 'Reflections of Reality'.

Also notable was John Murray with 'The Box in the Corner', 'In Focus', and '10 Lessons in Film Appreciation' (1966). The subject became part of the Higher School Certificate in the 1980s and is currently a strong component of the Victorian Certificate of Education. The VCE course covers Unit 1 - Representation, Technologies of Representation, and New Media; Unit 2 - Media Production, Australian Media Organisations; Unit 3 - Narrative texts, Production Planning; Unit 4 - Production work, Social Values, and Media Influence.

Media Studies also forms a major part of the Primary and junior Secondary curriculum and includes areas such as photography, print media, and television. Victoria has the leading Media body known as ATOM which also publishes Metro and Screen Education magazines. Other states that teach Media are South Australia, Western Australia, and Queensland. The subject does not appear to be taught in New South Wales.

GERMANY

In Germany two main streams of Media Studies can be identified. The first large flow of media studies based in humanities and cultural sciences as the Theater scholarship ("Theaterwissenschaft") and German language and literature studies widens since the 1960s. In this orientation, the Media studies in Germany today mainly developed and established.

As one of the first publications to this new direction is by Helmut Kreuzer, published the study *Literature Studies - Media Studies* (*Literaturwissenschaft – Medienwissenschaft*), summed up the units of the "Düsseldorfer Germanistentag" 1976.

The second stream is comparable to Communication Studies. Pioneered by Elisabeth Noelle-Neumann in the 1940s this stream studies mass media, its institutions and its effects on society and individuals.

Media studies is currently one of the most popular university courses in Germany, with many applicants mistakenly assuming that studying it will automatically lead them to a career in TV or other media.

This has led to widespread disillusionment, with students blaming the universities for offering highly theoretical course content.

The universities maintain that practical journalistic training is not the aim of the academic studies they offer.

INDIA

The media industry is growing in India at the rate of 20 percent per annum. Together, entertainment and media form the country's sixth biggest industry, with 3.5 million people working in it. Within the next 4-5 years, the industry is expected to gross eighty thousand crores (800 billion rupees) annually. Additionally, the third biggest media institute of the world, the Asian Academy Of Film & Television, is also based in India.

NEW ZEALAND

Media Studies in New Zealand can be regarded as a singular success, with the subject well-established in the tertiary sector (such as Screen and Media Studies at the University of Waikato; Media Studies, Victoria University of Wellington; Film, Television and Media Studies, University of Auckland; Media Studies, Massey University; Communication Studies, University of Otago).

UK

In the UK, media studies developed in the 1960s from the

academic study of English, and from literary criticism more broadly.

The key date, according to Andrew Crisell, is 1959: when Joseph Trenaman left the BBC's Further Education Unit to become the first holder of the Granada Research Fellowship in Television at Leeds University.

Soon after in 1966, the Centre for Mass Communication Research was founded at Leicester University, and degree programmes in media studies began to sprout at polytechnics and other universities during the 1970s and 1980s.

Media Studies is now taught all over the UK. The topics span from magazines to films. It is taught at GCSE and at A level, and the Scottish Qualifications Authority offers formal qualifications at a number of different levels.

It is also taught at University level. In the UK, Media Studies is regularly the victim of jokes and cynical attitudes, often being labelled as a Mickey Mouse subject. It receives many of the criticisms directed at sociology scholars during the 70s and 80s. In 2000, England's Chief Schools Inspector, Chris Woodhead suggested that media studies is a one-way ticket to the dole.

USA

Mass communication, communication studies or simply communication may be more popular names than "media studies" for academic departments in the United States. However, the focus of such programs sometimes excludes certain media — film, book publishing, video games, etc.

The title "media studies" may be used alone, to designate film studies and rhetorical or critical theory, or it may appear in combinations like "media studies and communication" to join two fields or emphasize a different focus.

Examples: Comparative Media Studies at MIT, Cinema and Media Studies at the University of Chicago, Rhetoric and Media Studies at Willamette University and Media Studies in Communication at Kennesaw State University. University of California, Berkeley has a long established and highly regarded interdisciplinary programme formerly titled Mass

Communications, which recently changed its name to Media Studies, dropping the pejorative connotations which accompany the term "Mass" in the former title.

Until recently, Radford University in Virginia used the title "media studies" for a department that taught practitioner-oriented major concentrations in journalism, advertising, broadcast production and Web design. In 2008 those programs were combined with a previous department of communication to create a School of Communication.

It is, by now, almost a commonplace to remark that the 20th century is an era of change, of change unprecedented in its scope, its pace, and its potential for violent effects on the fabric of civilization.

- For Kenneth Boulding, the changes which have taken place since 1900 are of such enormous significance that he marks the 20th century as the turning point in what he calls "the second great transition in the history of mankind"—that is, the transition from "civilization" to "post-civilization." According to Boulding, the impetus for that transition is provided by a radical shift in what he calls man's "image" of reality.
- Thomas Kuhn refers to the same kind of radical shift as a revolution in paradigms; Pierre Teilhard de Chardin calls it a change in the noösphere; Ervin Laszlo, Ludwig von Bertalanffy, and others call it simply a shift in man's world view.
- What each is referring to is an epochal change in the status, organization, and application of knowledge.

One of the consequences of the change to which Boulding and others refer, or, better perhaps, one of its hallmarks, is a movement away from the rigidly compartmentalized, uncoordinated specialization in scientific inquiry which characterized the Newtonian world, and a movement toward increasing integration of both the physical and the social sciences.

- One of the symptoms of this trend is the proliferation, in recent years, of "compound" disciplines such as mathematical biochemistry, psychobiology, linguistic anthropology, psycholinguistics, and so on.

- Another is the emergence of new fields of inquiry so broad in their scope that the word "discipline," suggesting as it does some well-bounded area of specialization, scarcely applies to them at all. Rather, they are perspectives, moving perhaps in the direction of metadisciplines.

One such perspective, or emerging metadiscipline, is media ecology—broadly defined as the study of complex communication systems as environments.

As a perspective, metadiscipline, or even a field of inquiry, media ecology is very much in its infancy.

Media ecologists know, generally, what it is they are interested in—the interactions of communications media, technology, technique, and processes with human feeling, thought, value, and behaviour—and they know, too, the kinds of questions about those interactions they are concerned to ask.

But media ecologists do not, as yet, have a coherent framework in which to organize their subject matter or their questions. Media ecology is, in short, a preparadigmatic science. —Christine Nystrom.

MEDIA ECOLOGY

Media ecology looks into the matter of how media of communication affect human perception, understanding, feeling, and value; and how our interaction with media facilitates or impedes our chances of survival. The word ecology implies the study of environments: their structure, content, and impact on people.

An environment is, after all, a complex message system which imposes on human beings certain ways of thinking, feeling, and behaving.

- It structures what we can see and say and, therefore, do.
- It assigns roles to us and insists on our playing them.
- It specifies what we are permitted to do and what we are not. Sometimes, as in the case of a courtroom,

or classroom, or business office, the specifications are explicit and formal.

In the case of media environments (e.g., books, radio, film, television, etc.), the specifications are more often implicit and informal, half concealed by our assumption that what we are dealing with is not an environment but merely a machine. Media ecology tries to make these specifications explicit. It tries to find out what roles media force us to play, how media structure what we are seeing, why media make us feel and act as we do. Media ecology is the study of media as environments.

Chapter 3

Media Selling: Perspective and Approaches

In popular usage, "marketing" is the promotion of products, especially advertising and branding. However, in professional usage the term has a wider meaning which recognizes that marketing is customer-centered. Products are often developed to meet the desires of groups of customers or even, in some cases, for specific customers. E. Jerome McCarthy divided marketing into four general sets of activities. His typology has become so universally recognized that his four activity sets, the Four Ps, have passed into the language. The four Ps are:

PRODUCT

The product aspects of marketing deal with the specifications of the actual goods or services, and how it relates to the end-user's needs and wants. The scope of a product generally includes supporting elements such as warranties, guarantees, and support.

PRICING

This refers to the process of setting a price for a product, including discounts. The price need not be monetary - it can simply be what is exchanged for the product or services, e.g. time, energy, psychology or attention.

PROMOTION

This includes advertising, branding, sales promotion,

publicity, and personal selling, and refers to the various methods of promoting the product, brand, or company.

PLACEMENT (OR DISTRIBUTION)

Refers to how the product gets to the customer; for example, point of sale placement or retailing. This fourth P has also sometimes been called Place, referring to the channel by which a product or services is sold (e.g. online vs. retail), which geographic region or industry, to which segment (young adults, families, business people), etc.

These four elements are often referred to as the marketing mix, which a marketer can use to craft a marketing plan. The four Ps model is most useful when marketing low value consumer products. Industrial products, services, high value consumer products require adjustments to this model. Services marketing must account for the unique nature of services. Industrial or B2B marketing must account for the long term contractual agreements that are typical in supply chain transactions. Relationship marketing attempts to do this by looking at marketing from a long term relationship perspective rather than individual transactions. As a counter to this, Morgan, in Riding the Waves of Change (Jossey-Bass, 1988), suggests that one of the greatest limitations of the 4 Ps approach "is that it unconsciously emphasizes the inside-out view (looking from the company outwards), whereas the essence of marketing should be the outside-in approach". Nevertheless, the 4 Ps offer a memorable and workable guide to the major categories of marketing activity, as well as a framework within which these can be used.

SEVEN PS

As well as the standard four P's (Product, Pricing, Promotion and Place), services marketing calls upon an extra three, totaling seven and known together as the extended marketing mix. These are:

PEOPLE

Any person coming into contact with customers can have

an impact on overall satisfaction. Whether as part of a supporting service to a product or involved in a total service, people are particularly important because, in the customer's eyes, they are generally inseparable from the total service. As a result of this, they must be appropriately trained, well motivated and the right type of person. Fellow customers are also sometimes referred to under 'people', as they too can affect the customer's service experience, (e.g., at a sporting event).

PROCESS

This is the process(es) involved in providing a service and the behaviour of people, which can be crucial to customer satisfaction.

PHYSICAL EVIDENCE

Unlike a product, a service cannot be experienced before it is delivered, which makes it intangible. This, therefore, means that potential customers could perceive greater risk when deciding whether to use a service. To reduce the feeling of risk, thus improving the chance for success, it is often vital to offer potential customers the chance to see what a service would be like. This is done by providing physical evidence, such as case studies, testimonials or demonstrations.

FOUR NEW PS

PERSONALISATION

It is here referred customization of products and services through the use of the Internet. Early examples include Dell on-line, but this concept is further extended with emerging social media and advanced algorithms. Emerging technologies will continue to push this idea forward.

PARTICIPATION

This is to allow customer to participate in what the brand should stand for; what should be the product directions and even which ads to run. This concept is laying the foundation for disruptive change through democratization of information.

PEER-TO-PEER

This refers to customer networks and communities where advocacy happens. The historical problem with marketing is that it is "interruptive" in nature, trying to impose a brand on the customer.

This is most apparent in TV advertising. These "passive customer bases" will ultimately be replaced by the "active customer communities". Brand engagement happens within those conversations. P2P is now being referred as Social Computing and is likely to be the most disruptive force in the future of marketing.

PREDICTIVE MODELING

This refers to algorithms that are being successfully applied in marketing problems (both a regression as well as a classification problem).

Companies wishing to reach potential employees on a global scale, while declaring a valuable employer promise worldwide, can benefit from incorporating international search engine marketing into their employer branding strategy.

MULTILINGUAL SOCIAL MEDIA

An effective way to deliver your employee brand to an international audience is through multilingual social media. Multilingual search engine optimisation for keywords relating to your employer brand is another useful endeavour.

Since you are essentially selling yourself to your workforce, you should approach global employer branding in much the same way you would approach global product or service marketing.

While some companies may cringe at the thought of spending more time and money on marketing, multilingual web marketing offers a cost-effective route to build a buzz-worthy employer brand.

KEYWORD AND SEARCH ENGINE OPTIMISATION COMPETITION

As the competition for English keywords rises, it is

becoming much more difficult to achieve decent return on investment in pay-per-click and search engine optimisation campaigns. However, the competition remains low internationally as many companies overseas have been slower to understand the branding benefits of search engine optimisation.

GLOBAL MARKETS

While the UK internet market nears penetration, more and more countries overseas are going online. The number of Chinese internet users has surpassed that of the US. There is plenty of room for this number to grow, as China's current internet penetration only represents one-eighth of its population.

There has been a 1,575 percent rise in the number of Arabic speakers online, along with an 800 percent increase in Russian internet users, over the past five years. Closer to home, the French and Germans are now spending more on online travel than the UK. These all represent significant markets for your employer brand.

WEB MARKETING STRATEGY & PAY-PER-CLICK

However, international audiences can be tricky to reach without a suitable international web marketing strategy. Brand recognition and perception varies widely according to the culture, so it is essential to really do you research before getting started.

I'll give you a few tips for how you can begin planning your strategy, according to your budget.

SMALL BUDGETS

Companies with a limited SEO budget should begin with market scoping. In other words, find out which international markets might be interested in your employer message. We at OBAN always take this first step with clients to establish just how much demand there is and then build a strategy. A low-cost entry point to begin taking your brand global would be to set up a pay-per-click campaign in different markets that leads to landing pages either in the local language or English. This can prove to be a great toe-in-the-water exercise.

If your budget allows it, have your website optimised for the keywords that your target culture is likely to associate with your brand. A recent study by Google and Enquiro research showed a 16 percent increase in brand association when the brand appeared in both the top ad and top organic listing.

MEDIUM BUDGETS

Companies with mid-size budgets should begin by building an international website with an international search engine optimisation strategy.

In addition, they should think about establishing a presence on social networking websites. As the popular social media sites differ from country to country, the companies that can afford the research should study their target markets to ensure they aim their employer brand message at the most popular websites.

There are also very niche social networking websites that can be used according to the nature of the company and its business strategies.

PR

Submission of press releases about the employer brand in local languages is something else that should be considered. Medium-sized businesses might want to collaborate with international PR companies to send their localised press releases through the effective channels in their target international markets.

LARGE BUDGETS

Larger companies will want to look at creating their own social media websites. Brand introduction is usually not an issue with this size of company, since they have their audience and usually benefit from good brand awareness. We recommend, in this case, that they create social media websites focused on their core business, to engage their audience and potential employees in different ways with their brand both directly and indirectly. Keep in mind that research shows that different cultures react differently (Jupiter, May 2008) to brand and social media and so what works in countries like the UK will not work in countries like Korea or Russia.

VIRAL ADVERTISING

Viral advertising is another area that large size companies can afford to invest in. This can be in the form of a short video or a game, relating to your employer brand. Viral marketing is a great way to generate a buzz about the benefits of working for your company.

INTERNATIONAL EMPLOYER BRANDING

Savvy companies with the potential to go global are beginning to think ahead, buying local domains and launching sites locally, allowing them better control of their international brand reputation. With over 70 percent of internet users not speaking English (around 900 million people), an employer branding campaign in English-only will mean that companies are greatly restricting their message in an increasingly competitive marketplace.

Your job as a salesperson for a radio or television station, a magazine, an Internet website, or any other medium is to sell time or space to display an advertiser's message. But what you are really selling is an estimate of the number of people who will be exposed to that message. The more people who see the advertising, the more money you get. Media sales are one of the few professions where the product you are selling is made by someone else–the research company that produces those estimates. To be an effective salesperson, you need to understand what the numbers mean, where they come from, their strengths and weaknesses, and the simple math that drives how you use them.

This chapter begins with research concepts that apply to all media–the general principles of media research that media planners and buyers use when they talk about a media plan. Then we will see how these concepts apply to each of the major media. We will take a brief look at the five "impossible" questions that every salesperson encounters in the course of their work - questions that media research cannot definitively answer. The chapter wraps up with an annotated list of media research resources available free on the Internet.

PRINCIPLES OF MEDIA RESEARCH

TARGET AUDIENCE

All media planning begins with a statement of the target audience, which is a description of the people an advertiser is trying to reach. The target audience is the most important marketing decision an advertiser will make because it drives all of an advertiser's subsequent decisions, and all of your decisions as you sell your medium.

Which programs have the largest audience for this target audience? Which programs have the greatest percent of the target audience among its viewers? When is the best time to reach them? What promotional materials, what colors, what style will be most appealing to this target group?

This core marketing decision is not always obvious; an advertiser may need your help. For example, everyone with a house needs carpets, but the carpet store's target audience is usually the person who makes the purchase decision. Customer research you have access to may reveal that women are the first to notice that the old carpet needs replacing, but it is a joint decision between husband and wife about which store to go to and which carpet to buy.

The same research may find that the majority of carpet buyers are between the ages of 35 and 54. So the primary target audience for this advertiser might be adults between the ages 35 and 54, expressed in media shorthand as A35-54.

GEOGRAPHY

When we think about where people live, it is usually in political or even postal terms: states, cities, counties and perhaps Zip Codes. For media sales, what matters is the geographic area where the advertising can be seen or heard, although for research purposes, that area must be adjusted to reflect the counties reported in the U.S. Census. For national television on the broadcast networks, cable or syndication, the coverage area is the entire country. For local radio it is the counties that are covered by a station's signal, generally the Standard Metropolitan Statistical Area (SMSA). For local television, it is the counties in the Designated Market Area (DMA), which Nielsen defines as all the counties where the stations of a given city get the plurality of viewing. More about DMAs later.

TARGET AUDIENCE UNIVERSE

Media coverage areas are defined in terms of counties because we need the census data to tell us how many people live there. This Universe Estimate (UE) is the denominator that will be used to calculate ratings. Knowing that 75,000 people watch the early news on a television station is interesting, but to be meaningful for comparison purposes, it must be expressed as a percent of the people living in the area. Rating services such as Nielsen and Arbitron report this UE for every age/sex demographic.

So, for instance, in 2007 there were 2,027,006 men between the ages of 25 and 54 living in television households in the Chicago television market (DMA). The age breaks are defined by the Census Bureau, so, for instance, there is no UE (and, therefore, no rating) for men age 27 to 42 – an group not defined by the Census Bureau. The television UE is expressed as the number of people living in households with a TV set because most, but not every, home has one.

ADVERTISING IMPRESSIONS

An advertising impression is a single exposure of a message to one person in the target audience. This sounds simple, but the exact meaning of exposure is different for each medium, and is governed by the way the medium is measured by the research companies. For television, it can mean the people who push a button on Nielsen's People Meter to indicate they are watching television. But, are they paying attention to the set? Do they watch every minute? Do they remember to punch out of the meter when they go to the bathroom or put the kids to bed? Do they continue watching during commercials? These are the kind of questions that are discussed at industry conferences, but the only thing that matters to you as a salesperson is the number reported by Nielsen. In smaller markets, a television impression means the viewer wrote in a time- formatted diary that he/she was watching a channel during a given quarter-hour of the day.

The diary cannot hope to accurately reflect the channel surfing usually associated with TV viewing, but this is the best Nielsen can do for smaller markets that cannot afford the expensive people meter methodology. Radio is measured by the Arbitron company with a quarter-hour formatted diary where listeners record the station they were listening to. Over the next few years, the radio diary will be replaced by the Portable People Meter that detects an inaudible code to identify the station. Note that the definition of impression will change from "listening to the radio" to "being within earshot of the loudspeaker."

GROSS IMPRESSIONS

Just as cooks never talk about one bean or one pea in a recipe, advertisers never talk about one impression. The concept of gross impressions begins with the total number of people watching a television programme or listening to a radio station at a given moment. This can easily number in the millions. In the average minute of the 2007 Super Bowl, 24.3 million men age 25-54 were watching the action. Thus, a single commercial in the Super Bowl was seen by 24.3 million men 25-54 and that commercial received 24.3 million impressions. But the concept of gross impressions is more than that. It is the simple addition of the impressions every time an ad is displayed.

GROSS IMPRESSIONS = The simple addition of impressions every time an ad runs.

In the 2007 Super Bowl, a Bud Light commercial ran 6 times. Each time it was watched by 24.3 million M25-54. By the end of the evening, Bud Light had accumulated 145.8 million gross impressions (6 X 24.3 = 145,800,000). Note that this does not account for duplication. Surely some of the men saw the commercial several times, but gross impressions reflect the total media weight for the game. The same concept applies over any period of time and any number of programs. Planners typically think in terms of weekly media weight.

RATING

Talking about hundreds of millions of impressions is mind-boggling. It is much more meaningful to think of the impressions as the percent of the target audience universe. This percentage is called a rating. To calculate it, simply divide the impressions by the target universe and multiply by 100 to get the percentage.

RATING = The percent of the universe that is watching or listening to a given programme.

According to the Nielsen national UE, 60.4 million men age 25-54 live in United States television households. And we know that 24.3 million of them watched the average minute of the 2007 Super Bowl. So, 24.3 million divided by 60.4 million = 40.3 percent. Ratings are always expressed in terms of the appropriate demographic, so a salesperson might say that the Super Bowl got a 40.3 rating against men 25-54. Expressed more precisely, 40.3 percent of men age 25-54 were watching (had their People Meter button pushed) during the average minute of the 2007 Super Bowl.

This is the Average Minute or Average Audience (AA) rating. Note that this 40.3 rating is for the Super Bowl, which is about the only programme on television to get such a high rating. The rating of most prime time network TV programs is less than 5, and cable ratings are generally less than 1. The same concept works in a local television market; although, because of the way a diary is formatted, ratings are expressed as an average-quarter-hour (AQH) audience instead of the average minute. As noted earlier, the Chicago DMA has 2.03 million men age 25-54. According to Nielsen, 951,000 of them watched the average-quarter-hour of the 2007 Super Bowl. So 951,000/ 2.03 million is a 47 rating. Expressed as a sentence, 47 percent of Chicago men 25-54 watched the average-quarter-hour of the 2007 Super Bowl. Since the Bears were playing, it's not surprising that the Chicago rating was higher than the national rating.

Because radio is still measured with a diary in most markets, a radio rating is also expressed as an average-quarter-hour (AQH) audience. Also, because local radio is sold by day part instead of by programme, a rating refers to an average-quarter-hour of the broad time period.

So if a Chicago radio station gets a 1.3 AQH M18-34 rating in morning drive time, it means 1.3 percent of the men age 18-34 who live in the Chicago metro area have written in their diary that they listened to that station during the average-quarter-hour (the average of the 80 quarter hours) Monday-Friday from 6-10 A.M.

Because radio advertisers buy spots that are evenly rotated through all the days and times in the daypart, the average is the most practical measure of a station's audience.

Magazine advertising is sold issue by issue, but there are several different ways of measuring how many people will see the advertising.

MRI shows its respondents a black- and-white rendering of the magazine's logo and asks if they are sure they have "read or looked into" it during the last publication period (a week for weeklies, a month for monthlies, and so forth).

Because this question can apply to any particular issue of the magazine, the result is a measure of how many people read the average issue – called the Average Issue Audience or AIA. Newspaper readership is also defined in terms of AIA (weekday or weekend/Sunday), but the measure is less important as a sales tool because newspapers are primarily evaluated in terms of the geographic area they serve. Although the math of an AIA is the same as for a rating, the word "rating" is reserved for broadcast audiences.

Another word for a magazine or newspaper's Average Issue Audience is its coverage. The concept of a rating is different when it comes to the Internet. When an advertiser runs a commercial in a television programme, instantly millions of people see the ad. By contrast, Internet advertising is bought one impression at a time at a price often based on cost- per-thousand impressions. That can be divided by the universe to get the same thing as a rating, but unlike broadcast, an Internet website's rating is determined by how many impressions the advertiser wants to buy, not by the medium.

Unlike broadcast, where advertisers must use a sample to estimate how many people are exposed to an ad and then what effect it has on sales, Internet advertisers know with great precision how many times an ad was served, how many times an ad was clicked on, and how many times people bought something after clicking on an ad, even if they don't know who saw or clicked on it.

Internet advertising is sold based on two different models— an impressions model and a performance model. For the time being, the term that has the most meaning for Internet advertising is gross impressions.

GROSS RATING POINTS

For planning purposes, advertisers add the ratings of all the programs where the advertising appears to get gross rating points or GRPs. This is the same concept as gross impressions, only expressed as the sum of the rating points.

GROSS RATING POINTS = The addition of rating points every time an ad runs.

Gross rating points are typically used to describe the message weight per week or per month, although it can be used for any period of time. Following is an example of a schedule that will deliver 120 gross rating points a week: Three commercials, each with a 15 rating = 45 GRPs Five commercials, each with a 10 rating = 50 GRPs Five commercials, each with a 5 rating = 25 GRPs Total weekly GRPs 120 GRPs Is it possible to have more than 100 GRPs?

Sure. Since GRPs are the simple addition of the ratings, there is no limit to the number of points that can be scheduled. Quick-serve restaurants, movies, and other heavy promotional advertisers typically run at least 250 GRPs in a week. Occasionally a television advertiser will run four or five hundred GRPs a week, giving viewers the feeling that they see the commercial every time they turn on a television set. Although it would be nice, no advertiser is going to buy all the planned GRPs on one station.

As a salesperson, you are concerned with getting your share of the buy.

You will probably not be told how many total GRPs are being bought or what the total budget is.

But those numbers exist, and are at the top of the buyer's mind as she works to buy the required GRPs for the budget she has been given.

The GRP concept can be extended to other media such as radio, magazines, and newspapers. In magazines, for example, gross rating points equals the average issue audience times the number of ad insertions.

For example: People magazine's average issue audience (coverage) of Women age 18+ = 25.4%

Number of ads to be placed in People = 5, thus gross rating points (GRPs) = 127.0

An advertiser who runs a single insertion in several magazines would calculate gross rating points by adding the target audience coverage of each insertion. W18+ coverage of People = 25.4% W18+ coverage of Reader's Digest = 19.6 W18+ coverage of Shape = 4.5 W18+ coverage of New Yorker = 1.7 Gross rating points 51.2 (rounded to 51 GRPs) For many years the Outdoor Advertising Association of America has used a showing as its basic unit of sale for the outdoor industry. A showing is defined as the number of poster panels needed in a market to produce a daily effective circulation (daily vehicular traffic past any of the boards) equal to a certain percentage of its population.

So a 100 showing would equal the number of billboards needed so that the daily effective circulation is equal to the market's population, 100 percent, or 100 GRPs per day. Other units of sale would be expressed as fractions of this basic unit: a 75 showing is 75 gross rating points daily, a 50 showing is 50 gross rating points daily, and so on. The outdoor industry is working to replace the showing concept with impressions based the number of people passing each billboard in a market every day. This would allow outdoor to be planned the same as other media; however industry observers expect it will be several years before such a fundamental change is implemented.

REACH AND FREQUENCY

It should be obvious that gross rating points do not account for duplication. In the magazine example, a reader of both People and Reader's Digest would be exposed to the ad twice, while a reader of all four magazines might see the ad four times.

REACH = The percent of a target audience that is exposed to an ad at least once.

FREQUENCY = The average number of times that a person who was reached sees an ad.

These three concepts are bound together with the equation: GROSS RATING POINTS = Reach x Frequency.

For example, a television schedule of 200 W25-54 GRPs in prime time is a collection of spots whose W25-54 ratings add up to 200. Computer models based on Nielsen data tell us this schedule will be seen by (will reach) 61 percent of these women an average of 3.3 times (61 x 3.3 = 200). Some will see the commercial only once, others will see it many times, but the average woman who was reached will see it 3.3 times. Conversely, 39 percent will never see the commercial.

The third home was exposed once, the fourth home three times, and so on. By the end of the week, the four telecasts have accumulated 110 GRPs, reaching 60 percent of the homes one or more times, and the average home that was reached saw the commercial 1.83 times. Other terms that are sometimes used to describe net reach are cumulative audience (referred to as cume), net unduplicated audience, or net reach.

Each is correct, but in popular usage media buyers are more likely to say, "The reach of these four programs is 60 percent." Note how GRPs and reach increase with each telecast. Frequency is calculated as GRPs divided by reach. So, in the last row of the table, 90/ 50 = 1.8 and 110 / 60 = 1.83. Four homes (40 percent) never saw the commercial–were never reached. Two homes (20 percent) saw the commercial only once. Three homes (30 percent) saw it twice. And one home saw it three times.

THE SALES UNIT AND MEDIA EFFICIENCY

Everything that is sold comes in some kind of unit. Meat is sold in pounds, gasoline in gallons, fabric in yards, and so forth. In television and radio the unit of sale is typically the 30-second commercial; in magazines, the page; and in newspapers, the column inch.

But the unit itself is meaningless without the associated audience that tells us how many people will see it. By long-standing convention, advertisers use cost-per-thousand impressions as the measure of media efficiency. It is calculated by simply dividing the cost of the ad by thousands of impressions.

Here is an example: A 30-second spot on "Boston Legal" costs $160,000. The average minute W25-54 impressions = 2,800,000 Cost-per-thousand (CPM) W25-54 = $160,000 / 2,800 = $57.14 At the same time, another channel is running "Law & Order: Criminal Intent."

A 30- second spot on this show costs $152,000 and is watched by 2,221,000 W25-54. This is less money but proportionally even fewer target viewers. The CPM for this spot is $152,000 / 2,221 = $68.44. The programme has a higher CPM and so is less efficient in reaching W 25-54 than "Boston Legal."

BROADCAST PLANNING WITH COST-PER-RATING-POINT (CPP)

CPM is useful for comparing the efficiency of different programs, schedules, or media, but for planning purposes the cost-per- rating-point (CPP) metric is more practical. CPP is used when planning spot television or radio. As we saw earlier, the 2.221 million W25-54 impressions for "Law & Order: Criminal Intent" can be expressed as a rating. There are 62.1 million women age 25-54 in the United States. The show's rating among this group is 2.221 million / 62.1 million = .0357, or expressed as a percent, or rating, 3.57. So the CPP of this network programme is $152,000 / 3.57 = $42,577. This seems like a lot of money, but for perspective, a 30-second commercial in the 2007 Super Bowl cost $2.4 million and was watched by 33 percent of W25-54, giving a CPP of almost $72,300. But that's the Super Bowl, and as they say, "If you have to ask how much it costs, you can't afford it." Local market cost-per-rating-point information is provided by SQAD, Inc.

The household CPP gives a general idea of the cost of a schedule, and is used here for illustration, but most planning is based on demographic costs-per-point that SQAD sells to its subscribers. A schedule of 200 GRPs per week for 4 weeks costs $1,499,200 (200 x 4 x $1,874). Note that the cost varies by market size. This is because there are more people in one percent (one rating point) of New York than there are in one percent of Atlanta. Although the CPM may be similar, the CPP reflects this population difference. Also note that the cost varies by daypart. Prime time programming has broad appeal and sets the tone for popular culture in America. Daytime television has a narrower range of programme types. The audience is much smaller and demographically less diverse. As a result, the cost-per-rating-point is lower. This is not unlike differences in the cost-per-pound for different cuts of beef.

RESEARCH ACCURACY

Research accuracy is determined by the size and representativeness of the sample and the methodology that is used to gather the data. As we consider these, we should keep in mind that research companies are first and foremost businesses. They must find buyers for their products and at the same time make a reasonable profit for their investors. This forces them to balance quality with cost as they determine the size of the sample, the way the sample is recruited, and in the way the data are collected. To a large extent, research is as accurate as the suppliers' customers can afford.

THE SAMPLE

Since a census (counting everyone) is not affordable or

practical for marketing purposes, research companies take a sample and project the findings to the entire population, or the universe.

This is totally acceptable as long as the sample is representative of the universe, that is, as long as the people in the sample behave in the same manner as the universe to which they are being projected.

There are three broad types of samples, presented here in order their cost. The *random sample* is the most expensive. It is used as the basis for ratings that serve as the currency for radio, television, and magazines.

It is the only type for which researchers can calculate a statistical margin of error. In a random sample, ideally everyone in the universe has an equal chance of being included –light viewers, heavy viewers, young, old, men, women, rich, poor, city, suburban, rural–people from all parts of the universe have an equal chance of being a respondent.

Conceptually, a random sample could be obtained by getting a list of everyone in the universe (the sample frame), sorting them by a random number, contacting every Nth name and then asking for their participation.

But getting an all-inclusive list is difficult, and then making contact is even more of a challenge these days with answering machines, gated communities, do-not-call lists, and general hostility to market research. Companies such as Nielsen Media Research use especially trained Membership Representatives who make multiple attempts to contact selected homes and convince them to join a sample.

Detailed rules govern the selection of alternate homes if the first, randomly chosen home, continues to refuse. Despite all the care taken to recruit a random sample, its final composition may still not look like the universe, because peoples' willingness to participate in a survey varies by age, income, ethnicity, and other factors.

Young adult males are especially hard to recruit. To correct for this problem, research companies weight the results to bring the sample demographics in line with the census. If the sample has a smaller percentage of young adults than is found in the general population, each person who does agree to participate will be given a larger weight (will count for more people).

At the same time, easily recruited older adults, who are over-represented, will be given a smaller weight. The sum of all the weights is the number of target audience people in the universe.

The *representative sample,* sometimes called a quota sample, is a less expensive alternative to the weighted random sample. From the Census, the researchers know what percent of the sample should fall into each demographic cell. The cells (quotas) for older adults are easy to fill. But the quota for young men is extremely difficult and may require contacting hundreds of candidates before enough are found.

Although the demographic cells may match the proportionality of the U.S. census, the shortcoming of a quota sample is that those people who quickly agree to participate may have different viewing/listening habits from those who only agree after multiple attempts to gain their cooperation.

The least expensive, and least accurate, sample is the *volunteer* or *convenience sample.* It is made up of people who respond to a mass mailing, are intercepted in a mall, or respond to an Internet solicitation.

Recruitment attempts are generally accompanied by some form of reward or payment for their participation. Because of its low cost, the Internet is becoming a popular convenience sample for research that does not require the discipline and accountability of research that will be used as currency for media sales.

ERROR IN MEDIA RESEARCH

There are two kinds of error in survey research: Sampling error and Non-sampling error. *Sampling error* exists solely because the research uses a sample instead of a complete census.

It is based on statistics and the mathematics of probability. The margin of error can be precisely calculated for surveys that take a random sample and project audience estimates to a universe. By projection, we mean that if 5 percent of the women age 25-54 in a Nielsen sample watch "Boston Legal," then Nielsen will report that 5 percent of all the 25-54 year-old women in America watch "Boston Legal."

The sampling error does not depend on the size of the universe (the market) being measured. Just as a nurse doesn't need to draw more blood from a tall man than from a short one to identify their blood type, a researcher does not need to talk to more people in a large market than a small one to know how many watch a given television programme. From a statistical point of view, a sample of 5,000 people in Missoula, Montana has the same margin of error as a sample of 5,000 people in New York City.

This is true as long as the samples accurately reflect the population. Sampling error is also affected by the size of the rating being measured. For surveys with a given sample size, the relative margin of error (the margin of error divided by the rating) is smaller for high rated programs than for low rated ones.

Sampling error can be reduced by recruiting a larger sample—the more people in the sample, the smaller the margin of error.

But it follows the square root law–it takes a sample four times as large to cut the sampling error in half. Since most of the cost of research is in recruiting the sample, this can be a costly option.

Sampling error can also be reduced by averaging the rating over a longer time period or more telecasts. The more measurements there are, the smaller the margin of error. The least accurate rating is for a single low rated broadcast.

Researchers acknowledge the statistical margin of error, but in practice it is viewed as a simple fact of life. Although the theoretical true rating can be larger or smaller than what is reported, it is of little day-to-day concern because the resulting rating estimate is satisfactory for media planning and buying purposes.

Non-sampling error is much more important because its bias, while understandable, cannot be quantified. It is caused by the messy reality of the research process. Evaluation of research suppliers focuses on how well they control the four kinds of non-sampling errors.

Sample Frame Bias

The sample frame is a list with the name, address, phone number or other way of contacting anyone in the universe from which the sample is drawn. Bias exists if some members of the universe are not listed, and so have no chance of being selected for the sample, and if their behaviour is different from the average person. For example, not so long ago researchers commonly used the list of numbers in a telephone exchange (the phone book) as the sample frame.

That is no longer acceptable because it excludes cell-phone-only households that tend to be younger, have higher income, and are more technologically sophisticated. Because of these consistent demographic differences, people in cell-phone- only homes are likely they have different media habits from those in wired homes, and as a result, the survey will undercount programs that appeal to that group.

Sample frame bias can be overcome by using an Area Probability Sample that divides a market into groups of addresses–perhaps one or two city blocks. These areas are numbered and randomly chosen.

Than an interviewer goes to the neighborhood and literally walks door to door in an attempt to recruit every Nth home. Alternatively, letters are sent to every address in the selected area. With an Area Probability Sample, selection does not depend on the characteristics of the household. This methodology is used by Nielsen, Mediamark Research & Intelligence LLC (MRI) and other research services whose reports are used as currency for media sales.

Non-response Bias

This bias results from households that have been selected at random but are unable or unwilling to cooperate with the survey. It results from simple refusals, language barriers, long-term not at home, access barriers such as apartment buildings or gated communities, unsafe neighborhoods, and incomplete questionnaires.

As with sample frame bias, non-response bias is important to the extent that the non-responders are different from the people who do cooperate.

By definition, it is impossible to know the demographics of people who refuse to provide that information, though researchers can get an idea by comparing the behaviour of people who readily cooperate with those who require multiple visits from the recruiter before they will join. There is an industry campaign to improve response rates, but it is an ongoing challenge.

Response Bias

This bias results from answers that do not reflect true behaviour, and there is a systematic effect. Examples are inaccurate diary keeping, channel confusion, magazine title confusion, and poor memory.

Modern electronic systems like Nielsen's people meter are subject to response bias if people fail to punch out when they leave the room, and if there are differences between demographic groups. Another example of response bias is seen in respondent's reluctance to accurately report their income, race, or education. Like the other forms of non-sampling error, this type of bias is impossible to quantify.

Processing Errors

These errors occur during the mechanical processing of the data. They include data entry errors, editing mistakes, and errors in the software when calculating or printing the reports. These errors occur more frequently these days as a result of new calculations that account for the effect of TV and other types of digital video recorders (DVRs) on the ratings.

An example of processing error occurred after Hurricane Katrina with the failure of the telephone system that transmits viewing data to Nielsen's Technology Centre in Florida. In another now classic example, a research company double printed one page of the report book and omitted the next. The embarrassing error was discovered at a sales call as the research sales rep was showing the rating report to a client.

THE MEDIA RATING COUNCIL

This discussion of research errors is not to imply that the ratings are deeply flawed, but to demonstrate that nothing is perfect. The research suppliers take great pains to minimize non- sampling error.

Their efforts are audited in detail by the Media Rating Council. The MRC is a non-profit industry organization that was established at the behest of Congress in 1964 to maintain standards in media ratings through the oversight of methodologies and implementation.

Its mission is to, "secure for the media industry and related users audience measurement that is valid, reliable and effective." It accomplishes this mission by setting standards and conducting detailed audits that are performed by an independent CPA firm to verify compliance.

Membership includes more than 100 broadcast and cable networks, magazine publishers, radio station groups, radio networks, advertising and media buying agencies, and other users of research data. The research firms themselves are not allowed to be members.

The key to the MRC's success is its stringent policy of non-disclosure. The audited research companies (Nielsen, Arbitron, and MRI, for example) allow complete access to their proprietary processes with the understanding that they will remain secret.

Upon completion of an audit, the MRC will only report that the service is accredited or not. In the latter case, no reason is given for the denial. The mere existence of the MRC and its accreditation process gives the industry assurance that the research is being conducted properly.

MEDIA RESEARCH CONCEPTS SPECIFIC TO THE MAJOR MEDIA

Up to now we have presented audience and research concepts that are common to all media. But in addition to these generalizations, each medium has its own research that salespeople will use every day as the tools of their trade.

Television

The broadcast ratings industry has been evolving for more than seventy-five years. In the early 1930s, radio advertisers decided they needed to know how many people were listening to their commercials, so they formed the Cooperative Analysis of Broadcasting (CAB).

This group commissioned the Crossley Company to conduct a survey of station listening. Crossley used a telephone recall methodology in which randomly telephoned individuals were asked to recall the stations that people in their household listened to over the past day.

In the 1930s, most radio listening occurred in a household or family setting; today's radio ratings are calculated for individuals and not households. In 1942 the A.C. Nielsen Company announced it would begin measuring commercial network radio audiences with a mechanical device, the Audimeter, which purportedly removed human error.

The result was the Nielsen Radio Index. This device used a stylus to make a scratch on a moving role of film that was mailed back to Nielsen's headquarters, then in Skokie, Illinois. The original Audimeters are on display today in many Nielsen offices.

The Nielsen Television Index began in 1950 using paper diaries. The Recordimeter, a mechanical device similar to the Audimeter, was introduced in 1956 to supplement the diary and record which channel the set was tuned to. This combination of a television set meter to record what programme was playing, and a diary to identify who was watching, continues to this day as one of the three ways Nielsen measures television audiences.

The Designated Market Area (DMA)

The most commonly used geographic area for local television is the Designated Marketing Area (DMA). There are 210 DMAs in the United States. Each is made up of all the counties that spend the plurality of viewing hours tuned to the TV stations of a given market. The majority of DMAs consist of whole counties, though some are split if a topographic feature such as a mountain range creates different viewing patterns.

For instance, the Sierras split El Dorado County between the Sacramento, CA and the Reno, NV DMAs. County assignments to DMAs are updated annually, resulting in minor revisions, mostly in the fringe counties where a few viewers can swing the audience.

The Total Survey Area (TSA) counts all viewers to the stations in a market, including viewers who live in counties outside the DMA. For local television sales, stations typically report DMA ratings and TSA (000) thousands of viewers. Television time is sold either by programme or by time periods know as dayparts.

NIELSEN METHODOLOGY

Nielsen uses three methodologies to measure television viewing: - Nielsen People Meter (NPM) for national television and the largest local markets - Integrated set meter/diary – mid-size markets – due to be replaced by the People Meter - Diary only – small markets The Nielsen People Meter (NPM) is the most precise and accurate method for measuring television audiences, and is used for broadcast network, cable, syndication, and spot TV in the top ten DMAs.

The NPM consists of two parts. The human interface is a small box that sits on top of each set in the house that has a screen five inches or larger. Household members use this to record who is watching. A row of lights on the front blinks red when the set is first turned on. Each person is assigned a button, and there is space to identify the age/sex of visitors.

Household members are instructed to push their button if they are "watching television." So if Dad is watching the football game, he would punch his button and his light would change from red to green. Mom, who may be in the room but is doing something else, would not punch hers. Her looking up from time to time, and even watching a commercial, would not be recorded. From the moment when someone's button is pushed, every channel the set is tuned to is recorded and sent by telephone to Nielsen's computers. The meter reports viewing in one-minute increments, allowing Nielsen to report the number of viewers in the average minute of the programme (the AA rating).

The second part of the People Meter is another, larger box off in a closet somewhere that identifies to which channel the set is tuned and sends the data by telephone line to Nielsen's computers in Florida. This is a challenge in today's 500 channel television environment.

The Active/Passive or A/P meter identifies the station being watched with an inaudible code imbedded in its audio signal (the "active" part).

A wire carries the signal from each set's loudspeaker or audio output jack to the meter. Passive digital signal matching is used to identify channels that are not encoded. Together they achieve almost 100 percent accuracy in identifying what the viewer is watching.

The A/P meter was specifically designed to handle today's digital environment, including cable boxes, satellites, digital video recorders (DVR) like TiVo, high definition television (HDTV), video games, PC viewing, and other forms of video delivery that have not even been invented. The largest DMA's below the top ten are measured by a combination of a meter (the Recordimeter) that electronically records how long the set is turned on and what channel it is tuned to. Respondents write down who is watching in a diary.

This meter/diary integration is the same methodology that has been used since 1956, and is scheduled to be replaced with the A/P meter in 56 markets (70 percent of U.S. TV households) by 2011. Although they are known popularly as Local People Meter (LPM) markets, the hardware and all of the procedures are identical to the way Nielsen measures national television – the only difference is that the sample is weighted to represent the local market's population instead of the nation's.

The LPM has minute-by-minute granularity that would allow reporting the average minute (AA) audience, but by long-standing practice all spot markets, even LPM markets, continue reporting the average-quarter-hour (AQH) audience. Nielsen is working on simpler, less expensive versions of the A/P meter for markets rank 57 to 125. But until it is released, and indefinitely for markets ranked 126 and above, all viewing will be captured in a diary.

Respondents write down what station/programme they are watching in quarter-hour increments, causing ratings to be defined in terms of the number of viewers during the average-quarter-hour (AQH) of a programme or daypart.

While researchers are quick to admit that Nielsen's diary is the least accurate methodology, especially in today's world, it is also the least expensive. Like all media research, the bulk of the cost is borne by the media that use the data to support their sales efforts. Buying agencies pay relatively little.

As markets get smaller, the fixed cost of research becomes a bigger burden on stations that have limited ability to raise their ad rates.

So, while the diary methodology is deeply flawed, it is all that stations in the smaller markets can afford. On the other hand, the diary has the advantage of providing a direct link to the viewers in the form of written comments on the last page. These are a popular source of information for station managers who make an annual visit to specially provided reading rooms in Nielsen's Technology Centre near Tampa, Florida.

RESEARCH IN SUPPORT OF SELLING TELEVISION

Television's unit of sale is the 30-second spot, but what you are really selling is an estimate of how many people will watch a programme at some time in the future. Television sales are all about predicting future ratings and coming to an agreement between the buyer and seller.

The following describes the process, the research, and the judgments that go into that prediction. The core arithmetic is: RATING = HUT x Share Homes Using Television (HUT): By convention, the following refers to the HUT which would be used to calculate a generic household rating. The same logic and arithmetic applies to Persons Using Television (PUT) which is used to calculate a demographic target (persons) rating. Almost all media sales are based on persons ratings. (e.g. W25-54). HUT = The percent of homes using television. It turns out that the percent of homes or persons watching television on a given day and time is relatively stable from year to year..

The HUT level does change from month to month, especially in prime time and early fringe when people are out of the house in the early evening hours of summer. Daytime and late fringe are much less affected. Each market has its own pattern of HUT level changes.

In Phoenix, for instance, the HUT level goes up in the summer when people stay indoors to avoid the extremely hot weather. But whatever the market, buyers and sellers generally agree on what the future HUT will be for any given daypart and month. That division of the pie is quantified as each station's share. SHARE = The percent of HUT/PUT that are tuned to a given programme. You know from the earlier discussion that a rating is the percent of the homes or persons in a market who are watching a programme.

The sum of the ratings from all the programs on air at a given time equals the HUT. And the sum of the shares is 100 percent. Sunday is a heavier-than-average night for viewing television.

On this particular Sunday, 69 percent of the homes were watching television from 8-9 P.M. Eighteen percent of the homes using television were watching "Desperate Housewives," or 12.4 percent of all homes were watching the programme (69.0 x 0.18). The same logic applies for all the programs on air at that time. These metrics are reported for national television in the Nielsen Television Index, and for each market by the Nielsen Station Index "Viewers In Profile" report. They are available for purchase in hard copy or from online systems provided by Nielsen and other suppliers. Projecting next year's ratings: If a spot on this November "Desperate Housewives" telecast in Chicago cost $32,000, the cost-per-rating point (CPP) would be $2,580 ($32,000/12.4).

Note that this is more than the $1,874 average CPP for Chicago prime time reported earlier. "Desperate Housewives," as a high-rated appointment viewing programme, carries a higher-than- average CPP.

How much should the station charge for that spot next June when the prime time HUT is 56.0 percent? It comes down to a judgment of how well the programme will perform next year – that is, what share it will get. If the share stays the same, the rating will be 56 x 18% = 10.08. At the same CPP, the station should charge $26,006 (10.08 x $2,580). But it is a judgment call to suggest that the share will stay the same. The Chicago ABC station salesperson would point to the growing success of the programme in Chicago, the introduction of exciting new characters, and the weakness of the competition. "Our research people project "Desperate Housewives" will get a 20 share next year – well worth the $28,896 we will charge." (56 HUT x 20 share = 11.2 rating X $2,580 CPP = $28,896).

The buyer, of course, sees it differently. "Oh, give me a break! By next June 'Desperate Housewives' will have gotten tired. The show may have new talent, but that's because they're replacing two of the favourite characters who are leaving to make a movie. And besides, next June the show will be in reruns. I don't think it will do better than a 14 – it won't be worth more than $20,227." (56 HUT x 14 share = 7.8 rating X $2,580 CPP = $20, 227). This example is simplistic in the sense that advertising is sold as packages of spots that are evaluated against the bottom-line cost and target audience GRPs. But the concept and the math are the same, and a judgment must be made about the future share and rating of each programme in the package.

RADIO

In all but the smallest markets, radio audiences are measured by Arbitron, Inc. Rural America is surveyed by Eastlan Ratings which provides low cost radio ratings based on a telephone survey. Unlike the television DMA whose composition is determined by viewing patterns, the geographic unit of radio ratings is the Metro Survey Area. This is a commercial construct that generally corresponds to the U.S. Government's Metropolitan Area. As a convenience to marketers who plan television on a DMA basis, Arbitron will report the number of listeners in counties that make up the DMA, but the primary geographic unit for radio is the Metro. Listening estimates are obtained from a one-week Arbitron diary placed in households by way of a random sample.

Unlike a Nielson television diary that is formatted by quarter-hour, an Arbitron radio diary is unformatted. Nevertheless, audiences are reported as an average-quarter-hour (AQH) rating. This is the same rating concept that was discussed earlier. A 1.0 M18-34 rating of a Chicago radio station in morning drive time means that the during the average-quarter-hour of that time period, the station is listened to by 1.0 percent of the men age 18-34 who live in the Chicago Metro Area.

In addition to AQH estimates (rating, persons and share), Arbitron reports each station's cumulative audience – the estimated number of people who listened to the station during one or more quarter-hours over the days included in the daypart listed in the rating report. These two estimates, the AQH rating and cume are the principal metrics of radio research. Although Arbitron reports the audience for each season, buyers generally use a four-book average because radio audiences are far more stable than television programs.

Buyers divide the cume persons by the AQH persons, to get an indication of the station's audience turnover. For WAAA, an all-news station, listeners tune in for a few minutes to get the latest headlines, weather and sports, and then move on. The M-F 6a-7p 4- book turnover is 14.3 (10521/735) compared to 9.8 (2100/215) for WCCC, a soft music station, that has much longer time spent listening, a lower cume compared to the AQH, and so less turnover. It takes more spots per week on stations with high turnover (shorter time spent listening) to achieve its cume potential. Note that Arbitron reports radio audiences in hundreds (00) compared to television audiences shown in thousands (000).

The time spent listening varies for different demographic

groups and different seasons. In addition to the AQH, Cume and Time Spent Listening, Arbitron reports an Exclusive Cume (people who only listen to a single station for the whole week), place of listening (home, work, car, other), the audience duplication between stations, and the demographic/ethnic composition of each station's audience. As it is for television, the diary is an imperfect methodology to report radio listening due to frequent dial switching and human error in reporting to what station the radio is tuned. After many years of testing, Arbitron has developed the Portable People Meter (PPM), a cell- phone sized device that "hears" an inaudible code in the audio signal.

A motion detector ensures the device is being worn. At night, the respondent puts the device in a docking station that charges the battery and at the same time transmits the day's data to Arbitron's computers. The PPM changes the definition from "listening to the radio" to being within earshot of the loudspeaker. It has been in used as the currency in Philadelphia and Houston since 2007 and has been accredited by the Media Rating Council in Houston. Arbitron plans to replace the diary with the PPM in the top 50 markets, but there have been bumps in the road that may delay these plans. Any change in methodology changes the numbers produced. Stations measured by a PPM report fewer average-quarter-hour listeners but more cumulative listeners than were recorded in the diary.

This difference is due to listening picked up by the PPM that a respondent may have failed to enter in a diary. Since a station's price is based mainly on the AQH audience, the lower PPM numbers are causing stations to scrutinize the sample's age/sex and ethnic composition compared to the census, and the respondent's compliance with Arbitron's rules. The station's reaction is a reminder that media research is a bread and butter issue for them. Local radio is sold by daypart in each market. National radio (network radio) is sold by both daypart and programme. The network radio audience is reported by Arbitron in a service called RADAR (Radio's All Dimension Audience Research). The report is essentially a roll-up of the local diaries from each market. RADAR reports the audience to individual networks for the daypart AQH, the audience to all commercials aired on network-affiliated stations, and the audience to commercials broadcast within network programs. Aside from these differences, the core metrics of network radio are the same as local.

MAGAZINES

The currency of consumer magazine media sales is circulation, or the number of copies printed. While not every magazine has subscribers, all the major books (industry jargon for a magazine) are audited by the Audit Bureau of Circulations.

The ABC was created in 1914 by advertisers, advertising agencies, and publishers as an industry organization to independently verify circulation. Its audits provide detailed information about how many copies are sold and the characteristics of those sales.

The ABC pink sheet publisher's statement is a standard element in the media kit of every audited magazine. Guaranteed circulation may be the basis for rates, but advertisers want to know how many people read the magazines and their demographic composition. A number of research companies provide this information, but the two largest (and intensely competitive) services are Simmons and MRI. Both survey a random sample of 25-30,000 people/year – Simmons by mail, MRI by personal interview.

These single source surveys capture media exposure, product use, attitudes about a wide variety of subjects, and a broad range of demographics for each respondent. Agency buyers use research to determine which magazines should carry the advertising of a given product. The key concepts for magazines are coverage and composition. Coverage is analogous to the broadcast rating – it is the number or percent of the target audience that is exposed to the medium – in this case, the percent of the target universe that reads the magazine. Composition is the percent of the magazine's readers who fall into various demographic groups.

This example shows that People magazine is read by 19.3 percent of all American adults (42,375 /219,581). It is read by 12.8 percent of men and 25.4 percent of women (28,863 / 113,753). The magazine covers 25.4 percent of all women age 18+ which is the same concept as a rating.

Those 28,863 female People readers are 68.1 percent of all adult readers (28,863 / 42,375). These numbers are interesting, but they are only meaningful when put in the context of total adults.

This is the value of the Selectivity Index. 51.8 percent of all adults in America are women, but 68.1 percent of People's readers are women. If you saw someone on the street reading People, chances are that person is a woman. Put another way, a selectivity index of 131 means that a People magazine reader is 31 percent more likely to be a woman than the average adult (68.1/51.8). Conversely, the reader is 34 percent less likely to be a man. This example used simple demographics, but the same concept applies to product users.

For example, instead of gender we could have used medium-heavy users of bottled water. A research report would tell us that 48 percent of all adults are M-H users of bottled water. 55 percent of *People* magazine readers are M-H users. And so, *People* magazine readers are 15 percent more likely to be M-H bottled water users than the average adult.

The Selectivity Index is a key metric. It tells a buyer how well the magazine delivers against a target audience compared to the base of total adults. This, in combination with the magazine's ABC circulation analysis, coverage and composition, its CPM target audience, and the magazine's contribution to total schedule reach/frequency form the primary research considerations in a magazine buy.

SPECIALIZED RESEARCH SERVICES (NATIONAL BASE ONLY)

MRI and Simmons are broad single-source services that have been characterized as a mile wide and an inch deep. While they cover virtually every product and service used by American consumers, they do not go into much detail, and they do not report on niche markets that take a special effort to recruit a sample. Other services are available that focus just on narrow target audiences.

- Monroe Mendelsohn surveys homes with $85,000 household income.
- IPSOS US Business Elite surveys corporate senior management
- KMR-Group's MARS studies the media behaviour of persons with various ailments for pharmaceutical advertisers
- Erdos & Morgan's Opinion Leader study reports the media behaviour of opinion leaders classified by industry such as immigration, the environment, healthcare, and aerospace.

QUALITATIVE MEASURES: ENGAGEMENT

In addition to the previously mentioned metrics, research services publish a wealth of data on various *qualitative* aspects of a magazine's circulation and the reading experience. The Audit Bureau of Circulations (ABC) reports newsstand versus subscription sales, the number of copies sold at full price versus at a discount, the number of copies sold for one year versus longer terms, copies distributed to public places, and many other characteristics of the circulation that *may* be related to the value that a reader places on the magazine.

One assumption is that the more a magazine costs readers, the more likely they are to be engaged with it, and presumably the more likely they are to be influenced by its advertising.

MRI offers a number of measures of reader quality, including: number of issues read out of four, place of reading, actions taken as a result of reading the magazine, time spent reading, interest in advertising, and overall evaluation of the magazine as "one of my favorites."

While all of these are *plausibly* related to involvement/ engagement, there have been virtually no studies that connect these measures to the effectiveness or memorability of the advertising. The few studies that do exist have failed to show any consistent relationship. At the most, these measures of engagement should be used as tie-breakers between publications that are comparable on the key metrics.

NEWSPAPERS

Readership of the national newspapers (the *Wall Street Journal, USA Today,* the *New York Times*) is reported by MRI and SMRB using the same measures as national magazines, their natural competitors.

Local newspapers are typically chosen on the basis of their coverage of a local advertiser's sales territory. However, in addition to geography, advertisers want to know how well papers reach people who shop at certain stores, visit local malls, or attend home games of the city's professional sports teams.

Scarborough Research provides this information in 81 DMAs. It uses a 16-minute telephone interview followed by a mailed self-administered questionnaire and TV diary. Another local service, Media Audit, competes with Scarborough, however it uses a telephone interview exclusively. Note that it is in the same format as the MRI example except that Scarborough reports the audience in hundreds (00), not thousands (000).

INTERNET

The currency of print advertising is circulation. For the Internet, advertisers buy a certain number of ad impressions that are served to a user's computer browser. These impressions might be purchased at a CPM of $20.00 per thousand.

A total ad buy is often tens of millions of impressions scattered over literally hundreds of websites. Delivering those impressions is the job of companies that are referred to as third party ad servers that keep track of which sites should get how many impressions. The ad-serving companies deliver (serve) ads as they are requested by users' browsers, and then bill an advertiser when the required number of impressions has been reached. Just as circulation doesn't tell a print buyer about the demographics of a magazine's readers, a count of impressions doesn't say anything about the demographics of the people who are moving the mouse – the website's visitors.

Two research companies provide this information: Nielsen NetRatings, a division of Nielsen Online, and comScore. Both use a panel of respondents who agree to allow the research companies to put tracking software on their computer. The respondent logs into the computer when first sitting down, then every keystroke is recorded and included in the tabulations.

A visitor to a website can go in and out many times, even in the same session. Each time will be recorded as an impression to the site, yielding a very large but inherently useless number. Web publishers use NetRatings or comScore to show the number of unique visitors, or simply uniques, over a 30-day period, counting each visitor only once.

This is roughly comparable to a cume in other media. Unlike other media where the base is essentially the total population in the geographic area served by the medium, an Internet rating can be calculated from three different bases:

- Total U.S. population. This base should be used when comparing an Internet rating to other media.
- Internet Universe. Persons age 2+ who had access to an Internet-accessible computer, whether or not they actually went online in the last month – roughly 85 percent of U.S. population.
- Active Universe. Persons age 2+ who have used an Internet-accessible computer in the last 30 days – roughly 65-70 percent of the U.S. population.

Typically Web publishers will report their audience in terms of the Active Universe in order to show the largest percentage. These include the number of page views (screens) seen by each unique visitor, the number of sessions over the month, the time spent with the site per person, and other metrics. Note that the report can be broken down by home and work samples. Active Reach is computed against the Active Universe. Universe Reach is computed against the Internet Universe. NetView does not calculate reach against the total U.S. population.

These reports give the buyer a complete picture of the size and demographics of a website's visitors, but there is a big difference between this information and a television rating. When a commercial appears on a television programme with five million viewers, we know that when it is finished, five million people will have seen it (or at least will have had the commercial displayed on their television set). But that number is meaningless to the Internet advertiser who decides to buy only one million impressions. And, unlike television that delivers the impressions all at once, it takes time for the impressions to be delivered on the Internet.

As each browser requests a page of content, the third-party ad server sends it an ad. But the server handles many advertisers, so those one million impressions do not all go to the first million browsers.

It takes time, days or even weeks for less popular sites, before there will be enough requests for pages that the server can deliver the one-million impressions an advertiser wants. In short, television exposures are immediate; Internet exposures are delivered over a period of time, possibly several weeks. The proper evaluative metric of a website for an advertiser is determined by the number of impressions that are bought, not by the total number of visitors.

Media buyers use the NetRating's WebRF programme or comScore's PlanMetrix Reach/Frequency system to show the net reach of an Internet campaign across many websites. Note that as a salesperson, you probably will not be privy to what other sites an advertiser is buying or how much the advertiser is paying. In the example, an advertiser is buying 50 million page views (impressions) against a target of M18-34, focusing on sports websites. The computer system tells the reach of that number of impressions on each site and the combined campaign statistics in terms of GRPS, reach and average frequency (OTS = Opportunities To See) to the base of the Active Universe.

THE AUDIENCE OF EMERGING MEDIA PLATFORMS

It seems every day there is an article in the trade press

about a new media form that has the potential to revolutionize electronic communications. We hear about video-on-demand, mobile advertising on cell phones, ads in cell phone video, advergaming (ads in video games), streaming video on the Internet, podcasting, advertising walled gardens on digital video recorders like TiVo, and others that will likely be developed after this book has gone to press.

All of these (yes, *all* of these) have research and developmental issues that go beyond the non- sampling errors discussed earlier. The particulars differ from medium to medium, but they include:

Irregular geographic coverage

- Privacy concerns
- Need for regulatory approval
- Technical limitations
- Copyright restrictions
- Competitive conflicts among similar services
- Lack of demographic data (impressions counted by the hardware, not by the person using it)

Salespeople cannot expect the definitive sort of research for these emerging media that is available for the traditional media. The research that is available can be used to *imply* advertising exposure, but most advertisers would not accept it as a currency measure.

As noted earlier, research companies are businesses that must deliver a profit to their investors. As each new medium appears, a research company's first consideration is whether it will draw enough advertisers to be successful. Only then will the research firms begin the long process of developing a service to measure its audience.

THE TOP FIVE IMPOSSIBLE QUESTIONS

Up to now we have discussed the general concepts and methodologies of media research and the concepts that are unique to each of the major media.

The methodologies that are based on a random sample have a statistical margin of error. All methodologies have non-sampling error caused by the real world challenges of producing research. But these sources of error can be identified and accounted for.

In the course of a salesperson's work, other questions come up for which there is no simple answer. These are the most important questions in media because they involve subtle judgments about what is best.

The following frequently asked questions cannot be definitively answered because they depend on what is happening in the mind of each consumer. They are presented here to characterize them as "impossible" questions, to sensitize salespeople to the inevitable day when one of them comes up in the course of their work, and to provide something to say and ways to think about helping the advertiser make a reasonable judgment.

How much is enough?

This is the most common question, and it takes many forms. What is the least I can spend and still have an effective campaign? If I have X number of GRPs against my primary target, am I delivering enough weight against the secondary target? My last campaign was wildly successful. I ran XX number of GRPs and actually had to turn away customers. Next time, how much weight can I cut back and still be successful? There are several approaches to answering the question that will put the advertiser in the ball park. If the advertiser has competitive sales and spending information, it is common to match the share of voice to the share of market.

An advertiser with a 10 percent share of a market should be spending at least 10 percent of the media dollars spent in that industry. Certainly an advertiser should look back at the experience with comparable products. For example, some industries have an historic advertising to sales ratio. An industry rule of thumb is that an ad must be seen three or more times for it to be effective. While this sounds like a reasonable prescription, it finesses the question, "How many people can I afford to reach 3+ times?" In the end, and unfortunately, many advertising budgets are simply what remains after all other costs have been accounted for.

Medium is Most Effective

Effective at doing what? Different media have different strengths. Effectiveness is heavily dependent on the creative quality. Many people think television is the most effective medium, but the question comes up when television is not appropriate or affordable.

There are virtually no independent, public domain studies of cross- media effectiveness. Advertisers who do conduct these studies treat the results as highly confidential. What publicly available research does exist comes from industry associations whose studies are designed to promote the value of their medium. As they say, "Don't ask your barber if you need a haircut." The best advice is to ensure the advertiser has matched the strength of the media to the marketing objectives.

The Best Environment

This question assumes there is a rub-off effect between the medium and the advertising message; however, as noted earlier, numerous studies have failed to quantify that effect, or even to confirm that it exists. We know that high-rated television programs attract more light viewers, but there is a heavy cost premium for these iconic programs.

The first position in a commercial break has a larger audience than mid-break positions, but pod position is usually beyond a buyer's control. In magazines, an ad on the back cover is more likely to be read than one inside the book, but advertisers pay a premium for that position. Some advertisers believe a magazine ad near the front of the book is preferable, but since most insertion orders request "Far forward, right hand page" these (assumed to be) desirable positions are more likely to be given to advertisers running a heavy schedule. At the least, salespeople should ensure that advertisers running multiple insertions are given a fair rotation.

Flighting or Continuity

This age old question concerns how a limited advertising budget should be scheduled over the year: in short bursts of heavy media weight followed by hiatus weeks of no activity, or continuous advertising at low weight. If the budget allows the advertiser to buy 1,600 GRPs a year, should they be scheduled in four 4- week flights (total 16 weeks on-air) of 100 GRPs/week?

Or would it be more effective to run for 40 weeks at 40 GRPs/week? For products that are sold more or less evenly throughout the year, advertisers are guided by the "recency theory of advertising" that was proposed by media guru Erwin Ephron.

In contrast to the theory that three exposures are needed, the recency theory is based on research that shows a single exposure close to purchase is most effective.

Since there is a steady demand for non-seasonal products, the advertiser should maintain a continuous presence on-air. The goal should be to maximize the total weekly reach points (the annual sum of each week's reach points). This is achieved by continuity scheduling. However, this ignores the effect of competitor's advertising that may be flighted. Also, there is a need for synergy between the advertising and seasonal consumer or trade promotions. Finally, there is a reluctance to go below a perceived minimal level of about 50 GRPs per week. Most advertisers appreciate the importance of continuity, but given this minimum, they find continuity scheduling to be an ideal that is beyond their brand's budget.

When is my commercial worn out?

It is hard enough to know what a commercial "does" when it is fresh. Commercial wearout is really a variation of the "How much is enough?" question. An industry rule-of-thumb is that a commercial is worn out when the heaviest viewers are exposed 26 times – somewhere around 1,000-1,500 GRPs. This has become a benchmark against which to judge a given situation, but many questions remain. Does that rule apply to a single execution or to an entire campaign of similar but different creative executions? Over what period of time? What is the effect of hiatus periods? Is that target rating points or household points which are usually larger? One researcher sees a political agenda behind the question. The agency wants to make a new commercial and the advertiser doesn't, or vice versus.

People who are closely involved with the lengthy creative process may be so close to the commercial that they will think it is worn out when in fact it hasn't even been on air. It should be clear by now that there is no simple answer to these "How much is enough" questions of effective frequency, fighting versus continuity, minimum GRP levels, maximum hiatus weeks, media effectiveness, wear out, and so forth.

Research can provide guidance, but in the end, it requires buyer and salesperson judgment to apply these general findings from the past to specific plans for the future.

MEDIA RESEARCH RESOURCES ON THE INTERNET

There is a wealth of information available on the Internet. The research companies, the media, and industry associations all have websites that offer helpful information about their service, methodology, and the media they cover. This is provided at no charge, although some require registration with name, company, and e-mail address. What they do not give is current information about the audience to specific media vehicles – television programs, magazines, radio stations, and so forth. This data, the product they sell, is password protected and limited to paying clients.

Chapter 4

Attitudes

Let's return to those years of yesterday when I made my first sales call and ask what I did wrong. The answer is easy – everything. But everything is not a helpful response, so we will put the responses into a context of a selling system to help you understand the elements of a successful sales call and a successful sales system. To begin with, I did not plan my call properly did not have a framework, or a method for breaking down the sales call into component parts in order to analyse it. The AESKOPP system of selling provides such a framework. The AESKOPP system is a generalization, a simplification of some underlying, universal sales principles and provides a framework for coaching, planning, and evaluating sales thinking and action.

It posits that successful selling requires Attitude (A), Emotional Intelligence (E), Skills (S), Knowledge (K), Opportunities (O), Preparation (P), and Persistence (P): *A x E x S x K* x O *x* P x P = *Success* Notice that each element in the above formula is multiplied by the others. Just as in a mathematical formula, if any one of the elements is not present, then the result is zero success; any element multiplied by zero is zero. Thus, all of the elements must be present for a successful result – getting customers and keeping them.

Before making a sales presentation to a prospect or customer, salespeople should get into the habit of asking themselves the seven AESKOPP questions, and they should also evaluate their overall sales approach and performance by regularly asking themselves these questions. In addition, managers should continually ask these questions about their salespeople and their performance in order to coach them effectively.

THE SEVEN AESKOPP QUESTIONS

- Do I have the right mental Attitude to solve problems and get results for my customers?
- Do I have the Emotional Intelligence to understand people and build rapport with them?
- Do I have the Skills necessary?
- Do I have the Knowledge necessary?
- Do I have the Opportunities?
- Do I have sufficient Preparation?
- Do I have the Persistence to never, never, never, never give up?

If the answer to all of the above questions is yes, you will make lots of sales. However, if you put a priority on closing a sale above all else, you put establishing and maintaining relationships, solving problems, and getting results in a subordinate position. This means that sooner or later your customers will know you care more about yourself and your income than about their problems and their desired results.

THE AESKOPP SYSTEM

- Attitude: *Attitude* is having the desire and motivation to be a salesperson and having the proper mind set to do it. If you have the skills, the knowledge, and the opportunities to sell but have no desire to do so, you will not be successful.
- Emotional Intelligence: *Emotional intelligence* is the ability to understand yourself and others so you can develop empathy and rapport with people and manage relationships successfully.
- Skills: *Skills* are the ability, improved through practice, to use your knowledge of techniques, methods, and tools. For salespeople, it understands the techniques of prospecting, identifying problems, generating solutions, presenting, negotiating and closing, and servicing.

- Knowledge: *Knowledge* means knowing the product you are selling in depth – knowing more about it than your customers do so you can educate them. For salespeople, it means having information not only about their product, but also about research, about marketing and advertising, about customers' businesses, and about competitive media.
- Opportunities: *Opportunities* are the circumstances in which you can use your tools. Even if you have the tools and know how to use them, you cannot accomplish anything unless you have opportunities to put them to use. Salespeople may know how to solve problems and have a storehouse full of product, marketplace, and competitive knowledge, but if they do not make sales calls and find prospective customers, they will lack the opportunities to put their skills and knowledge to work.
- Preparation: *Preparation* is getting organized to solve customer problems. Even if you have the attitude, emotional intelligence, skills, knowledge, and opportunities to sell, you will not solve problems or make many sales if you forget your presentations and if you do not know anything about clients' businesses or personalities.
- Persistence: *Persistence* means never giving up. Salespeople need to continue working on prospects past any initial uninformed "no" they might encounter.

COMPETENCIES OF THE AESKOPP SYSTEM

Each of the seven elements of the AESKOPP system is made up of a group of core competencies – building blocks – that, linked together, lead to successful performance on that element. The core competencies are subject to change, depending on the media selling job involved. Some sales positions, such as in a large-circulation national magazine – *People*, for example – require a high level of knowledge, especially about national advertising, the product, and magazine research, plus very strong relationships with major advertising agencies and advertisers. Other sales positions, such as in a local television station, might require an understanding of retail businesses – an automotive dealership, for example – and skills in negotiating with advertising agencies. Below is a list of core competencies for each of the elements the AESKOPP system.

- Core Competencies Attitude: Honest, positive/optimistic, committed, confident, courageous, competitive, coachable (open/non-defensive), self-motivated, assertive, flexible, cooperative, and nurturing.
- Emotional intelligence: Self-awareness, self-management, social awareness, and relationship management (internal and external).
- Skills: Communicating (internal and external), listening, understanding people, creating value, presenting (to individuals and groups), negotiating and closing, and servicing.
- Knowledge: Financial/economic/business/category, marketing/advertising, market, product, and competitive media.
- Opportunity: Prospecting/getting appointments, and identifying problems (discovery).
- Preparation: Strategic thinking, creativity/problem-solving, organization, planning, and time management. Persistence: Determined/never giving up, and follow-up. Each of the seven AESKOPP elements will be defined and explained much more thoroughly in subsequent chapters.

CORE COMPETENCIES

The next step in effectively using the AESKOPP system is to evaluate yourself based on your degree of expertise on each of the core competencies. I have assigned a percentage to each of the seven AESKOPP elements according to my perceived importance each contributes to a salesperson's ultimate success. These AESKOPP elements and their corresponding core competencies will change with the type of media selling job as will the percentages I have assigned, but the AESKOPP elements and core competencies are a good place to start in order to define and evaluate a media salesperson's job. I recommend that salespeople and sales managers go over the list together and add or delete core competencies and put weights on each according to the needs of the medium they sell and the company they work for. Then, salespeople should study their modified and weighted list, evaluate themselves, and then develop a plan to improve those competencies in which they lack experience or have a deficit. Note the title "Salesperson Core Competencies."

The term salesperson is used because it is inclusive of a wide variety of titles salespeople in the media are assigned by their organizations: sales representative, account executive, account manager, sales consultant, radio marketing consultant, business development director, director of new business, and many more. The preferred title is Account Executive or Account Manager, which implies managing customers' accounts, schedules, and campaigns according to what is best for a customer. Also, titles that include "consultant" should be avoided because customers need results more than advice. In this modern age of solutions selling, Results Generator might be a suitable title. But this euphemism is akin to calling a janitor a Maintenance Engineer, so Account Executive or Account Manager are more appropriate titles. However, in this book, to avoid confusion, salesperson will be used in order to encompass all titles.

Whoever tells the stories defines the culture. That isn't new. What is new is that we have delegated more and more of the storytelling function to mass media. Some of the media take the art to new heights. Too many, however, specialize in dishing out heaping servings of violence, mayhem and degradation. In this presentation we will discuss the role of the media in creating and nourishing a "culture of disrespect" among young people. Combining the latest discoveries in brain science with cutting-edge research, we will discuss how media stories of disrespect, sex, and violence in television, video games and online affect our kids and what we can do to help our kids become MediaWise.

Advertisers spent $267 billion in 2005 to get their message out to the American public and the business sector, but a pressing question remains: given the dramatically changing media and cultural landscapes, what is the best way for firms to communicate messages to key audiences? This report examines consumers' attitudes towards television, Internet, radio, print, and public advertising. Using exclusive consumer research, extensive analysis is devoted to how TiVo, DVRs, Internet video, and other technologies and trends have affected consumers' receptivity to commercials. This report also identifies which media channels are suffering as a consequence of these changes, and which media channels hold opportunities for advertisers seeking to reach various constituents.

Specific topics include:

- Groups most and least receptive to television commercials
- The emergence of new opportunities on the Internet
- Opportunities for reaching select groups via traditional media outlets

This report also features lengthy discussion on important trends in advertising in 2005 and 2006, along with related changes in the cultural fabric, such as the "iPod Effect" and the decline in leisure time. This report analyzes how demographic changes are reshaping the American population, the affluence of various sectors of the population, and snapshots of what the country's population will look like in 2012.

The media sector plays a crucial role in shaping public attitudes and perceptions around globalization, sustainable development and corporate citizenship. According to a comprehensive study released this year ("Good News & Bad: The Media, Corporate Responsibility and Sustainable Development"), media understanding – and, most importantly, sustained intelligent coverage – of these issues is a necessary precondition for real progress. However, there exists a major disconnect: while these issues are arguably the most important of our time, many media watchers – and media representatives themselves – say that the press is generally abysmal at covering critical – but "slow burn" – issues, instead opting for sensational events and "headline-grabbing" news stories.

The big media story of the late 1990s was globalization – or, more accurately, anti-globalization. However, many observers believe that the anti-globalization movement is on its back foot as a result of September 11. Still, the issues remain real and urgent. They demand action, both in terms of coverage and corporate accountability mechanisms. The media have a critical role to play in the transition towards the objectives of the sustainability movement, and in the fair and intelligent coverage of globalization issues so that citizens can make more informed decisions that influence policy making in positive ways. For example, the media-sector study revealed that many media appear to be missing one of the biggest stories of our times, that of the progressive undermining of global ecosystems – with profound social and economic consequences.

The assumption is that if the issues are real, we will have time to adapt. But the sudden discovery of the ozone hole shows how even global problems can take us by surprise. There is a trend towards increased coverage of the corporate responsibility movement by media – some leading journalists are beginning to show interest in the "triple-bottom-line" agenda. In general, European interest in CSR – both in the public mind and in the media – has been sustained at higher levels than in the U.S., Latin America and Asia. Among the issues that have driven the debate: child labour, climate change, and GM crops. One striking aspect of U.S. media coverage has been its "CSR blind spot".

Despite clear evidence that growing numbers of U.S. corporations are embracing CSR, U.S. media have largely ignored the trend – with the exception of widespread coverage of "corporate responsibility" in the wake of many high-profile business scandals. However, recently more U.S. media outlets have been showing interest in larger CSR and development issues, including Fortune, BusinessWeek and The New York Times. Partly in the defence of media coverage, one of the findings of the sector study was that governments, companies, CSR groups and others interested in responsible globalization do a poor job communicating to media in an effort to raise awareness about pressing issues.

Many editors surveyed expressed a desire for more information. Interestingly, the NGO community is perceived as being much more effective in leveraging the media to communicate their messages. Another important finding was that, editorial coverage aside, media companies as businesses are among the least accountable institutions in the world. While the sector is arguably poised to become the most powerful institution on earth, accountability mechanisms are generally weak. Few media companies, for example, produce CSR or sustainability reports. However, it is predicted that media will come under growing scrutiny as its influence grows.

And expect the spotlight to pick up other parts of the media ecosystem, too, including advertising agencies, PR firms and lobbyists. Finally, one must consider the impact of "new media". Technology – the Internet in particular – has given a powerful new platform to these agendas. Niche electronic newsletters and websites convey a wealth of information that might otherwise fail to make it into the mainstream. And powerful search engines help people find them. Thus, new technology has changed the both how – and by whom – news is captured as well as how it is distributed. S hopping has indeed become the great American past time.

The number of consumers participating in this activity on an average day at a large mall overwhelms attendance at even the greatest spectator sports. America's continuing love affair with shopping is great news for retailers. However, "branding" their products and services on the minds of consumers is still a great challenge for them. The competition for consumer attention and dollars is stronger than ever. Now retailers have to sell harder and smarter to increase brand awareness and market share. Much of this strategy relies on the best medium or combination of media to deliver advertising messages. But the measure of a medium should include its ability to impact consumer buying decisions as well as reach wide and targeted audiences.

An advertising medium needs to help consumers decide where and when to shop, and what to buy. It's important to know some of the drivers that impact shopping behaviour. For example, almost four out of 10 consumers (38%) shop for the best price. So, it's important for a medium to enable shoppers to easily compare store prices. Almost half (49%) of shoppers go where good sales are. Thus, it's vital for a medium to proficiently bring sales information to the attention of consumers. The following data shows that newspapers are clearly more favorable among consumers when it comes to various attitudes toward media advertising. This is where newspapers have an opportunity to shore up these strengths and maintain a competitive edge over other media.

In categories, such as service/utility, convenience, credibility and core values, newspapers are more challenged by other media. In these areas newspapers need to closely examine the attributes that are less favored by consumers, to see where their product needs to be re-shaped to build consumer confidence. The graphs in this report were created using data culled from NAA's 2000 "How America Shops & Spends" study and NAA's 2000 "Media Usage Study". They provide snapshots of consumer attitudes toward media's role in advertising, service/utility, convenience and credibility. There are also charts illustrating consumer attitudes toward different core values among media.

POWER OF THE PRESS

This year's campaigns are being more widely covered by the media than in any other election in U.S. history. Studies and reports continue to show that more people are tuning in and turning on their televisions, radios, and computers to receive, view, and respond to news about the race and the candidates. The cable news MSNBC reported that, in February, more than 8 million people tuned in to watch a debate between

U.S. senators and Democrat presidential candidates Hillary Clinton and Barack Obama; the usual audience for the same time period is only one-tenth that number. Foreign news agencies are also offering unprecedented, in-depth coverage of the elections to their own and U.S. expatriate markets.

According to a recent national survey, current public interest in the campaigns is vastly outpacing comparable periods in previous presidential elections run-ups.

What is fueling this phenomenal interest is the subject to debate. Some experts chalk up the increased public interest in the election to media coverage that is more sensational and dramatic than in past campaign periods.

Others contend that the news media's interest in the issues of race and gender because of the Clinton-Obama contest has generated greater levels of interest among a broader number of audiences.

According to historian and author Lee Edwards (a Hoover media fellow), the influence of mass media within any country—the United States included—cannot be discounted. In an article written for *Hoover Digest,* Edwards explains the mass media have become an "essential component of national power, as important to a nation's viability as natural resources, population, economic strength, military might, and political will." Likewise, in an article published in the Hoover Institution's *Policy Review,* author and international affairs expert Robert D. Kaplan notes journalists and news show executives, because they control the "spin" and have ultimate authority over which stories are presented to the public, possess immense influence and power in today's society—more than the politicians they often cover.

TURN ON AND TUNE IN

In the United States and other industrialized nations, the pervasiveness of digital information has made media more accessible now than ever before. The National Telecommunications and Information Administration (the president's principal adviser on telecommunications and information policy) reports the number of people using broadband Internet connections grew 1,100 percent between 2000 and 2006. Broadcast news now cycles endlessly on a variety of 24-hour news channels; talk radio continues to be a rallying point for millions of Americans; and the Internet has spawned an entirely new culture of sites called "blogs" that allow anyone— from professors to athlete, scholars to politicians, stay-at-home moms to celebrities —to post information on myriad subjects.

Compared to only a few years ago, capturing and distributing audio and video files has become relatively simple and inexpensive. Video-hosting websites, such as YouTube, allow people to broadcast amateur videos to a worldwide audience. As a result, once-unknown individuals and groups have been able to reach vast audiences and rocket to fame (or infamy) virtually overnight. Video clips of the Reverend Jeremiah Wright's fiery and controversial sermons have been extensively broadcast on YouTube, which led to Obama publicly addressing his relationship with the pastor. Activist organizations and individuals, taking advantage of the anonymity of the Internet, often use digital media to coordinate their efforts or broadcast their messages to supporters and the public at large.

Audio or video clips routinely appear on sympathizers' websites with messages from Osama bin Laden and like-minded extremists warning Westerners, non-Muslims, and noncompliant Muslims of impending doom. Print media are increasingly following the digital trend. Many of the world's largest and best-known newspapers and magazines have created online presences, and almost as many use bloggers to scour the net and report on news that the print venue does not allow. Each year, the number of people who read their morning news from a monitor rather than the newspaper increases. A national report released in late 2007 showed that newspaper subscriptions fell 2.6 percent during the previous six-month period. Data released by Nielsen/Net Ratings show that the number of visitors to online newspaper sites has increased from 41 million visitors in one month in 2004 to more than 63 million one month at the end of 2007.

PRESSING ISSUES

While print media becomes less utilized, alternate/new media outlets are gaining wider audiences. Coverage of the 2008 presidential primaries illustrates this shift; more people than ever are relying on nontraditional forms of media for news and information about the race and the candidates.

A recent nationwide study found that 26 percent of Americans receive information about the 2008 presidential campaign via the Internet on a regular basis, nearly twice that of the previous (2004) election. Political candidates increasingly turn to alternative means to reach out to supporters and potential voters.

All three top presidential hopefuls have created "MySpace" pages, where supporters can become virtual "friends" of the candidates, follow the campaign trail, download digital campaign images and slogans, and post and receive messages from the candidates and other friends. These sites garner thousands of hits every day. Many of these new media outlets, especially blogs, openly espouse a particular political view, and attract readers who share similar views.

In contrast, traditional media outlets have generally touted their offerings—editorial content aside—as unbiased, balanced, and fair, a claim often challenged by politicians, pundits, and academics who question the objectivity of any given news source. Accusations of unfairness, interest pandering, preferential politics, and flat-out personal bias are plentiful. Charges that mainstream media reflect a liberal or conservative slant are common among academics and politicians.

Thomas Sowell, a Hoover senior fellow, agrees that many journalists are guilty of "filtering and spinning the news" according their own political agendas or that of the candidates they support. Such bias, according to Sowell, hurts the public that depends on "journalists to tell them the truth as they see it and to offer their honest opinion as to what it means." Hoover senior fellow Morris Fiorina points out that bias in the media is to be expected because the experiences of journalists are limited to surroundings that are not representative of mainstream America. Thus, according to Fiorina, those providing the information cannot help but offer skewed observations.

CRITICAL MASS MEDIA

In today's media-saturated worlds, news outlets constantly vie for market attention. In an article written for the *Hoover Digest,* American legal history scholar and Hoover media fellow Morton Keller states "journalism is by nature contentious and opinionated. Gossip, sensationalism, and exposure are inescapable tools in the business of inducing readers to read (or viewers to view) media output."

Hoover research fellow and former journalist Robert Zelnick chalks up frivolity in today's news to an overriding shift in priorities. Zelnick believes many news outlets are forced to rely on "the shock value of things" to constantly feed the never-ending news cycle. To this end, news producers have a "tremendous need to break new information when there's no new information to break."

Zelnick argues that the news consumer is not a helpless bystander but rather is in control and, ultimately, responsible for media content. During a conversation with host Peter Robinson on *Uncommon Knowledge,* Zelnick remarked, "I think that the discipline that has to be exerted on the market has to be exerted by individuals who care about news. They have to seek out the better programming, they have to seek out the more erudite coverage, and that's the only type of noise that has any resonance in the rooms where decisions are made."
—Michelle Bussenius, Editor

Chapter 5

Emotional Intelligence

In the last few decades, researchers have been identifying specific things that make people successful and it's clear that the world's achievers see life and behave in ways that we can learn. They use a set of skills that *we* could loosely call *intelligence* - emotional intelligence.

Broadly speaking, our emotional intelligence is our ability to manage ourselves and our relationships. One study (by Hay/ McBer) showed that emotional skills were twice as important as intellectual skills in determining excellence. Many observers say that your intellectual abilities, technical skills, qualifications and experience may get you the job, but your emotional intelliegence will determine how far you are promoted,

Researchers disagree on how much the emotional skills contribute to success, but even the most skeptical we've come across recently, thinks they are probably as valuable as your intellectual and technical skills. You can't do much about your I.Q. but your can certainly increase your E.Q. (Your Emotional Quotient.) Studies of major organisations in the United States show that the need for emotional intelligence grows with the complexity of the work. For success in the top levels of leadership, emotional skills are virtually the entire difference between outstanding leaders and mediocre ones.

At Media Associates, we prefer to focus on skills rather than emotional intelligence. It's partly so that we don't get distracted by the debate over the definition of intelligence, but mostly because it allows us to concentrate on a range of communication and emotional skills that we know are closely linked with success in business and in life generally. Notice that, with a few exceptions, the list of skills that make up what we could call a kind of intelligence, are relevant to every part of your life. Some are disciplines, such as having initiative and being conscientious. Most are skills you can learn or enhance.

Self-awareness

For example:

- Knowing your feelings at the moment
- Knowing how those feelings affect your performance
- Having a realistic picture of your abilities
- Having a well-founded self-confidence

Self-management

For example:

- Having the ability to manage disruptive emotions including handling stressful situations well
- Being open about your mistakes and expecting the same of others
- Being conscientious
- Being adaptable
- Having initiative
- Being optimistic as you strive to perform better

Social awareness

For example:

- Being able to show empathy
- Giving good service to others
- Being aware of what's going on in your organisation

Relationship management

For example:

- Developing other people's abilities
- Influencing others (persuasion)
- Communicating effectively
- Managing conflict so that you achieve a win/win outcome
- Leading effectively

- Building bonds with others
- Being an effective catalyst for change

Emotional intelligence predicts exam success. This is the finding of a study into the relationship between emotional intelligence and educational achievement, presented today, 1st November, at The British Psychological Society's Education Section Annual Conference. At the start of the five year study, 628 Year 7 students were tested on an objective measure of emotional intelligence - the ability to identify, assess, and manage your own and others' emotions. These measures were then compared to each student's English and Science results at Year 9 SAT and again two years later at GCSE.

A significant relationship was found between boys' emotional intelligence and their SAT and GCSE English scores, with boys with higher emotional intelligence scores doing better in these exams. While for girls, a relationship between emotional intelligence and their SAT Science scores was discovered; girls with higher emotional intelligence scores did better in this exam. Dr Pamela Qualter, from the University of Central Lancashire, said: "IQ does result in better academic test results, but our results suggest that emotional intelligence is another key predictor of academic success.

"Further detailed analysis of the results suggests that emotional intelligence may moderate the effects of IQ on academic achievement. Faced with failure, a student low on IQ but who is emotionally intelligent will be able to manage their emotions surrounding failure, reconcile poor performance and work to improve; a student low on IQ and low emotional intelligence may find failure more difficult to deal with, which undermines their academic motivation." One implication of this research is that opportunities to develop students' emotional intelligence could be a way to improve their educational achievement. Thus, engagement in current UK educational strategies (SEAL) are likely to be important for children's future academic progress.

The British Psychological Society's Education Section Annual Conference is taking place at Kents Hill Park Conference Centre, Milton Keynes from 31st October to 2nd

November 2008. The term emotional intelligence has been used in academic circles since the late 1980s, but it took American psychologist and journalist, Dr Daniel Goleman, to release his best-selling book Emotional Intelligence for the concept to capture the public's imagination. Goleman, a former Harvard graduate and behavioural science contributor to the New York Times, has since written a second book, Working with Emotional Intelligence in which he argues that workplace competencies based on emotional intelligence play a far greater role in high performance than do intellect and technical skills.

Moreover, Goleman claims that individuals and companies both benefit from cultivating these capabilities. Drawing on research from some 500 leading businesses, he concludes that emotional intelligence is twice as important as IQ plus technical skill combined. When IQ scores are correlated with how well people perform in their careers, the highest estimate of how much difference IQ accounts for is 25 per cent. By contrast, says Goleman, emotional intelligence accounts for more than 85 per cent of star performance. What EI is Interest in emotional intelligence in the workplace has grown dramatically in recent years, particularly in America where EI has spawned a movement in schools, home and the community as well as the corporate environment.

A similar level of enthusiasm is evident in Europe and interest is increasing rapidly in Australia, New Zealand and Asia. But what do psychologists really mean by emotional intelligence? Is it just another term for so-called people skills and, if so, why all the hype? Some psychologists describe emotional intelligence as street smarts of sorts. Goleman defines it as "the capacity for recognising our feelings and those of others, for motivating ourselves, and managing emotions in us and in our relationships". These are soft skills, but he insists there are hard consequences if they are ignored in the corporate world. To illustrate his point, he cites the example of global consumer products firm that was not assessing emotional competence as part of its recruitment process. Within two years of hiring, some 50 per cent of all division heads left the firm after initial search costs of $4 million. When the firm started assessing potential candidates for emotional intelligence, only 6 per cent of the division heads left within two years.

Why emotions are different While such general attributes, as maturity, commonsense and people skills have long been associated with effective managers and employees, Goleman claims to be among the first to draw on recent scientific research to link emotional intelligence to high performance.

He says that while cognitive and technical skills evolve from only one area of the brain - the neocortex - emotional intelligence involves an integration of several areas of the brain including the higher thinking centres.

"The thinking brain, which regulates technical skill and cognitive ability, can operate without involving emotions," he says.

In other words, emotionally intelligent behaviour requires all the brain power used for intellect plus more. Our thinking and feeling need to be integrated. "When you are facing a decision, the sense of right or wrong is as important as any other data you might bring to the table," he says. "If it feels right it probably is . . . feelings are fact". Who needs it? It is generally recognised that managers and leaders need high emotional intelligence because they represent the organisation to the public and they interact with the highest number of people within and outside the organisation. Moreover, they set the tone for employee behaviour and morale.

In a recent paper in the Harvard Business Review titled What Makes a Leader, Goleman argues there are certain competencies within the emotional intelligence framework that are particularly desirable at the corporate executive level. These include self-awareness, self-management including being able to handle our emotions and keep our impulses under control (Bill Clinton take note) achievement drive and empathy. This last competency is considered essential for leaders who operate in today's diversifying and global marketplace. "Cross-cultural dialogue can easily lead to miscues and misunderstandings," says Goleman. "Empathy is an antidote.

People who have it are attuned to subtleties in body language, they hear the message beneath the words being spoken." Increasing emphasis on matrix structures and cross-functional teams is another reason why empathy is so important. "A team leader must be able to sense and understand the viewpoints of everyone around the table," he says. There is not a single recipe for success in a leadership role. Nor is cloning the means to attaining an emotionally intelligent organisation. Rather, highly effective leaders can demonstrate quite different competency profiles. What is clear, however, is that successful leaders possess a balance across the four key components: self-awareness, self-management, social awareness and social skills.

TEACHING EI

Are people born with certain levels of emotional intelligence or do they acquire these personal qualities as a result of life's experiences? Goleman claims research and practice clearly demonstrate that emotional intelligence (unlike IQ) can be learned; but not through a how-to-manual or a brief seminar. Nor does he recommend a twist on the popular white-water rafting experience or the executive pow wow in a remote mountain retreat. "Developing an individual's emotional intelligence (or that of an organisation) requires a different sort of approach," says Goleman who argues that such one-off programs are a waste of money. "American companies are wasting between six and 15 billion dollars a year on development programs in this area which simply do not work. They have no transfer of learning to on-the-job performance." Goleman recommends an emphasis on multi-level development and coaching initiatives, rather than one-off workplace programs.

The aim is to produce sustained improvements in performance and create an emotionally intelligent organisation. In particular, a business that is more collaborative and cohesive than its competitors. Based on his analysis of successful development programs, he advocates using the working environment as the "classroom" for learning. While initial exposure to the concepts of emotional intelligence might take place during an external workshop, and would typically include some assessment of participants, change in behaviour can only be tested in the workplace. The challenge for organisations is to help managers understand what they need to change and to motivate them to try out new things.

For this to be effective, the organisation needs to be supportive and there should be coaching and mentoring available. Often, participants work in mutual support groups to act as sounding boards and advisers for one another. In other cases external coaches play this role to help individuals monitor their progress against their improvement agenda. Air New Zealand has started such a programme, which focuses more on the internal culture and operating climate to ensure delivery of the brand promise. Air New Zealand believes that it is critical that they integrate EI competencies into all aspects of the management of their people

ASSESSING EI

When it comes to recruiting the best people, it is not surprising that Goleman believes that IQ tests are a poor indicator of career success. He cites a Harvard study on entrance exam scores of people in the business school, the medical school and the law school. In each case entrance exam scores had zero correlation with how the students did in their field. It is relatively simple to assess IQ, and technical skills can be ascertained from past performance and referees reports. Assessing emotional intelligence is not yet quite so easy, though there are several tests available and more in development.

Many of these are reliant on self-assessment, and thus assume possession of one of the crucial emotional intelligence competencies (accurate self-assessment). Others are designed to measure the underlying psychological construct and, as with IQ, depend upon hypothesised or predicted links to performance. Identification of demonstrated emotional intelligence requires evaluation by a third party, typically involving 360-degree assessment or in-depth interviewing by a skilled practitioner. This latter technique was utilised by the global consumer products company to reduce turnover in senior managers.

Goleman says it is still important to hire technically-minded executives. But these are mainly threshold abilities; they're entry level requirements most executives already have. They may get a person through the door of a company, but abilities like leadership, collaboration and teamwork, self-confidence and initiative - the emotional intelligence-based abilities - ensure that he or she will thrive.

Chapter 6

Effective Communication, Effective Listening and Understanding People

Active listening is a powerful way of listening and responding to customers, that improves mutual understanding. It is the foundation of effective communication and demonstrates real respect. According to Nancy Kline, author of the book 'Time to Think', when you are listening to someone, much of the quality of what you are hearing is your effect on them. Giving good attention to people makes them more intelligent. Poor attention makes them stumble over their words and seem stupid. Your attention and your listening is what is important. When we are in conflict, we can sometimes contradict the customer, denying their description of a situation.

This tends to make them defensive and they will either lash out or alternatively, withdraw and say nothing more. However, if they believe that we are really tuned in to their concerns and want to listen, they are more likely to explain in detail what they feel and why. This in turn gives sales people a much greater chance of being able to develop a win-win solution. Your role in the sales situation alternates between sender and receiver of messages. The very best sales professionals devote a large portion of the sales interview to listening, because sincere listening demonstrates sincere interest. Ultimately, good listening is the shortest distance between you and more sales; better sales, faster sales.

How often has a customer said something that has been misinterpreted by you? If you accept the view that everyone is unique, then every word has a different meaning to different individuals? What we say can be different to what we actually mean, because we all have to edit our thoughts in order to communicate them in words. We do this by a combination of deletion, distortion and generalisation

Communication involves four steps:

- Sensing the message and the stimuli that goes with it
- Interpreting it (to be sure you understand)
- Evluating it (never judge before you understand)
- Reacting (either verbally or non-verbally)

That's why it pays to listen with your eyes as well as your ears. Frequently, a gesture, an expression, will reveal as much or more than words. Therefore, effective listeners seek to understand the meaning behind their customers' words. This requires giving the other person full attention and demands conscious practice.

To become excellent at listening, there are three main techniques:

- Build high levels of rapport and trust your instincts.

When two people have established high levels of rapport, they unconsciously pick-up on the feelings of each other. At this point the sales person may get an instinct about something the customer 'feels', which is important feedback that is driven from their unconscious mind. Trusting these instincts can sometimes prove to be a challenge for people who work in a corporate, logical environment, yet the ability to 'listen' and act upon these instincts can make the difference between a good listener and a great listener. If for example, you have created rapport and start to feel nervous, then chances are so is your customer. Imagine the impact of asking, "I'm getting a sense that you're feeling nervous about this, what specific concerns do you have?" will have on your customer.

- Demonstrate that you are paying attention.

This really encourages the customer to continue talking and helps put them at ease because they can see that you're interested in what they are saying. Using noncommittal words with a positive voice tone that neither agree or disagree with what is being said, will ensure that the customer remains motivated to want to continue talking. For example, "I see"/ "Uh-huh"/ "That's interesting" are great ways to achieve this. Nodding your head and taking written notes are also effective when demonstrating your interest.

- Clarifying your understanding.

Adopting a consultative approach means that it's vital to fully appreciate your prospect's requirements. Even if you think that your prospect has made them very clear, it's good practice to summarise your understanding of them. For example: "So what you're saying is (requirement)." "You obviously value (requirement) as being very important to you." These summaries will strengthen your relationship and demonstrate a genuine desire to really understand what they want. Rephrase their main points at regular intervals and 'play them back' to them. This helps them see if they have said exactly what they wanted to say and to make sure you understand. Put their feelings into words. This will help them evaluate and perhaps modify their statement...and it gives further evidence of your understanding.

Understanding what others are trying to communicate to you is essential for building open and strong relationships, whether face to face or by telephone. More and more organisations are recognising the value of effective communication through effective listening and questioning techniques in increasing productivity and sales. This course is for staff of all levels who wish to enhance their communication skills.

LEARNING OUTCOMES

By the end of the course you will be able to:

- Gain new information through effective questioning techniques
- Pick up on hidden messages
- Listen for feelings as well as meaning and respond to them

- Use techniques to check and build understanding
- Use support to minimise stress
- Increase your confidence when communicating face to face or by telephone

The benefits of good communication:

- Avoiding confusion and misunderstanding
- Reducing frustration, stress and sickness levels
- Capturing new ideas and initiatives facilitating change
- Gaining an understanding of others perspectives
- Meeting customer needs
- Increasing productivity and sales

Good listening skills:

- Empathy - listening for feelings
- Absorbing unpalatable messages
- Appreciation of the other person's point of view
- Listening, not just hearing
- Body language and its impact on communication

Good questioning skills:

- When and how to ask a question
- The purpose of questions
- Techniques to gathering information
- Using information effectively

ACTIVE LISTENING

According to a google web definition, active listening has many different definitions. "Active listening is a way of listening that focuses entirely on what the other person is saying and confirms understanding of both the content of the message and the emotions and feelings underlying the message to ensure that understanding is accurate."

"Communication technique that stimulates open and frank exploration of ideas and feelings and enables trainers to establish trust and rapport with participants. In active listening, the trainer accepts what is being said without making any value judgments, clarifies the ideas or feelings being expressed and reflects these back to the participants."

There are several ways to be an active listener, as

demonstrated through this list of "Keys to Effective Listening":

Stop working. Stop watching TV. Stop reading. Look at the person. Keep a good distance between you and the speaker. Don't turn away from the speaker. Sit-up straight. Nod your head and make statements such as "uh-uh," "I understand," and "I see what you mean" to show the speaker you truly understand what he/she is saying. If you don't understand, let the person know that. Don't fake listen! Repeat back phrases to clarify what the person is saying. Act like you are interested and ask questions to show that you are interested in what the person is saying. Don't interrupt the speaker.

According to Thomas Gordon, "active listening involves carefully attending to and demonstrating understanding of what another person says". A teacher can use active listening by nodding their head and then reflecting back to what the student is saying. It is a process of mirroring back what students are trying to say. No judgment or evaluation is made, but it is important for a teacher to use active listening because it confirms that the teacher is attentive and understand the student's message.

In the classroom, active listening is the process of summarizing back to a student his feelings and problem being expressed as the teacher understands them. Active listening is the most important step in Thomas Gordon's T.E.T. model because it improves communication and allows the teacher to hear what the student is attempting to communicate. Active Listening is a main technique that is used in Cognitive Coaching. It really makes a person feel like they are being heard and understood. You do not agree with the person, but validate by paraphasing what you hear them saying to you.

Furthermore, it is a practice that is encouraged to be utilized by applicants at a job interview. The same principles of active listening apply, but "because job interviews are more progressive and fast-paced than leisurely social interactions, it's often necessary to apply a more streamlined version of active listening principles". In sum, active listening is a skill that good teachers need to develop. Active listeners listen to the person speaking instead of thinking about what they are going to say next. They reiterate what the person is trying to say in an effort to clarify and clear up any misunderstandings. They seek to understand the person and their needs before their own concerns are heard. ("Seek first to understand, then to be understood"-Covey) Using specific emotions helps to identify how the other person feels and help the two parties come to some kind of "win-win" solution.

APPLICATION IN THE ONLINE CLASSROOM

Active listening as described above is very face to face oriented, if not exclusively. What happens when listening (and speaking) takes place at a distance? Can the varied physical cues discussed above be implemented in a virtual environment? Does the virtual environment lend itself to new forms of active listening? Recent research indicates that the use of back channeling in the listener-speaker feedback loop improves as technology tools make more and more functionality available.

One study from focused on synchronous learning environments and explored the use of audio feedback via microphone (the "uh-huhs") and newer digital backchannels such as IM and text messaging. The presence of varied backchannels where participants can indicate acceptance or understanding increases the notion that there is someone else out there or a "copresense." As long as the "mechanisms for creating common ground in the enactment of online interactions" are there, we can infer that the environment can support some sort of active listening (or "processing" if the medium is text).

EVIDENCE OF EFFECTIVENESS

Research shows that teaching active listening skills (along with critical listening, note taking and applications for life transfer) can improve students' listening skills and behaviour. Teachers surveyed in this study indicated the majority of students have poor listening skills, while less than half of teachers taught listening skills to their students. Students and teachers alike agreed that listening at school is an important skill. Students on average are expected to listen in elementary school 57.5% of the time. Clearly, time teaching listening skills is time well spent. Teachers need to model active listening and give children the skills and opportunities to do so. They also need to give students time, experiences and purposes to do so. Once active listening is taught, transfer to other classrooms can occur if that instructor provides an environment for students to do so.

Graves' research, published the month following Engraffia's, looked at ways of teaching active listening to students. This study included first and third grade students in two schools in the same school district in a low to middle income community in central Illinois. To implement a programme of teaching active listening, teachers first need to be trained in active listening. They then should model it in the classroom and be aware of and monitor whether their students are actively listening. Students can be taught active listening through a variety of required active responses while listening. Habits for giving verbal and non-verbal feedback while listening can be developed.

Students should also practice clarifying what has been said. Listening journals can be quite helpful. The study used journals, standardized tests and KWL charts to assess progress. Students in this study learned that active listening is something you do, not something that just happens. Not only did the study show that teaching active listening increased student use and understanding of active listening skills, but also indicated "the possibility of the existence of types of listeners". Three categories of active listeners occurred, as during the process of the study many students expressed a liking to certain strategies and frustration with use of others. Students tended to be visual, bodily kinesthetic or verbal.

CRITICS AND THEIR RATIONALE

Signed Life Experiences and Testimonies and Stories

This article is a terrific wake up call to teachers, parents, and professional persons. Active Listening is such an important skill. It used to be a natural occurrence in society, where you would actually sit down and have tea and talk one on one on a frequent basis, talk over the fence, have family discussions regularily. I personally am so mentally overloaded with teaching responsibilities, home, and paperwork that my mind is often racing. I have been working on taking a deep breath when the phone rings or someone addresses me. I have attempted to stop Multi-tasking(no emptying the dishwasher when I am on the phone) or thinking of what I have to do when talking with another teacher.

As a computer lab teacher, I think one of the reasons the children love it so much is that they put on their headsets and listen to the prompts, and they are then praised when they make a decision and corrected when they make an error. I think they feel "listened to ". I am happy to say that Active Listening is now a part of my daily life.

Active listening is really about slowing down and taking the time to value other people and their ideas. In our world of multitasking, we are constantly thinking ahead. As teachers, it is important to stop what we are doing and listen to our students, even if we have to tell them to wait for about a minute, finish up what we are doing and then give them our full attention. Remember, we are teaching students by example, and if we take the time to listen to their concerns, give them our full attention and listen to what they have to say, hopefully they will do the same when they interact with other people.

I find that active listening is sometimes difficult for me when I am interacting with a student especially if they are arguing over a grade or trying to get permission to turn in an assignment late. I am usually trying to think of what I need to say next instead of fully listening to what they have to say. I know this is something I need to work on, but it is sometimes difficult when I am trying to respond to the student with an understanding but firm answer.

Craig Johnson- Active listening is one of the most important skills a person can learn. It involves not only the understanding of what the person has said but also allowing them through your body language etc. to realise that you are actually listening to what they are saying. There is nothing more frustrating then to have someone say repeat that or did you say something. Teaching students better active listening skills will make them better learners as a whole

Bret Helms - Active listening is a very important skill to learn. I spend many class periods a year teaching kids listening skills. I teach a class called quest which spends a lot of time working on these skills. It is amazing how much the kids will change while you are discussing this topic. The key is to continue the listening skills throughout the year. Someone who becomes a good listener really increases their chances of being successful.

Brandon Correa- "I'm sorry, did you say something?" is one of the most demeaning phrases you can say to someone else. I think the key to being a good listener is humility. If all you think about is yourself, than you won't show any care for what someone else has to say. I think women definitely are better at being good active listeners than men are. They can instinctively tell somehow when you are really listening to them or to the ESPN report on TV. Someone should do a study on how men can just tune people out. It must have to do with the inability to multi-task that hinder the active listening in men.

Rhonda Hall—I think active listening is a great skill. I first learned in depth how to be an active listener in some post graduate courses I took in a counseling programme. It was something I've always remembered and I really try to use that skill, especially with my students. I don't how I would fit teaching that into an already full day.

Ralph Alexander- I was fortunate enough to attend a seminar on listening skills and was fortunate to see how effective listening skills can be. My boss at the time asked(demanded) each of his employees to take a Sunday to attend this seminar he was paying for. Needless to say none of us were very excited about the prospect. I was living in Peoria, Illinois at the time and traveled to Champaign, Il to listen to Dr. Elaine Gregory. We spent the day practicing listening skills and how to practice practicing listening skills. After the seminar our communication between each other improved and more importantly the communication with the customer improved, thereby increasing our sales dramatically and putting money in the bosses pocket and our own. I can testify to the power of listening closely and well to another person, it can make incredible differences in personal and business relationships.

Scott Cebulski- I recall feeling that I had had an epiphany when I used active listening almost unconsciously early in my teaching career. Mostly from a lack of knowing what to say, I remember pausing while talking with a student about a discipline issue privately.

The student saw it immediately as a signal to discuss the underlying causes of the problem and felt more comfortable with me as a result. I unknowingly went from the traditional "I talk — you listen!" stance to one that expressed a concern for the student, a concern that I had but had never been able to express.

It occured too long ago to recall whether the particular instance was better handled as a result, but I definitely remember how it affected the way I was percieved by the student and our future relationship. I felt it was a positive step, and I have become much better at actively listening to my students as a method of understanding discipline problems as a result.

Steve Hetzel- Active listening is about bringing your full self to an enounter with someone else, and committing yourself to them during the time of your interraction. You're there to listen and respond to what they have to say, not to talk about yourself or push your own agenda. You are listening to them under the premise, the mantra, of, "Yes, I am here to listen to what you have to say." You're not thinking about what you really want to say, or where you have to go, what you have to do, or where you'd rather be, but you're fully committed to that person at that moment. This is not to say that you disregard your own needs, only that you bring them to a level of importance equal to the other person's. Non-judgement is also key, as is understanding where the person is at with what they're talking about.

Ting Hsiao- I think active listening is also important to successful family interactions. Through active listening, teachers are able to understand different family culture, concerns, and priorities, and know how to make positive impact on studenets' learning based not only on students' but also on families' needs. Through teachers' activie listening, families feel they are welcomed and valued and will be more cooperative with teachers.

Jasmine Johnson- I'd never heard of 'active listening' before reading this post, and I wondered what the difference would be between active listening and just plain listening...? I definitely think I have a problem with active listening, or listening, and sometimes have a tendency to "tune out" or drift into other thoughts instead of focusing on what someone is saying. Although I don't believe it has dramatically affected my school performance, I do think that it must have affected it somewhat (although taking notes—no matter what—seems to help). I'd be very interested in taking an active listening class, and I wonder where I might begin to look for some.

In Sociology 480, we are learning how to do research and the different types of research methods. Active listening is such a big step in the research process that you do not realise how much valuable information you gain until you realise this is a strategy to utilize. Just as when you are interviewing someone on your research topic, using active listening is beneficial to draw the person out and get deeper more meaningful information. This same strategy would be useful when talking with students because you would not be talking at them but rather talking with them and understanding where they are coming from to develop a more meaningful and somewhat more respectful relationship. MJB

Janet Vallowe- It seems like such an easy thing to do when you read a description of active listening. However, in the world of a busy teacher where there never seems to be enough time and we excel at multitasking, this is an aspect of teaching that takes a lot of conscious practice and effort. When a student walks into my classroom I immediately recognize their presence and stop what I am doing. Many times the student simply has stopped by to say "Hi" or to talk about something. All they are looking for is someone who will listen. After 28 years of teaching, this is something that I still have to consciously think about and do.

When I read this post, I immediately thought about how often adults don't listen (actively) to their children. A lot of children aren't always aware of how valuable and appreciated they are and a lot of this stems from their relationships with adults. Children absolutely love when they know they have the full attention of an adult. Students are more respectful of teachers who *listen* to them. Parents, teachers, and other adults, keep this in mind when you are interacting with young people.

I think active listening is most important for effective communication between children and adults. The younger the children the more difficult because they still have to learn quite a deal to express themselves appropriately. To be patient and show them through active listening that you care about their problems will help them to learn these skills very well. When they are adults no one listen to them when they have not learned to communicate and express themselves appropriately. That is why it is so important to take always the time to listen when children want to talk to you .

I did not realise how much I did not actively listen until I was confronted by my children. On day my son stopped me and said "you always complain that we don't listen it is you mom who doesn't listen" My reply was of course I listen. He then asked the real question: "then what did I just say?" I was speechless. Since our encounter, I am doing better. I have enlisted many of the active listening strategies to ensure I fully understand a conversation. I have quit filling in the gaps with my own information. Also, because of my new awareness I know when someone is really not listening to me. I believe this will be a great tool for both all parts of life. c. yeoman

I have noticed since I started working as a teacher how important active listening is. I always thought of myself as a good listener until I experienced the life of a teacher. Some days my mind is working on several tasks at once. One day a student came into my room to talk about an assignment while I was in the middle of prepping a lab. I kind of rushed through the explanation and the student left. The next day the student turned in the wrong assignment. I clearly recognized my error and have made efforts to always stop what I am doing and give each student my full attention.

It wasn't until my years as an undergrad in college that I actually learned "good" communication skills. My COMS100 class really taught me how to be an active listener and from then on, I have taken those skills with me. I also read an excellent book the summer before I began my professional teaching career on how to effectively communicate with students, though I don't remember the name of it. Believe me, I would have been lost without that book!

Anyway, I use active listening all the time not only when talking to friends about issues they are facing but also with my students. I think my students are surprised when once they have been misbehaving I ask them to go in the hallway and I have a one-on-one discussion with them. I think students are expecting me to yell at them and issue an immediate consequence; however, this really isn't the case at all. Instead, I talk to them and get their input as to why they have been asked to leave the classroom. I ask them if something is bothering them that may be the cause of their misbehavior or inattentiveness. Once I have this talk with students, they return back to the classroom and are usually more likely to stay on task from that point on. If not though, the students know there will be a consequence. As a result of our talk, I know their side of the story and they know mine.

Active listening is an art! I am a student in the Ed.M. programme and I find that active listening is crucial to the amount of contributions I make in class discussions. When I feel that the professor is intrigued and that the students in the class are genuinely interested in the subject, I am more apt to share. I found that in undergraduate classes, the professors taught the material with the expectation of little discussion and class participation. Active listening creates an environment where individuals want to share and feel like their thoughts matter.

Craig makes a good point about Active Listening being a very important skill to be learned in life. By paying attention, asking questions and contributing to what someone is saying shows the speaker that what they say matters to you. I try to do this with each of my athletes I coach. My athletes have seemed to gain respect for me, and are more willing to come and talk with me. They know I really care about what they are saying, not just they're putting in time to collect a paycheck. This also helps with personal relationships. I know my wife really appreciates it when she has had a bad day at work, and while telling me about it, that I participate it he conversation. Let her feel like I am interested in her life and her job.

I often find myself very distracted in class. I either can't keep my mind off other things, or I fall asleep. I often wonder if I have ADHD. One thing that I find helpful is to really try to make eye contact with the teacher as much as possible and sit in the front row. I try to relate the material somehow to my own life, and usually if I think hard enough without becoming distracted, I can. Being an active reader is something that I also need to work on for material that doesn't immediately interest me.

Active Listening sounds like such a simple concept, but it's importance is often overlooked. I look back at my past year of teaching and I am pressed to find examples of times when I was completely focused and concentrated on repsonding to show that I was listening. This is becuase there is constanly so much going on in the classroom, that it is difficult to stop and concentrate on one thing. However, I look at my like and can tell you the difference it makes when I speak with people who show Active Listening skills. I feel validated and affirmed and confident to share. What a powerful thing it would be if we could provide the same feelings for our students.

Lack of Active Listening skills is what makes working with children with mild autism and Aspergers challenging for me. I can't tell without indication that a person is listening and comprehending. There are times that these students are listening, show no evidence and can answer questions about the topic; this is just a difference in their social skills as part of the condition. There are other times these same students prove to not be listening. Indications of Active Listening really help the teacher, but there are always those students that can "fake" active listening that are just as, if not more difficult to teach.

This reminds me of a student in one of my college courses in SPED. He was the ultimate Active Listener. He nodded his head during lecture, would just audibly agree with the instructor with a "yes," or "I firmly agree," and felt he needed to interrupt lectures to prove that he was listening.

The entire class of 200 was annoyed twice a week for a full hour. This "excellent" active listener went too far. It was funny when he came to class late for the first time ever.

He quickly began nodding, taking notes, agreeing under his breath, and then raised his hand to 'prove' he was listening and make up for being late. We had a guest speaker that day. She was blind. Yes, he would have known this if he had arrived on time, but he could not have really been listening to her speak about *BEING BLIND* since he kept his hand up *the entire time she spoke ABOUT BEING BLIND* and was showing signs of great frustration at not being called upon. Pretending to be Actively Listening is a coping skill many master, and others just don't get.

"Verify-Clarify" It is sad that the skills of active listening seem to have been tossed aside as our society changes. I remember as a young boy going to grandma's house and there we would sit in her living room and talk for hours while sampling her fresh baked cookies (which was a great motivation for being there).

And as strange as it may seem, I still remember some of those conversations. We were taught active listening, although it wasn't called active listening at that time. We called it respect; valuing what someone has to say. Since then our society has moved into a media rich world where we are bombarded constantly by every type of media competing for our attention. Maybe as a way of self-preservation we have been forced to learn the skill of listening without really hearing.

Years ago I was taught a concept called "verify-clarify' which I have found to be extremely helpful in active listening.

Basically, when listening to a student explain their view on a point, I will take what I have just heard, rephrase it and ask them, "Let me see. If I understand you correctly you are saying .... Is that correct?" This little skill helps me to "verify" that I am understanding what they have stated. Sometimes I can be concentrating so hard on the words that I miss the meaning. This ensures that I am understanding both. It reassures the person speaking that I am listening and hearing what they have said. It also gives them the opportunity to further "clarify" a point if I did not restate in a form acceptable to the speaker. This little skill has been an excellent skill to help me, in every area of my life, to be a better active listener.

I have found the teaching students how to actively listen has improved their ability to take in information as well as respond in seminar/discussion type settings. Conscious thinking to myself that I need to actively listen to something prior to the experience is still something that I try to reinforce myself with beforehand. In my classroom, I have run into instances that, due to the needs of the child, precludes the child from using what would normally be considered "standard" active listening skills. ADHD, certain behavioral or emotional disorders, and other conditions can cause issues. It is, however, possible to use interventions/modifications that allow, in most cases, active listening to occur.

Active listening is a skill that everyone needs to learn. As teachers, we need to let our students feel that we are listening to them and hearing what they are saying. Also, we need to use active listening with our colleagues. It is important to listen and show you are listening, even if you do not agree. Students need to be taught active listening skills. In a programme we are currently using called Making Meaning, students talk with other students and use prompts to talk to each other. Some of the prompts are "I heard you say...Did I get that right?" By having students practice this kind of discussion, we promote active listening skills. Active Listening is definitely something we all need to work on.

I can see its usefulness in every aspect of my life (my marriage, with my toddler son, my students, my co-workers, my friends, etc.). Since learning about Active Listening I've been focusing more on using this skill. I was lucky to have the opportunity the other day in my study hall class. I have a student in the middle school that has become socially self-destructive. After yelling at a fellow student I sent her to the hall. She was clearly upset with the other student and with me for reprimanding her by sending her out of the room. When I went out I asked a few simple questions and just listened...and summarized. The student shared some problems she's been having at home, started crying, and sounded remorseful for things she's been doing to her friends. At the end of the conversation I felt really good about knowing WHY the student was behaving the way she was (although I didn't excuse her behaviour). That was a nice start for me, I need to keep on working though.

A common activity in my classroom is to call on students at random during discussions and have them summarize different comments their classmates are making. This forces the students to actively listen to the comments their peers are making, and I then provide them with class rewards (class money, called greenbacks), which are redeemed weekly for participation grades and candy. Additionally, the students participate in a job interview unit. The students truly enjoy and are engaged by this unit, which sees them creating resumes, cover letters, and practicing proper job interview techniques in preparation for their future introduction into the workforce. A human resources employee from a Chicago company visits the classroom and instructs students in the proper ways to actively listen.

The practice revolves around such non-verbal communicators as sitting up straight, mimicking the posture of the job interviewer, proper dress, smiling, eye contact, speed, silence, and think time. Think time occurs when a difficult question is asked and the interviewee must "summarize what [he or she] thinks [the] interviewer wants to know and ask[s] for confirmation before proceeding"

(Active Listening for Interview Success). The students are instructed to believe periods of silence are okay, and that simply lets the interviewer know that the questions was truly heard, understood, and that the proper response is being formulated.

Active listening is an important skill that many people lack. After learning more about active listening, I have increased my efforts in having students discuss problems with one another and really listen to each others views. The benefits have been great and I feel that my students are getting along better with each other. Active listening is a skill we must all reflect on to improve our relationships. Hopefully I am modeling this skill for my students.

Active listening has been an asset in several situations with my students. I like how it forces teachers to listen attentively to their students and vice versa. Asking a young child what they heard or understood allows for self reflection and understanding. Once students understand the concepts of active listening they can use this skill in all aspects of their learning. Even though the majority of us have ears that test in the excellent category for hearing, most of us have not developed the necessary skills or aural skills as the academics call it to be used effectively to listen well.

Many experts have tested listening skills through numerous activities focused on how well people remember the information presented. This has been tested in different environments, different time frame and different types of presentations and communications. The consolidation of results from this myriad of research convinces me that people have very short memory spans. Results have proven that we only remember on average about 50% of the information presented immediately after the presentation. The more time that passes, the less we remember. Research at Florida State University suggests that after 60 days have passed we will only remember a maximum of 25% of the information presented. In fact, the predominant amount of that memory loss occurs within the first eight hours after listening to the information. Many people may believe that a person's listening ability is directly related to their intellectual ability; smart people listen better.

Personally I believe this is a myth. Of course someone with exceptional intelligence may be able to retain more information than someone with a very low IQ. But..... For most of us that have average to above average intelligence, our listening abilities are directly related to certain skills that are acquired through experience and training. Keep in mind, being alert, learning to read and being present alone does not automatically increase our listening abilities.

LISTENING IS A UNIQUE ACTIVITY

Listening is different from reading. Listening is about communication, understanding and comprehension. I have known people who are excellent readers that can capture your attention just by the way they form the words that flow through their lips and yet if you ask them to explain exactly what the information means they fall short of expectations. We must be aware of the factors that affect our listening abilities. These factors include:

- Concentrating on the material at hand – remember we think at a much faster pace than we talk. (average talk = 125 words per minute) We must be careful not to get ahead of ourselves. Since our thoughts are faster we can often get distracted or we begin to sandwich in personal thoughts that may or may not be relevant to the information presented. We also may often wander off with a different line of thought and then hurry back to the listening mode when we feel something is relevant.
- Interest which creates a motivation to learn - Additionally this has a tendency to create opportunity for our wandering thoughts to wander in the direction of anticipating what the presenter is leading up to. This keeps us focused on the material at hand improving the quality of our listening.
- Weighing the evidence -Utilizing our listening and rationalization skills we can focus on weighing the

facts presented to determine the validity of the information presented. This also keeps us focused on the material presented thus improving our listening ability.

- Mentally summarizing the points made by actually taking notes reinforces the listening process. Note taking is an essential ingredient to improving our listening abilities. Research has proven that the physical act of writing down information improves our ability to remember and comprehend the information.

EFFECTIVE LISTENING SHOULD SPUR CREATIVITY AND NEW IDEAS

A key technique you can use to improve your listening skills is simply looking for new ideas to utilize in your business or personal life. Ask yourself this question repeatedly throughout the listening process. "How can I apply this (fact – theory – information) to my specific business or challenge?"

Raise your expectations when it comes to what you expect to do with the information that is being presented. Listening to a "motivational speaker" may make you feel good but if you don't come away with some actionable items to work on in your personal environment it is simply a waste of time.

MEMORIZING IS NOT EFFECTIVE LISTENING

You may take pride in getting all the facts and memorizing them considering yourself a good listener. Getting all the facts seems logical to effective listening. However, memorizing all the facts presented in any presentation is often a virtual impossibility for most people. Often we miss critical pieces of information that can often lead to more harm than good. To be an effective listener we must strive to understand the ideas that are being presented. That is why it is much more effective to ask a listener what he intends to do with the information you presented instead of simply asking them if they understand. Grasping the idea behind the information being presented is a key skill that must be developed to become an effective listener. If you understand the idea behind the material presented, the facts often follow naturally.

CLEAN THE EMOTIONAL FILTER

Our listening ability is definitely affected by our emotions and the environment we grew up in. Realistically we often tune out when information threatens a preconceived notion, a belief or when we hear something that strikes a painful emotion from our past.

We simply turn off our listening skill when what is being said is something we just don't want to hear. Adversely, we really focus and turn up our listen skill when we hear something that we especially want to hear. Unfortunately, this emotional trait is often taken advantage of by scam artists and "Free Lunch Schemes" you often find on the internet. We have a tendency to believe anything whether it's fact or fiction.

So..... It is clear that our emotions can act as listening filters. They can both shut out information or they can enhance it. In fact, we must be careful when we begin to hear something that strikes a positive emotion to avoid hearing only what we want to hear.

It is imperative that we clear our minds when listening to prevent our inner emotions from distorting the information being presented both positively or negatively. That means we should withhold evaluation of the information presented until the presentation is complete and we can rationalize our thought process without emotional influence. I'll end this article with the following tips that may help improve the listening skills in your organization.

Tips to Improve Listening Skills:

- Actually conduct a learning session or seminar devoted to improving listening skills. There are many DVD's and exercises available that can be used to support this learning activity. Mini case studies are also an excellent tool used a breakout session with open discussion.
- Study communication skills as they are an integral part of effective listening.

- Hire a consultant to help your group improve listening and communication skills.
- Create a definitions file for industry terms, acronyms and key phrases specific to your business and planning process.
- Make sure you have a well defined and documented orientation programme for new employees. Create a system to have all employees participate at various times with new employee indoctrination. The most effective way to have someone learn something is to have them teach it.
- Create a session of "Team Role" playing that addresses specific listening challenges.
- Develop a listening critique that can be employed after a specific meeting or session that has been recorded. Have the group actually make suggestions for improvements and identify potential miscommunications as a result of ineffective listening.

Chapter 7

Skills: Generating Proposals

By completing this unit, candidates will be able to multi-skill in audio, text, visual and moving image based media. They will be able to work safely in studios, offices and on location. Candidates will understand that the success of media products is based on feasible and clear proposals and effective research. They will gain awareness of their own strengths and how to develop further their specific and transferable skills.

KNOWLEDGE, UNDERSTANDING AND SKILLS

Develop basic specific skills to use in text/visual based and audio/audio visual products create a file of work to demonstrate cross media skills:

Two text/visual skills eg:

- Writing copy
- Producing computer graphics
- Word processing
- Taking photographs
- Editing

Two audio skills eg:

- Recording speech/sounds/music
- Mixing sounds
- Editing

Two audio visual skills eg:

- Recording moving images
- Vision mixing • designing sets
- Organising lighting
- Editing

Skills must include:

- Generating ideas e.g. mood board, storyboard, mind map
- Editing e.g. dubbing music, cropping photographs

Develop basic transferable skills to use in text/visual based and audio/audio visual product. Demonstrate transferable skills which must include:

- Saving, storing and indexing work
- Presenting work showing creativity and good organisation
- Using digital equipment
- The ability to work without supervision
- The ability to follow instructions
- The ability to support other team members
- The ability to meet deadlines

Demonstrate two safe working practices e.g.:

- Lifting heavy objects correctly
- Using cable mats to prevent trips
- Storing sharp/electrical equipment appropriately
- Showing awareness of personal safety when interviewing
- Wearing appropriate clothing
- Present proposals for text/visual and audio/audio visual products. Make a proposal for one audio/audio visual product and one text/visual product from:
- Audio: speech based radio, music based radio, recorded music
- Audio visual: films, fictional and factual television programmes
- Visual: photography
- Print: newspapers, magazines, books
- Electronic media: games, websites
- Advertising: posters, leaflets, commercials, websites

Proposal includes:

- Contact details
- Title
- Type of product
- Purpose
- Content

- Target audience

Conduct research for text/visual based and audio/audio visual products Research for one audio/audio visual product and one text/visual product into eg:

- Target audience
- Content
- Similar products

Demonstrate one example of primary research and explain its purpose:

- Questionnaires
- Interviews

Demonstrate one example of secondary research and explain its purpose:

- Print products
- Audio visual products
- Internet Explain and present research findings

Review progress in practical skills Evaluate skills in terms of:

- Creativity
- Working accurately
- Use of equipment
- Saving/storing material

IDENTIFY STRONGEST SKILLS, SKILLS THAT NEED DEVELOPING

ASSESSMENT

This unit is centre-assessed and externally moderated. In order to achieve this unit, candidates must collate a portfolio of evidence showing that they can meet all the assessment objectives. Portfolios of work must be produced independently. They will need to be made available, together with witness statements and any other necessary supporting documentation, to the OCR Visiting Moderator when required.

GUIDANCE ON ASSESSMENT AND EVIDENCE

This unit prepares the candidate for the production work they will do in Unit 3, although some centres may choose to integrate it with some of the optional units. Candidates are not expected to make complete products in this unit when demonstrating their skills. Tutors may find it useful to introduce this unit at the same time as Unit 1, so that candidates are able to absorb theoretical concepts through practical work. Planning is usually considered to be an important part of pre-production.

However, in this unit, candidates will not necessarily be making one product but possibly parts of lots of products, so for the purposes of this qualification planning has been incorporated into unit 3 in which candidates make a specific media product. The purpose of Assessment Objectives 1 and 2 is to enable candidates to develop and experiment with a range of basic skills in both print and audio/audio-visual areas.

It is important that candidates develop technical, visual and auditory skills and gain competency in using digital equipment across media areas. Audio skills can be developed and demonstrated through use of radio, music technology or moving image digital technology. Candidates will become aware of how some skills such as teamwork or good presentation of work are useful in all areas. They will then be able to use these skills in other units. It may help candidates if they carry out some form of initial skills audit at the beginning of the unit and periodically review their own progress as they proceed. These records can then be referred to as part of the review to be carried out for Assessment Objective 5.

Candidates should demonstrate these skills through producing small pieces of evidence, the best of which they should store and index in a work file could be both paper based and electronic or all electronic. A tutor witness statement should be included to support this evidence by confirming what digital equipment was used, what level of support was given, how well the candidates followed instructions and whether they were able to support other team members. A proforma may form the basis of a witness statement but it must refer to an individual candidate rather than to a group. The witness statement or media products eg photographs may be used to evidence safe working practices. It is expected that most of this work will be individual work though the candidates must have the opportunity at some point to work in a group. Some media tasks such as writing copy for hard news are solitary tasks; others such as studio filming rely heavily on teamwork.

Candidates should have the opportunity to experience both types of work. They need to be able to follow instructions accurately and meet deadlines. For Assessment Objective 3, candidates are expected to make individual proposals for both a new text/visual based product and an audio visual based product.

These products may form a starting point for products made in other units. For example they may make a proposal for a magazine which they intend to make in Unit 3 or Unit 10 and a proposal for a radio advertisement which they intend to make in Unit 4 or Unit 7.

If candidates are working on an integrated project (for example a combined radio and print advertising campaign) they should produce one proposal but this should clearly distinguish between the two products. Making proposals will emphasise to the candidate that the media industry is a business that has to sell its products. Candidates must realise a proposal is a feasible business idea and must identify who the proposal is from and to whom it is going. Some candidates will want to make up a company name to add to the proposal. It is acceptable for a proforma to be used for the proposal as long as it does not limit the candidate.

The production of proposals requires preliminary research into audience preference and market competition but once the proposal has been developed the research will need to be more specific. For Assessment Objective 4, it will help if candidates' research is focused and narrow (eg how long do magazine readers like articles to be or which colour do readers find most attractive for a title) rather than general and wide (eg what do readers expect to find in a magazine). The review may take the form of a written or verbal report but it must include feedback from the tutor/teacher or technicians who have supervised the candidate's practical work. Candidates may find it helpful to refer to tutor feedback when referring to their skills.

SIGNPOSTING TO KEY SKILLS

The unit contains opportunities for developing the Key Skill, and possibly for generating portfolio evidence, if teaching and learning is focused on that aim. Assist with the research of specific requirements of the design brief Research requirements based on the design brief Co-ordinate the art department Liaise with team members to assist the production process Contribute to good working relationships Ensure your own actions reduce risks to health and safety Production Film & TV (Skillset) P5 Identify sources of information and present findings.

RESOURCES

This section provides suggestions of suitable resources. The list is neither prescriptive nor exhaustive, and candidates should be encouraged to gather information from a variety of sources. Some suggested resources are intended for tutor use. The resources in this section were current at the time of print. Develop basic specific skills to use in text/visual based and audio/audio visual products Candidates demonstrate they have developed specific skills in generating and editing material to a basic level possibly with support. Candidates demonstrate basic specific skills in generating and editing material effectively and confidently. Candidates demonstrate basic specific skills in generating and editing material effectively, confidently and creatively to a high standard without support.

AO2

Develop basic transferable skills to use in text/visual based and audio/audio visual products Candidates demonstrate safe working practices and transferable skills to a basic level possibly with support. Candidates demonstrate safe working practices and transferable skills effectively without support. Candidates demonstrate safe working practices and transferable skills effectively and creatively to a high level showing initiative.

AO3

Present proposals for text/visual and audio/audio visual products Candidates complete proposal forms for the products, providing only brief details. Candidates complete proposal forms for the products, providing comprehensive detail. Candidates complete detailed proposal forms and use media terminology correctly.

AO4

Conduct research for text/visual based and audio/audio visual products Candidates carry out general primary and secondary research for the products. They may be unclear on the purpose for carrying out research and its presentation is basic. Candidates carry out relevant primary and secondary research for the products. They describe the reason for carrying out research and it is well presented. Candidates carry out relevant and detailed primary and secondary research for the products. They explain clearly the reason for carrying out research. The research results are effectively analysed and presented.

AO5

Review progress in practical skills Candidates identify their skills in general terms, eg editing and explain their strongest skills in simplistic terms. Candidates identify skills in general terms, eg editing and justify the identification of their strongest skills. Candidates review specific skills eg cropping and sizing photographs and justify the identification of their strongest skills and suggest how they might improve their skills Assessment This unit will be centre-assessed and externally moderated. In order to achieve this unit, candidates must collate a portfolio of evidence showing that they can meet all the assessment objectives. Portfolios of work must be produced independently. They will need to be made available, together with witness statements and any other necessary supporting documentation, to the OCR Visiting Moderator when required.

GUIDANCE ON ASSESSMENT AND EVIDENCE

Candidates should gain knowledge, understanding and skills through practical tasks so that they can effectively decide where their strengths and interests lie. The focus of this unit is to develop candidates' practical skills. This may help them choose to follow a specific or general pathway within media. Centres are strongly advised to integrate this unit with others so that the skills developed and the proposals presented may act as starting points for products made in other units. This may be the production work candidates will do in Units 3 and 4 though some centres may choose to integrate it with some of the optional units.

Candidates are not expected to make complete products in this unit when demonstrating their skills. Tutors may find it useful to introduce this unit at the same time as Unit 1, so that candidates are able to absorb theoretical concepts through practical work. Planning is usually considered to be an important part of pre-production. However, in this unit, candidates will not necessarily be making one product but possibly parts of lots of products, so for the purposes of this qualification planning has been incorporated into unit 3 in which candidates make a specific media product.

The purpose of Assessment Objectives 1 and 2 is to enable candidates to develop and experiment with a range of basic and more complex skills in both text/visual based and audio-visual areas. It is important that candidates develop technical, visual and auditory skills and gain competency in using digital equipment across media areas. Audio skills can be developed and demonstrated through use of radio, music technology or moving image digital technology. They will become aware of how some skills such as teamwork or good presentation of work are useful in all areas. They will then be able to use these skills in other units. As different candidates will have different skill levels at the beginning of the unit, it may help if each carries out some form of initial skills audit and then periodically reviews progress as the unit proceeds. These records can then be referred to as part of the evaluation to be carried out for Assessment Objective 5.

Candidates should demonstrate these skills through producing small pieces of evidence, the best of which they should store and index in a work file that could be both paper based and electronic or all electronic. A tutor witness statement should be included to support this evidence by e.g. confirming what digital equipment was used, what leadership qualities were shown, what technical support was given.

A proforma may form the basis of a witness statement but it must refer to an individual candidate rather than to a group. The witness statement or media products e.g. photographs may be used to evidence safe working practices. For Assessment Objectives 1 and 2 candidates could be given a series of small discrete production tasks e.g. writing a feature article, filming a short sequence to include a tracking shot. They could be given an overarching task that demonstrate a number of skills e.g. producing a 10 second television advert which includes print activities such as storyboarding and writing copy and audio-visual activities such as filming and editing special effects.

It is acceptable for a product such as a web page to be considered as either a text/visual based product or, if it includes animation or video clip, as an audiovisual based product. It is expected that most of this work will be individual work though the candidates must have the opportunity at some point to work in a group.

Some media tasks such as studio filming rely heavily on teamwork whilst writing copy for hard news can be seen as a solitary task. Although some media tasks are completed independently, almost all media employees have to function as part of a team with regular meetings, e.g. the journalist writing hard news needs to liaise with an editor. Candidates should have the opportunity to experience both types of work. They need to be able to follow instructions accurately, show leadership qualities and meet deadlines. Candidates can observe media teamwork if they visit a television studio as a member of a studio audience. Talks from visiting speakers from the media industries can highlight how job roles operate.

For Assessment Objective 3, candidates are expected individually to make proposals and treatments for both a new text/visual based product and an audio visual based product. They may for example make a proposal for a magazine which they intend to make in Unit 3 or Unit 14 and a proposal for a radio advertisement which they intend to make in Unit 4 or Unit 26 or 27. If candidates are working on an integrated project (for example a campaign for the release of a piece of music which incorporates a promotional video and a poster campaign) they should produce one proposal but this should clearly distinguish between the two products and offer specific detail, primary and secondary research and treatments for each.

Making proposals and treatments should emphasize to the candidate that the media industry is a business that has to sell its products. Candidates must realise a proposal and treatment is a business idea and should present it as fit for purpose as a commercial document. It must identify who the proposal and treatment is from and to whom it is going; it should be word processed with clearly presented story boards, drafts and sample copy; and descriptions should be clear and concise whilst also being original and attractive to the commissioning body. They should also be feasible and legally and ethically appropriate. Some candidates will want to make up a company name to add to the proposal. It is acceptable for a proforma to be used for the proposal as long as it does not limit the candidate.

Some media organisations expect ideas to be submitted using their submission forms and it is acceptable that if candidates have access to these that they can use them. The research activities related to Assessment Objective 4 will need to be carried out simultaneously with the production of the proposal. There will need to be preliminary research into audience and the market, and, as the proposal develops, the research should become more focused. It will help candidates if their research is specific (eg which topics attract magazine readers most or which colour do readers find most attractive on magazine front covers) rather than general and wide (e.g. what do readers expect to find in a magazine).

The evaluation may take the form of a written or verbal report but it must include feedback from the tutor/teacher or technicians who have supervised the candidate's practical work. Candidates may find it helpful to refer to tutor feedback and their own skills audits when referring to their skills. It will be useful for candidates to be able to recognise their strengths so that they can select appropriate roles to work in for Unit 3. Explaining how their skills can be further developed may be addressed in a number of ways e.g. by looking at higher education courses or through making a career plan.

Chapter 8

Skills: Servicing

Broadcast writing demands a special set of skills and knowledge from the journalist. Broadcast copy is written to be read out loud by a news reader rather than to be read silently by a news consumer. The words and sentences must be constructed so they are accurate and clear. They must also complement the pictures, video and audio that accompany a story.

SHORT VIDEOS ON BROADCAST WRITING

For those interested in teaching or learning to write in broadcast style, you should listen to or watch four short video clips about broadcast writing produced by my friend and colleague Mark Harmon, a professor of journalism and electronic media here at UT. They can be found at this Volcasting link. The four clips concern news judgment, attribution, broadcast style and active voice. (All four videos will take less than 10 minutes to watch.) They are well worth the short amount of time it takes to view them.

COURIC TAKES OVER

In the long history of the CBS Evening News, there had been only three permanent anchors: Douglas Edwards, Walter Cronkite and Dan Rather. Now there is a fourth. Katie Couric (CBS biography) debuted as the newscast's latest anchor. Couric is a legitimate journalist who was part of NBC's news team covering the Pentagon and the Gulf War in 1991. For the last 15 years she has been the host of NBC's Today Show, and her work has not been considered to be on the front lines of reporting. Her main job at CBS is not to deliver the news but to deliver an audience (preferably one that is a little younger than the one CBS has). Here are a few stories and reviews of her first night: New York Times, Washington Post, NPR.

News orgs discover web's immediacy. A couple of stories from Romenesko's blog on today show that big time news organizations are discovering the immediacy of the web. One comes from Westworld, which reports that when the Denver Post stumbled onto a scoop last month about beer magnate Peter Coors being arrested for drunk driving, the Post nailed the story and then put it on the organization's web site – despite some grousing from the traditionalists. These folks thought a story like that should be saved for print first, which was several hours away. The paper's managing editor said the web would be "our breaking news platform." Then there is the story about CBS streaming its nightly news programme simultaneously with its over-the-air broadcast. This, apparently, has come about only after painstaking negotiations with affiliates. One is tempted to ask: "Where have these folks been for the last 10 years or so?" *(Posted Aug. 17, 2006)*

Off again, on-again. The general manager of the public radio station in Lexington, Ky., caused a minor flap late last week by announcing that he was pulling Garrison Keillor's Writer's Almanac off WUKY. Tom Godell expressed some dismay at the language that was cropping up in some of the poems that Keillor had read on the programme and fear that his station would be fined by the Federal Communications Commission. Keillor was certainly no Howard Stern, Godell said, but "the FCC has been so inconsistent, we don't know where we stand."

That was Friday. By Saturday Keillor was back. The station received so many phone calls and emails from its listeners that Godell was forced to relent. One of those who protested was Leonard Press, the founder and long-time director of Kentucky Educational Television who called the cancellation "an overreaction" and said, "This is a man who is one of the premier writers and performers of our time. I think he's generally recognized for his tastefulness." according to a report in the Cincinnati Post. Godell said he decided to cancel the show after an increasing number of "language advisories" had been sent to produces. Such advisories alert stations to the possibilities of language that might not be suitable to all audiences. In this case, there were references to the female breast and in one poem to getting "high." While many (including Keillor) are castigating Godell for his decision, we might want to examine whether or not the FCC has created a climate where such fears are legitimate. The heavy-handedness of the FCC should be remembered along with the names of Janet Jackson and Howard Stern.

Put your news on the pod. Podcasting is one of the new terms in online journalism. It simply means putting news and information into an audio MP3 format and making it available to folks who own MP3 players – millions of them. News web sites, particularly broadcast sites where this is a natural, are beginning to use this method to reach those who want to do more than just listen to music on their MP3 players, according to Jonathan Dube, Cyberjournalist.net. (In addition to the MP3 players, there are lots of cellphones that have MP3 capability.) Dube cites an article in Digital-Lifestyles.info that says the BBC used this method for extending one of its programs late last year, and the file got 100,000 downloads. The technology and technique are not confined to broadcasters, of course. Any news outlet can create these files and offer them to an audience that might not otherwise be exposed to its content. (Podcasting comes from Apple's iPod, which dominates the world of MP3 players.)

Update: Cyberjournalist has posted more information on the growing phenomenon of podcasting. As a result of the success of podcasting for the radio show On the Media, WNYC is going to start making another of its shows available as an MP3 download. The WNYC news release announcing this plan says the podcasting of On the Media has added significantly to the show's audience:

"Podcasting is a remarkable boon for local radio broadcasts," added Phil Redo, VP of Station Operations and Strategy. "This easy-to-access, easy-to-use technology allows local programming to transcend the limitations of both traditional radio and online streaming, by allowing users to plug into great programming from far-flung places, anytime, anywhere."

WNYC launched the first podcast of an NPR programme in January 2005 to great success. NPR's On the Media, the station's nationally-broadcast media analysis show, has doubled the amount of listeners it reaches online in just four weeks. OTM's podcast audience now rivals the number of individuals that would enjoy the programme in a mid-sized media market like St. Louis or Kansas City.

CBS and the Bush National Guard memos. The big media story of the week was a report of an internal investigation that CBS News conducted on a story aired in September concerning George W. Bush's service in the National Guard in the 1970s. The report cited memos written by Bush's superior officers showing that Bush has received favorable treatment both in getting into the Guard and during his service there. The story aired on Sept. 8, 2004, on CBS's 60 Minutes Wednesday just as the presidential campaign was getting intense; it had originally been scheduled to air on Sept. 29. Soon after the show, many people called into question the authenticity of the memos CBS reporters used as the basis for the story. Initially, CBS and Dan Rather, who reported the segment, defended the story, but they eventually had to back down because the memos had not been properly investigated. CBS suffered a storm of criticism and launched its own internal investigation. The report of that investigation was released this week, and five people from CBS News were fired. (Rather was not one of them.) The report did not clear up the questions about the authenticity of the memos; nor did it specify who at CBS News made the decision to move the broadcast up by three weeks.

A note on format. CBS News put the report on its web site in a PDF format rather than simply having it in HTML. Consequently, if you wanted to look at the 200-plus page document, you had to download the whole thing onto your computer and then either print it out or try to search through it in Acrobat. Either way, it did not make things easy for the reader. Breaking in. Want to get into broadcasting? The Poynter Institute (which has a whole section on broadcasting journalism) has a timely article on tips on getting started in broadcast journalism. Here's how it starts:

Dig hard, write well, and maybe even sweep a few floors.

Broadcast professionals say that's what young journalists should do if they're serious about pursuing a career in the competitive field of news broadcasting. Television and radio students who want to stand out from the crowd must become enterprising, information-sniffing archaeologists, said Al Tompkins, Poynter's broadcast journalism group leader.

Broadcast professionals say that's what young journalists should do if they're serious about pursuing a career in the competitive field of news broadcasting. Television and radio students who want to stand out from the crowd must become enterprising, information-sniffing archaeologists, said Al Tompkins, Poynter's broadcast journalism group leader. Tompkins said that for students to be great storytellers, they must dig up information no one else is looking for, and then produce the package with clarity and cohesiveness. To uncover well-hidden journalistic gems, Tompkins said students need to talk with the people no one else is interviewing.

"If a crowd of journalists is going somewhere, I'd go wherever they are not going," he said. "Break the habit of talking to your friends. Seek out people not like you and learn to listen and not talk." In addition to being a good listener, broadcast students also must be outstanding writers. "It doesn't hurt to look good, but in the long term it doesn't matter. I've seen too many average-looking and sounding people who are great writers do very well in this business. Mike Wallace and Morley Safer are not pin-ups, but they're fine journalists."

Gayle Sierens, veteran co-anchor and reporter for Tampa's WFLA-TV, also said honing writing and editing skills is a top priority. In addition, she tells budding reporters to "develop a thick, thick skin" and "be yourself." Sierens said students need to work hard while being patient. Getting comfortable in front of the camera or behind a microphone "takes a while and doesn't happen overnight," she said. To get a head start on the competition, Sierens said broadcast-minded students should seek volunteer or internship positions with local stations.

"Be willing to start small," Sierens said. "Get your foot in the door and make a nuisance of yourself. Do everything and anything beyond the call of duty. Any shred of experience will only help you." CBS News Radio's Peter King agreed. "The best thing you can do is visit radio stations in your area," said King, a national anchor and reporter. "Visit more than one. Get an internship or part-time job sweeping the floors. You can learn a lot just by hanging around. Be curious and ask a lot of questions.

Don't just ask what; ask why." While a great face may help in TV and a fantastic voice won't hurt in radio, broadcasters agree that it's what's between the ears that counts. "Good reporters know a little bit about a lot of things," King said. "A good voice helps, but that's not necessarily what's going to keep you going. Being a good human being, having common sense and curiosity — those are the traits that make a good journalist."

Chapter 9

Skills: Negotiating and Closing

Between 1996 and 2002, the Rhode Island Coalition Against Domestic Violence (RICADV) moved from media obscurity to become the primary information source about domestic violence for Rhode Island reporters. This change was not part of a general trend. During the same seven-year period, most state domestic violence coalitions did not improve their media standing appreciably.

RICADV's success, therefore, merits analysis. This longitudinal study employs both qualitative and quantitative methods to explore how the collective actor, RICADV, working with the university-based collective actor, the Media Research and Action Project (MRAP), strengthened its standing in the Rhode Island media market which ranks in the top quartile of U.S. media markets (43 rd of 200).

Beginning with qualitative approaches, we reconstruct how the collective actor RICADV parleyed growing media standing into expanded media opportunities. We then assess RICADV's media standing quantitatively via a content analysis that measures shifts in RICADV's ability to influence media coverage of domestic violence murders over a seven-year period. Finally, we tentatively conjecture on the impact of media standing on political standing.

In 1996, two collective actors, the statewide Rhode Island Coalition Against Domestic Violence (RICADV) and the university-based Media Research and Action Project (MRAP) * initiated a common project. To further RICADV's mission of ending domestic violence, we wanted to strengthen its media standing, e.g., we wanted Rhode Island reporters to recognize

RICADV as an indispensable source for news and background information regarding domestic violence. RICADV and MRAP saw media standing as a prerequisite for achieving a second objective—to open new opportunities to promote RICADV's framing of domestic violence as a social problem not a private problem, requiring social not individual solutions.

This paper assesses one aspect of our collaboration—RICADV'S efforts to alter the Rhode Island reporters' representation of domestic violence murders as unpredictable, private tragedies. Our project's focus on domestic violence murders emerged from our joint work. In spring 1996, a month into our collaboration, a cluster of three domestic violence murders occurred within a six-week period. First, an elderly man brutally beat his wife to death. Then, a young man killed his girlfriend, his two-year-old, and himself.

Three weeks later, a middle-aged man killed his wife, two children, and himself. Print news presented the murders as inexplicable, private family tragedies. Coverage of the first case stressed the elderly couple's failing health.

In the second case reporters quoted a shocked neighbour describing the perpetrator as "a really nice kid. . . . Things like this don't hap- pen around here supposedly". Print coverage of the third case similarly conveyed shock and denial. The victims were a "model family," insisted their minister. The perpetrator's sister added, "I guess he loved them so much, he just took them with him". RICADV did not influence this 1996 coverage. While comfortable calling press for a planned event, RICADV then lacked the capacity to leverage an unexpected incident such as a murder into a media opportunity. "We waited by the phone, but no call came," recalled one RICADV staff. To our surprise, the same reporters and media outlets that had covered RICADV education campaigns supportively failed to recognize the murders as domestic violence.

RICADV asked MRAP to analyse news coverage of domestic violence murders systematically; MRAP's preliminary study confirmed that reporters in the Rhode Island media market routinely treated domestic violence murder as an isolated and unforeseeable event—a slasher movie cum morality play in which modern man inexplicably unravels. Domestic violence murder coverage was sensationalized, decontextualized, and fixated on the perpetrator's motive, findings that replicated those of other studies described below. In 1999, just as MRAP completed our study, a second cluster of three domestic violence murders occurred.

By this point, RICADV had strengthened its capacity to respond rapidly to unexpected events. Its spokespersons, now quoted widely, shifted news accounts of the murders from the previous framing of domestic violence as a private, unpredictable tragedy to the advocates' social framing of domestic violence as a community responsibility. RICADV subsequently published a handbook for journalists summarizing recommendations from survivors, reporters, advocates and MRAP (2000). When a third cluster of three domestic violence murders occurred in spring 2002, RICADV was even better positioned; it had consolidated its rapid response capacity and strengthened working relations with member groups and a broad network of allies all of whom it rapidly mobilized.

At a packed press conference, Deborah DeBare, Executive Director of RICADV flanked by domestic violence survivors and leading politicians, called for social not private responses to domestic violence. The over-flow audience included film crews, photographers, and reporters from every major news outlet in Rhode Island, candidates for Attorney General, elected officials, law enforcement officers, and domestic violence advocates. Reporters had labeled the press conference a "must attend" event, and its coverage topped the evening news and the next day's headlines.

In contrast to domestic violence advocates' silence in 1996, news accounts in 2002 opened with RICADV's messages of community responsibility for domestic violence. Reporters high- lighted the testimony of RICADV's domestic violence survivor group, Sisters Overcoming Abusive Relationships (SOAR). SOAR's Rosa DeCastillo described fleeing with her children barefoot in the snow and urged the audience to "work together to ensure the safety of victims." A friend of Barbara Lombardi, a recent victim, also stressed social responsibility: "Tragically, our present system failed Barbara and should be held accountable—anything less would be an injustice."

RICADV's DeBare then linked these experiences to a major policy initiative; in ten days following the third murder, an RICADV-initiated coalition had crafted a seven-point plan to close gaps in the safety net of domestic violence services. A few months later, the Coalition and its allies shepherded the plan through the Rhode Island legislature. Thus, a seasoned RICADV turned the 2002 cluster of murders into a catalyst for policy change, not only a media opportunity but also a political opportunity. After the bill's passage, RICADV and MRAP agreed to enter a period of reflection to distill the lessons from RICADV's intentional capacity-building and strategic intervention in the Rhode Island media market. From that reflection, came the study that follows.

THEORETICAL BACKGROUND

Since the founding of Mobilization, social movement theorists have debated whether opportunity is primarily exogenous—a structural opening caused by forces beyond social movements' control—or more negotiable—a strategic tug of war in which unequal contending forces wrestle for advantage amidst shifting historical conditions. Mapping thirty variables appearing in these debates, Gamson and Meyer warn that opportunity "threatens to become an all-encompassing fudge factor for all the conditions and circumstances that form the context for collective action". Eight years later, Meyer finds more variables added while previous variables have yet to be "disproved, refined or replaced," a tendency he finds "both completely understandable and frustrating". Since different studies focus on distinct theoretical issues and movements, Meyer continues, "analysts talk past each other".

For instance, studies stressing "big" opportunities (shifts in relatively stable structures and values) do not engage with those focused on "small" opportunities (shifts in more volatile attitudes, policies, and practices). Diverging methodologies further complicate debates; comparative studies of social systems and movements tend to highlight big opportunities, while studies tracking single movements over time, highlight small opportunities. More fundamentally, theorists begin with divergent definitions of collective action and collective actors. Some focus only on collective acts of protest, others on action in the political arena, while others include cultural and economic dimensions. In defining collective actors, some studies vaguely refer to challengers while others may focus on individual activists, social movement organizations, coalitions, or whole social movements.

Without much uniformity regarding what constitutes collective action or actors, it remains hard to generalize about intentional agency—how collective actors share perceptions, reach common cause, act and reflect together as a collective force: The presumption underneath a political opportunity approach is that the development of movements reflects, responds to, and sometimes alters the realities of politics and policy although most work gives short shrift to how. Criticizing theorizing that ignores collective actors' intent, Flacks (2005) agrees, It is surprising how rarely the historical studies that constitute the canon of the political opportunity (PO) perspective focus on the ways activists, in the movements being studied, understood and determined their own opportunities. Indeed, how organizers figure out their opportunities, and how movements expand on them is largely unstudied and untheorized.

As yet, he concludes, "the concept of 'political opportunity' provides little help in deciding what opportunities may actually be germane to what sort of mobilizing effort". To ground the debate over the nature of opportunity, Flacks urges that theorists follow the collective actor, a proposal resonant with Morris' (2000) suggestion that theorists study the processes that form and sustain collective actors. In line with both Flacks and Morris, Alimi (2003, 2004) demonstrates how Palestinian framers in the occupied territories in the years preceding the "first" Intifada utilized both print media and grassroots mobilization to construct a shared Palestinian perception of growing divisions in Israel regarding the continued Israeli occupation.

Alimi argues that this internal Palestinian discourse was a critical component of Palestinians' reassessment of opportunity and that this discourse contributed to Palestinian mobilization; Palestinian organizations' shifting assessments of opportunities catalyzed increasingly overt conflicts with the Israeli state.

We share Alimi's interest in tracking how small opportunities, strategically nurtured by collective actors over time, can expand into bigger opportunities for more permanent structural changes. This longitudinal study of the Rhode Island Coalition Against Domestic Violence, a statewide organization representing opponents to domestic violence, tracks how they negotiated media opportunities by strengthening their internal communication capacity and broadening relationships. As RICADV negotiated with media outlets to strengthen its media standing, it expanded opportunities to promote its oppositional frame via mainstream news outlets.

MEDIA OPPORTUNITY

Mass media form the "master forum" of our historical period. Yet for social movements, U.S. corporatized mass media markets offer limited access. To gain media standing, actors raising counterhegemonic perspectives as well as actors marginalized by inequalities such as race, class, gender, sexuality, citizenship or age must overcome barriers institutionalized in news gathering routines; pressured to produce fast, interesting stories that avoid legal controversies, journalists gravitate toward sources widely deemed "reliable," and avoid marginalized constituencies. Sourcing decisions are political; in choosing sources, reporters decided whose accounts count. When accounts count, their sponsors gain visibility and options to press for added power. When accounts do not count, their proponents remain beyond the public eye; they lack credibility and their framings of reality remain marginal.

Individual activists and informal groups can master the skills and resources needed for occasional media appearances. Becoming a routine source in a market-driven mass media system, however, requires the sustainable energy of a collective actor with social and material capital far exceeding that of an individual activist or an informal group.

To sustain a routine working relationship with media outlets, e.g., function as a routine source, a collective actor must invest over time in communication capacity building so that media strategies can enhance political strategies (Ryan 1991). Movements' often paltry success establishing media capacity and gaining media standing provides anecdotal support for "strong hegemony" approaches that document how modern mass media structures con-strain democratic discourse. While fully accepting these structural constraints, RICADV and MRAP build their work on weaker hegemony approaches that stress agent-focused opportunities for changing media.

In adopting a weaker hegemony model, collective actors strategically assess their options and weigh their resources and networks against the dangers and pressures of structural inequalities. Raymond Williams calls this reflexive strategizing, "options under pressure".

Applying a similar approach to media-movement interactions, weaker hegemony adherent Barker-Plummer calls for a dialogic approach to relations between movements and reporters that can acknowledge collective actors' reflexivity: A dialogic approach looks for two-way influences from any interaction, and it assumes the participants in any interaction can learn about and use the resources of the other— especially if those resources are discursive knowledge resources. . . . Seeing the media- movement relationship as two-way does not preclude it from being an imbalanced interaction, nor deny that one organization holds more power than the other. A dialogic model comes with no guarantees. . . . But to say that a relationship is difficult, complex, subtle and unbalanced is not to say that its outcomes are inevitable.

Highlighting intentional interactions embedded in historically shaped inequalities, Barker- Plummer's dialogic approach resonates with theorists stressing relationships and coalitions, discourse, power, strategy, reflexivity, and collective processes and infrastructure. Like Steinberg's historically embedded discourse analyses, Barker-Plummer's dialogic approach recognizes that, at heart, social change involves actors communicating—developing strategies by airing grievances, testing challenges, negotiating conflicts, lobbying allies, evaluating accomplishments, and sharing lessons.

As relations deepen and collaborations widen, the collective actor extends its power, gaining standing in widening circles. Like Klandermans (1992) and Gamson and Meyer (1996), Barker-Plummer calls for longitudinal studies of media opportunity: Movement and media interactions play out over time.

> Only by studying these interactions across time can we track the influence of one discourse on the other. Short term studies that declare a critical movement or discourse to have been marginalized and thus to have 'failed' in the short terms, may be missing some of the most important effects. (1996: 32)

DOMESTIC VIOLENCE AS AN ISSUE CULTURE

Meyer (2004) flags the value of an "issue-specific conceptualization" of opportunity, an insight of particular importance for the collective actor negotiating media opportunities. Historically rooted framing contests start with the existing issue culture. Domestic violence advocates today build on previous decades of organizing that successfully established domestic violence as a social problem worthy of public and media attention. While the movement against domestic violence has established public awareness of domestic violence, media coverage does not consistently adopt the movement's framing of the issue—that ending domestic violence requires social intervention. To the contrary, researchers have identified the following recurring problems with existing coverage:

- News suggests victims, at least partially, are responsible for their fate.
- Inscribed as crime news, domestic violence reports

focus on the sensational. Reporters revert to predetermined framings such as "tragic love goes awry".

- In an exculpatory search for perpetrator's motive, domestic violence is psychologized and individuated.
- Coverage focuses on perpetrators' motives and victims disappear.
- Coverage obscures social dimensions of domestic violence—ways that society produces and promotes violence against women.

Coverage patterns also vary by beat. A Living Page reporter may describe a new domestic violence shelter sympathetically, yet, re-assigned to the crime beat, may revert to traditional crime reporting lacking substantive insight into underlying issues.

Crime news' common severing of problem from causality undermines efforts to change public policy and consciousness, leaving past and potential victims isolated; atomized victims struggle for protection while the social roots of domestic violence remain obscured.

To address these problems, advocates and researchers have urged:

- Changes in news practices;
- Changes in journalist training;
- Journalistic guidelines regarding domestic violence coverage.

Though practical and compelling, the recommendations do not address the barriers to change inherent in a market-driven news industry. While some argue that newsgathering practices can change, media critics generally concur that corporate mass media systems bedevil reform efforts unless grounded in strong collective efforts.

Thus, despite their practicality, the reforms proposed above remain a critique. It would take a collective actor to translate the critique into an intervention strategy, to develop the relational ties and networks needed to implement that strategy and distill lessons. In 1996, RICADV decided to attempt such an intervention.

METHODS AND FINDINGS

MRAP's preliminary study found that existing news coverage sensationalized domestic violence murders while framing them as private tragedies. RICADV was eager to replace this individuated framing with its frame conceptualizing domestic violence as a social problem, "everybody's business." To negotiate wider opportunities for promoting this social frame, RICADV worked to improve its media standing as a routine news sources for reporters, a goal involving internal strengthening and external relation building. Positioning ourselves as theorists and activists working with RICADV, we tracked RICADV's decision making and strategizing, its actions and reflections. We wanted to explore how intentional collective actors strategize to gain opportunity, an issue on which many studies remain "agnostic".

Conceptualizing the Research

To conduct an actor-centered, longitudinal study, we needed to resolve questions of scale, scope, and duration, and to identify outcomes that would serve as measures of media standing. Regarding scale, RICADV represented a collective actor working within interacting political and media arenas; as a statewide coalition, RICADV was mandated to work for change in Rhode Island social policy, its political catchment area coinciding with the geographical area covered by the Rhode Island media market. The research's scope was RICADV's communications work driven by two goals—solidifying media standing and expanding media opportunities in the Rhode Island media market.

To track the development of RICADV's growing communication capacity, we coupled qualitative methods with quantitative content analysis assessing RICADV's shifting influence on domestic violence murder coverage. Our estimates of duration were informed by previous MRAP research that it took years not months for a social movement organization to become a routine source. Collective actors need to train staff and spokespersons, develop and refine internal and external communications systems, prepare messages and establish standing with reporters as a consistent and reliable source; while added resources can speed some processes, relation-building occurs in real time and the process can not be rushed.

Qualitative Approaches

As do individual activists, collective actors have life histories. To track the collective actor RICADV's growing communication capacity, we broadened life-history methods, which are gernerally understood as: Oral in-depth interviews conducted by a researcher within the framework of a research project. Thus life histories involve interaction between the interviewer and the interview and involve a scientific intention in the telling of a story.

Our collective life history approach involved thirty hours of oral in-depth group interviews with staff, survivors, coalition members, interns etc. These were transcribed, reviewed by participants, and augmented by archival research, participant observation, and individual interviews. The resulting collective life history tracks RICADV's conscious efforts to establish good working relationships with journalists (media standing) and, how it turned that standing into new opportunities in its media market.

Qualitative Findings

We began our life history of the Rhode Island Coalition Against Domestic Violence (RICADV) in 1996 when the organization, rooted in the Rhode Island women's movement, crafted a strategic plan to forward its mission of ending domestic violence in Rhode Island. In winter of 1996, RICADV hired a full-time communications coordinator, Karen Jeffreys, and charged her with developing and overseeing RICADV communications initiatives, including both mass media and grassroots outreach. A seasoned community organizer, Jeffreys took a movement-building approach to communications. She reasoned that those directly affected by domestic violence—victims and survivors—should be at the heart of setting the movement's directions. Starting there, Jeffreys worked to establish diverse networks of communication and support. "Everyone is a communicator," was our slogan. To ensure group participation, Jeffreys translated MRAP's framing work into a collective process, dubbed as the "media caucus" at RICADV.

Other media systems included a communication plan, media protocols, and a rapid response team at the organizational level. Jeffreys began to build RICADV's communications infrastructure and then worked with staff and members to map a communications strategy resonant with its overall strategy. Jeffreys called what she did "public relations," but her approach was far from the popular understanding of "PR" as sound-bite-driven marketing. She conceptualized public relations as genuinely relating to one's publics, i.e., creating working relationships with all constituencies relevant for RICADV's mission of ending domestic violence in Rhode Island. Jeffreys also brought to RICADV her existing ties to the Media Research and Action Project (MRAP). Based on prior experience, MRAP estimated it would take five to seven years to establish RICADV as a routine source.

To establish a baseline of information, the partners began to monitor existing news coverage of domestic violence. RICADV interns combed the news clips to identify reporters covering domestic violence-related beats. Using the same news clippings, MRAP analyzed media framings of domestic violence. At the same time, Jeffreys and other staff with roots in the Black Liberation and feminist movements began to strengthen RICADV's ability to make decisions collectively through solidarity building practices focused on core values and world view, diversity and conflict resolution practices. With internal capacity to dialog and resolve differences reinforced, RICADV then developed a communications plan, a collective framing process dubbed a media caucus, media trainings and other media systems.

As internal and external communications capacity grew, RICADV gained media standing. In 1996, RICADV had not gained access to media coverage when an external crisis—a cluster of three domestic violence murders—occurred. Three years later in 1999, RICADV could influence media coverage of a similar murder cluster. By 2002, RICADV turned a murder cluster into a media opportunity, and then a political opportunity, a legislative campaign to reform Rhode Island's domestic-violence laws. Furthermore, on a state and national level, RICADV was functioning as a small agency-laden institution supporting other collective actors' media capacity building.

QUANTITATIVE APPROACHES

While increased calls from reporters suggested that RICADV's media standing had grown, we hadn't assessed that growth systematically. To do so, we decided to measure shifts in RICADV's rapid response capacity—its ability to influence unplanned events. The obvious beginning point was RICADV's 1996 decision to intensify communication work. As a closing point, we chose 2002 when RICADV concluded that, within the Rhode Island media market, it had achieved its goal of becoming an indispensable source of news and information regarding domestic violence.

To measure ability to respond quickly to outside, unpredictable events we looked for possible critical discourse moments. We settled on three comparable clusters of domestic violence murders. Each cluster involved three independent domestic violence murder cases that had occurred in a compressed time period—five to seven weeks. Moreover, the three murder clusters had occurred at three-year intervals at the beginning, middle and end of our proposed study. We measure growth of RICADV's media standing in terms of its capacity to use the critical discourse moment to introduce the domestic violence movement's perspectives via the language and the sources that reporters use.

Study Design and Methods

MRAP's preliminary frame analysis of domestic violence murder coverage RICADV 2000), found that coverage stopped framing domestic violence murders as "private family tragedy" or "love gone awry" when the murder was labeled as domestic violence and when domestic violence advocates or experts were quoted. Based on these findings, RICADV decided to urge reporters to adopt two changes in journalistic practice: first, to use the words, 'domestic violence' if speaking about violence between intimates in order to set context; and second, to downplay or use selectively sources who stress the personal, tragic aspects of domestic violence (family, neighbors, random bystanders). Instead, RICADV urged reporters to seek sources who discuss domestic violence murder—and its prevention—in its social context. In short, police, domestic violence survivors, advocates, or other experts can frame domestic violence more broadly than family and bystanders.

To analyse RICADV's progress vis-à-vis these changes, we measured the use of domestic violence language and sourcing patterns after three comparable clusters of domestic violence murders. The first cluster in 1996, serves as a baseline occurring before RICADV established systematic communications infrastructure and practices. The 1999 cluster and the 2002 cluster provide measures at three-year intervals. Sample Selection Using a news-clipping service, we surveyed all weekly and daily papers, in the Rhode Island media market for coverage of any domestic violence murder that occurred between 1996 and 2002. Crosschecking the sample against Lexis-Nexis, we identified 275 stories addressing the 22 domestic violence murder cases that occurred in Rhode Island between 1996 and 2002. From this sample we selected a subset of murder cases that occurred in comparable conditions; in each case, a cluster of three murder cases in less than two months.

Spaced at three-year intervals, the clusters represent the seven-year time period over which RICADV established a communication staff, strategy and infrastructure. Thus, the clusters permit us to contrast changes in coverage against the incremental growth of RICADV's communication capacity. We treated each cluster of murders as one critical discourse moment. We focused on murders rather than incidents of domestic violence more generally for several reasons. Use of murders ensured that the issue met news criteria. Murders could be identified irrefutably as domestic violence (as contrasted to domestic violence incidents that are contested by either party). Finally, murder stories represented a clear example of unplanned crisis coverage. As such, murder stories were a good measure of RICADV's ability to take advantage of an external, unanticipated media opportunity.

Moreover, a cluster of murders occurring in close proximity, we hypothesized, might create a media opportunity; reporters might be more open to domestic violence advocates highlighting the murders' common features: in domestic violence murders, usually there is a history of violence, others besides the victim know about it, and existing prevention systems fail. Our focus on local print media reflects communications scholars' findings that local news provides the most common journalistic venue for domestic violence crimes since they are usually deemed of mostly local interest. National media, covering only the most egregious or unusual domestic violence murder cases, offer a less reliable arena for evaluating coverage patterns.

Our focus on print media grows from Kaniss' (1997) finding that local print news outlets serve as kingmakers directly impacting politicians, police and other institutions. Broadcast news, Kaniss finds, generally trails print coverage, the longer print accounts providing raw material for broadcasts' shorter "headline" versions of events.

Coder Training and Content Variables

We trained two teams, each comprised of three coders, to identify both the patterns of sources and the kinds of domestic-violence language used in the newspaper articles. Post-training, intercoder reliability averaged. We compared the reporters' choices of lead and key sources and articles' use of domestic violence language. Removing advocate/activist sources from the sample, we looked for use of domestic violence language by nonadvocate sources and reporters. This article compares media coverage of each of the murder clusters in relation to our two key variables—journalists' choice of language to describe the murders and journalists' choice of sources.

To analyse journalists' choice of language describing domestic violence murders, we first reviewed RICADV press releases for each murder. From these press releases we created a glossary of common phrases used by advocates vis-à-vis the murders. Each news article was then coded for reporters' incorporation of language that corresponded to the advocates' domestic violence message. Coders documented where and how often the term appeared. Each story was coded three times, each time by an independent coder.

A final coding reviewed all cases for consistency, data entry errors, etc. Intercoder reliability exceeded. Positing that journalists use sources to shape the story line, we also studied source patterns. We coded articles for all quoted sources, identified by relationship to the crime (e.g., police, domestic violence advocate, bystander, victim, victim's family, friend, co-worker; perpetrator; perpetrator's family, friend, coworker, and so on). The police category included court professionals. The advocate category included survivors and all others involved in domestic violence work or activism. We focused this analysis on sources used in lead quotes and key quotes.

CONTENT ANALYSIS: FINDINGS

A comparison of news coverage of the 1996, 1999, and 2002 murder clusters reveals significant changes in reporters' use of domestic violence language and sourcing patterns.

Domestic Violence Language

In news articles covering the first cluster of domestic violence murders, there were only 0.57 references per article to domestic violence, i.e., on average, less than one reference per article. By 1999, news stories, however, were averaging five references to domestic violence per article, roughly a seven-fold increase. After the publication of the handbook for journalists, subsequent dialogue and relation building, references to domestic Violence rose to ten per article. This doubled the reference per article rate from 1999. Measuring change from the baseline year of 1996, however, 2002 figures represent a sixteen-fold increase.

Sourcing Patterns

To analyse trends in sourcing patterns, we studied shifts in lead source and shifts in key sources. The lead source was the first source cited in the article. No news story covering the 1996 cluster of murders quoted a domestic violence advocate as lead source. The majority of lead sources at this point were police, victim's relations (family, friend, coworker), perpetrator's relations (family, friends, coworkers) and bystanders (the proverbial "man on the street" interview). Police and victim's relations, tied for the most common lead source; 28.6% of the 1996 stories lead with a quote from the police or from victim's family, neighbors, or coworkers. Similarly bystanders and perpetrator's relations split second place at 7.1% and 7% respectively.

By 1999, the situation had changed. In print coverage of the second cluster of murders, advocates rose from invisibility to become reporters' most common lead source; 30.8% of articles quoted an advocate (A) as their lead source. Reporters continued to use police as the lead source but to a lesser extent (P = 19.2%). Reporters dramatically decreased their use of victim's relations and perpetrator's relations as lead sources; by the second cluster of murders, use of victim's relations (V) had dropped to 7.6% and no perpetrator's relations were quoted. Reporters, however, continued to solicit reactions from random by-passers. (B = 11.5%) 2002 coverage demonstrates further changes. Advocates and police have remained the two most common lead sources.

Reporters' preference for advocates as lead source has continued to rise (40.3%) but reporters' use of police sources has increased as well; in the third cluster of murders reporters cite police as lead source almost as frequently as in 1996 (24.8%). The additional visibility garnered by advocates drew, therefore, not from police but from bystander sources. A graphical representation of trends in lead source citation can be found. Besides lead sources, we analyzed all key sources—sources quoted in the first three or last paragraphs or quoted for at least one paragraph—coding them again by their relationship to the murder. Changes in sourcing patterns for key sources were virtually identical to those cited for lead sources above.

Changes in the Culture

Since advocates routinely use domestic violence language, we expected an increase in use of domestic violence advocates as lead or key sources might result in a concomitant increase in domestic violence language. This would tell us that domestic violence advocates had become more visible in public discourse but would not mean that other public voices had embraced domestic violence language. To test whether reporters and/or other sources— police, bystanders, victim's families—increased their use of domestic violence language over the six-year period, we created a dummy variable that removed all articles citing advocates as sources. Using the resulting "nonadvocate" subsample, we conducted an independent sample T-test to determine the means for domestic violence citations when advocates are not quoted.

In other words, when advocates are removed from the 1999 sub- sample, reporters average one reference to domestic violence in every four articles. Thus, most domestic violence language in the 1999 clusters—five references per article on average— was attributable to advocate sources. For the 2002 cluster, however, the mean number of domestic violence citations grew to 5.75 per article—even with advocates removed from the sample. Thus, by 2002, reporters and nonadvocate sources had increased use of domestic violence language ten-fold. In sum, our findings suggest that by the third cluster of murders in 2002, reporters adopted the newsgathering practices suggested by the Rhode Island Coalition Against Domestic Violence in several critical ways.

Articles identifying the murder of intimate part- ners as domestic violence rose. Sources representing domestic violence advocates increased in both relative and absolute terms as did reporters' use of police and other expert sources. And while reporters continued to use neighbors, family, friends and co-workers as sources judiciously, they curtailed their use of casual bystanders. As a result, bystander and family sources dropped in frequency. In perhaps our most notable finding, even when advocate sources were removed from the sample, reporters and nonadvocate sources had increased their use of domestic violence language ten-fold between 1996 and 2002.

Over seven years, Rhode Island domestic violence advocates achieved media standing, moving from obscurity to become routine sources for Rhode Island reporters. RICADV, working with MRAP, strategically negotiated this rise in media standing. When the 1996 murders occurred, RICADV did not have the capacity to respond. By 1999, RICADV had established a solid communications infrastructure that helped it navigate its media market; its systems facilitated rapid responses to crises and working relationships with reporters were growing. Building on MRAP's initial analysis of domestic violence murder coverage, RICADV opened dialogs with reporters. As RICADV consolidated its communications infrastructure and built relationships, it became a routine source. Whereas, domestic violence advocates were invisible in newspaper coverage of the 1996 murders, domestic violence advocates were the most prominent sources in the 1999 coverage.

As sources changed, frames changed. By 2002, RICADV's efforts in the Rhode Island media market over the previous six years had shifted the public discourse; nonadvocate sources, police for instance, and reporters themselves had begun to adopt domestic violence language. With broader constituencies framing domestic violence as a social issue, the state's residents and political leaders were readied for the RICADV-led Seven-Point Plan that reformed state policy vis-à-vis domestic violence. The use of domestic violence language by sources other than domestic violence advocates, therefore, suggests a broadened awareness of domestic violence and a culture shift supporting the proposed political change. RICADV's expanded ability to transform comparable unforeseen events—murders—into media opportunities and ultimately political opportunities suggests that conceptualizing opportunity primarily as external is insufficient.

As Klandermans (1992) and others suggest, seen from a longitudinal perspective, the process is more interactive and allows for conscious collective actors to expand their power. RICADV's intentional decision to develop a media strategy resulted in its hiring skilled staff who developed its internal and external communications capacity. This helped RICADV take advantage of existing media opportunities. These media opportunities, well utilized, built media standing. Reporters came to trust RICADV, deeming its events "must-attend." As its media standing grew, RICADV's ability to negotiate broader media opportunities grew beyond its original boundaries of the Rhode Island media market. RICADV has already shared its approaches with 37 states.

Its public awareness campaigns have been adopted nationally for three years and it is now working with a national coalition to replicate its communications systems nationally. If RICADV had over-emphasized the very real structural barriers to gaining media standing, it would not have taken its first steps. If it had under-emphasized the structural barriers, it would not have sustained a seven-year labour—a sprinter ill-prepared for a test of endurance. Believing that it could make its accounts count, RICADV worked incrementally to strengthen its capacity to respond to unfolding events. Its ability to navigate the Rhode Island media market helped RICADV deepen its network of relationships with allies and reporters. As RICADV proved useful, reporters' estimation of the group as a valued news source—its media standing—grew. To the concept of media opportunity, therefore, the concepts of media capacity and media standing add recognition of the advantage of the organizationally stable collective actor over individuals and less formally organized challengers.

A collective actor's media standing is not so easily lost as to be called "volatile," nor are existing hegemonic structures so impermeable that collective actors must wait for opportunity as if it were a state lottery. While individual, isolated challenges to corporate mass media rarely succeed, a collective actor operating strategically and reflexively over time can accrue media standing if it builds sustainable communication infrastructure and relations suited its media market(s). This study also suggests the importance of locating structural challenges at local, state, or national levels depending on the collective actor's level of development. In our case, a statewide collective actor successfully breached structural barriers in a state-level media market. Had RICADV, as a state-level collective actor new to media organizing simply entered the national media fray without attention to analyzing market structures or its resources, they would have found the barriers facing them insurmountable.

Breaking structural critiques of the corporate-dominated media arena into its component markets makes local, state, and regional challenges viable. Replicated, challenges in individual media markets provide the infrastructure to sustain a national challenge. Thus, our work moves us to define opportunity not as residing in structure or agency but in historical conjunctures—strategic fits that allow the intentional collective actor to craft a challenge to relations of domination suited to its resources and historical position. While in our case, the right fit was a regional challenge in a regional market by a regional actor, the question of scale is historically variable. In the early stages of a social movement, smaller collective actors working on a limited scale may dominate.

If theorists ignore how these early stages accrue to catalyze political sea changes, the theories they manufacture may miss how collective actors identify strategic opportunities appropriate for their historical moment. They may present institutionalized power as impenetrable rather than understanding that social relations and processes are vulnerable to challenge and change over time. We have noted that by 2002, RICADV used the third cluster of domestic violence murders not only as a media opportunity, but to launch a successful political initiative, the Seven Point Plan. As political leaders look to the media to reach their constituents, media opportunity becomes inextricably linked to political opportunity. While here we emphasize media opportunity, political opportunity forms the ever-present background that, like an M.D. Escher drawing, shifts to the foreground with the blink of an eye. Since RICADV's 2002 media strategy represented one of many strategies used to pass the Seven-Point Plan—legislative lobbying, grassroots mobilizing, coalition-building—we hesitate to conjecture too broadly regarding the impact of media standing on political opportunity apart from a full analysis of the campaign.

Social movements and their participating collective actors start with seemingly impossible goals—to create macro shifts in social structures. By organizing strategically with support from agency-laden institutions, collective actors gain tensile strength over time—despite pressure from existing structural arrangements, they find opportunities and turn them into bigger ones.

For an intentional, reflexive strategic actor, a little meeting on creaky chairs in a musty, echoing church basement can represent an increase in opportunity; its participant's respected allies. In challenging hegemony lived, in learning and growing from experiences even on a small scale, a collective actor creates tantalizing tastes of counter- hegemony lived. Critical to the collective actor's growth is the formation of a strategy and infrastructure that will guide and support action over time; intentional actors, social movement organizations channel the limited resources of many to mount focused challenges to existing structures. The reflective collective actor grows as it reflects on its experience, a process in which theorists may be useful.

This article represents the collaborative reflections of RICADV and MRAP working within a one media market to nurture internal and external communication capacity and leverage that growth into broader media standing and opportunity. That reporters bestowed media standing on RICADV fits our historical times. In the wake of the civil rights movement and other counter-hegemonic movements and now, with the rising tide of conservative mobilizations, reporters recognize social movement organizations as recurring players in American life. U.S. residents today may not be startled to hear their nation labeled a "social movement society".

The 1996 launching of Mobilization signaled a parallel emergence of social movement studies as an institutionalized field of social science. Ironically, social movement theorists may work with social movements less than reporters. While reporters recognize social movements as permanent features of American society, social movement theorist remain relatively isolated from activists, an isolation all the more troubling because activist-theorist collaborations might provided insights into outstanding theoretical tangles. To illustrate the opportunities such collaborations present, we offer our experience. In the coming decade of Mobilization, this opportunity beckons all takers.

Chapter 10

Business and Finance

As organizations are growing and expanding to all the corners of the globe, their information needs are growing at the same speed thus for an enterprise it is imperative to improve or replace old systems. Enterprises, instead of investing loads of money in to small software applications are moving towards ERP solutions which can be more parameterized according to their day to day needs and in the event that some customization is required and if the parameterization does not support it, it is not a problem for the enterprise to organize a small team of IT professionals to achieve the said task in some other tool. This guide will give the readers an insight to current global economic and technology business trends and show them the path forward towards success in the field of IT, which is considered to be totally recessed.

CAPITALIST GLOBAL TRENDS

The global advancements in business and technology are making enterprises larger and stronger (don't forget what happened with Microsoft). The true concept of capitalist controlled economies is emerging. The enterprises are in more control of economies today and we are all well aware of the famous capitalist approach. Even in Pakistan, the richer are growing richer and the poor are falling towards poverty! Companies are either being deeply affected by the global recession and shutting down or are growing into large enterprises. A small example (though not relatively small) may be Unilever Pakistan, which has the power to buy off any small company that tries to compete Unilever products in the local market. No More IT! In spite of all this, most of the times we think about what is going to be the future of IT, with the burst of the Dot Bomb; the industry has seen a lot of disasters. A majority of end users developed a fear that forced them to block further investments in to IT and this did not save them money, originally their needs have come to a point where they have been provoked to once again move towards the inflow of IT but with a more intelligent and planned approach.

SMALL SOFTWARE APPLICATION OR BIG ONES

Enterprises still need software applications, which can streamline multi-type relationships with customers, partners, suppliers and employees. New concepts like Intelligent Relationship Management have been evolved in order to achieve total business process streamline. Nowadays it's not about just saving money and increasing efficiency, it's about making the customer stronger and stronger through the use of scalable and robust technology.

Enterprises are moving towards solutions, which cater to the need for content management, eCRM, and eFulfillment solution markets (combining to form the intelligent relationship management market). Large Software game players have aligned themselves in order to provide technological solutions that are more coherent, easier to implement, and that could ideally support and enhance both B2C and B2B type 'enterprise to individual' relationships. The days for small-scale development companies aren't over yet but at the same time new entry points for such companies have been blocked by the large enterprises that can completely automate any small or large organization within no time. Now we are talking of Enterprise Solutions with large game players.

ERP-THE NEW WORLD ORDER

These large players have suddenly taken over the enterprise technology and ERP scenario leaving the small companies dazzled in the take over. Not so far away, large corporations like ARAMCO, Saudi Arabia have contracts ranging to 350 million dollars with SAP and Foxboro for streamlining processes and automating their projects. A great demand for Chartered Accountants, MBAs, Developers with business knowledge are required in order to build and manage these solutions.

So this directs us towards the new world order today, i.e. ERP, yes Enterprise Resource Planning is where business is moving. As this shift to ERP moves forward, our IT Professionals have to make that divide between the ordinary techi and the true professional and ERP draws that boundary.

Our professionals have to be trained in ERP in order to cater to this great need, especially under the present Pakistani business environment, where the process of globalization has been initiated, large ERP projects are nearing completion (Unilever, ICI, Packages, KMLG, local governments etc), and it is expected that the whole business system will undergo a major shift.

Thus by being adequately skilled, Pakistani IT Professionals can accommodate to the changing business world and run inline with modern management systems and secure their futures. Most of you might have never heard of ERP products but the truth is that these products are the in things today. If one wants to survive and make a break through in the IT arena today, then without the knowledge of any one of these products, he/she won't be successful. So now I would like to take the liberty of introducing our readers to "ENTERPRISE RESOURCE PLANNING!"

ERP is a high-end sophisticated software solution that reduces the pressure and workload off the Managers and provides accurate, timely information for taking appropriate business decisions. Managers with knowledge of ERP will be able to achieve their targets and goals by proper implementation of ERP system in their organization. In fact Managers are expected to translate the business rules and requirements for mapping them into ERP software. Implementation of ERP solutions is one of the largest drivers of growth in the consultancy business. Why do organizations need ERP? The emergence Large organizations across the globe have realized that in rapidly changing environments, it is impossible to create and maintain a custom designed software package that will cater to all their daily business needs. Realizing the requirement of user organizations some of the leading software companies have designed Enterprise Resource Planning software which will offer an integrated software solution to all the functions of an organization.

According to the current growing global business environment, organizations are trying to meet heavy demands of:

- Aggressive cost control and reduction initiatives
- Need to analyse costs/revenues on a product or customer basis
- Flexibility to respond to changing business requirements
- More informed management decision-making
- Changes in ways of doing business
- Reaching out to the Customer
- Bringing the Customer more nearer to the enterprise
- Customization of products according to Customer needs

CURRENT TRENDS

Enterprise Resource Planning is the latest high-end solution, information technology has lent to business application. The ERP solutions seek to streamline and integrate operation processes and information flows in the company to mix the resources of an organization namely men, material, money and machine through information.

SPREADING OUT

Initially implementation of an ERP package was possible only for MNCs and Infrastructure Companies due to high cost of implementation involved. Today many companies in Pakistan have gone in for implementation of ERP and it is expected in the near future that 40% of the companies will be implementing one or the other ERP packages since this will become a must for gaining competitive advantage over competitors or for entering in to global markets and bringing the customer closer to the enterprise.

THE GREAT CHALLENGE

The introduction of such large and complex software like ERP, enables an organization to integrate their manufacturing, finance and marketing operations at all levels, is in itself a challenge, since it calls for technical and functional skills and a change in user mindsets. Managers as representatives of the Organization have to coordinate with Vendors, Consultants, Auditors etc., for a proper implementation of ERP package thus without IT and Business & Finance knowledge, they may not be of any help to the organization.

FEATURES OF ERP SOFTWARE PACKAGES

Some of the major features of What an ERP do for organizations are:

- ERP facilitates company-wide Integrated Information System covering all functional areas like:
  - Manufacturing
  - Selling and distribution
  - Payables
  - Receivables
  - Inventory
  - Accounts
  - Human resources
  - Purchases
  - E-Commerce
  - E-Business
- ERP performs core corporate activities and increases customer service and thereby builds the enterprise's Corporate Image.
- ERP bridges the information gap across the organization and interconnects all the departments to single information access point across the companies under the same management.
- ERP is the only solution for better Project Management.

- ERP allows automatic introduction of latest technologies like:
  - Electronic Fund Transfer (EFT)
  - Electronic Data Interchange (EDI)
  - Internet
  - Intranet
  - Video conferencing
  - E-Commerce
- ERP eliminates the most of the business problems like:
  - Material shortages
  - Productivity enhancements
  - Customer service
  - Cash Management
  - Inventory problems
  - Quality problems
  - Prompt delivery etc.
- ERP not only addresses the current requirements of the company but also provides the opportunity of continually improving and refining business processes.
- ERP provides business intelligence tools like:
  - Decision Support Systems (DSS)
  - Executive Information System (EIS)
  - Reporting, Data Mining

Early Warning Systems (Robots) for enabling people to make better decisions and thus improve their business processes

ERP COMPONENTS

In order to enable easy handling of the business management systems the ERP has been divided into the following core sub-systems:

- Accounts Payable/Receivable
- Asset Management
- Bill of Materials
- Capacity Requirement Planning
- eBusiness

- Financial Accounting
- General Ledger
- Human Resource Management
- Logistics
- Master Scheduling
- Material Requirement Planning
- Payroll
- Purchasing & Sourcing
- Sales and Marketing
- Shop floor control

ERP Benefits [t]

The benefits accruing to any business enterprise on account of implementing are unlimited. According to the companies like ICI, Shell, Philips, Unilever, Saga Sports, Packages, Service Industries, KMLG, Rupali, etc., following are some of the benefits they achieved by implementing ERP packages:

- Gives Accounts Payable personnel increased control of invoicing and payment processing and thereby boosting their productivity and eliminating their reliance on computer personnel for these operations.
- Reduce paper documents by providing on-line formats for quickly entering and retrieving information.
- Improves timeliness of information by permitting, posting daily instead of monthly.
- Greater accuracy of information with detailed content, better presentation, fully satisfactory for the Auditors.
- Improved Cost Control 6. Faster response and follow up on customers
- More efficient cash collection, say, material reduction in delay in payments by customers.
- Better monitoring and quicker resolution of queries.
- Enables quick response to change in business operations and market conditions.
- Helps to achieve competitive advantage by improving its business process.

- Improves supply-demand linkage with remote locations and branches in different countries.
- Provides a unified customer database usable by all applications.
- Improves International operations by supporting a variety of tax structures, banks like Deucthe Bank, invoicing schemes, multiple currencies, multiple period accounting and languages.
- Improves information access and management throughout the enterprise.

ERP Implementation

Implementing an ERP package is pretty long and cumbersome process. It has to be done on a phased manner. Step by step method of implementing will yield a better result than big-bang introduction. The total time required for successfully implementing an ERP package will be anything between 18 and 24 months. The normal steps involved in implementation of an ERP are:

- Project Planning
- Business & Operational analysis including Gap analysis
- Business Process Reengineering
- Installation and configuration
- Project team training
- Business Requirement mapping
- Module configuration
- System interfaces
- Data conversion
- Custom Documentation
- End user training
- Acceptance testing
- Post implementation/Audit support
- Online Support

The above steps are grouped and sub-divided into four major phases namely:

- Detailed discussions
- Design & Parameterization

- Implementation
- Production.
- Detailed Discussion Phase:

Task: Project initialization, Evaluation of current processes, business practices, Set-up project organization. Deliverables: Accepted norms and Conditions, Project Organization chart, Identity work teams

- Design and Parameterization Phase:

Task: Map organization, Map business process, Define functions and processes, ERP software configuration and Build ERP system modifications. Deliverables: Organization structure, Design specification, Process Flow Diagrams, Function Model, Configuration recording and system modification.

- Implementation Phase:

Task: Create go-live plan and documentation, Integrate applications; Test the ERP customization, Train users Deliverables: Testing environment report, Customization Test Report and Implementation report

- Production Phase: Task: Run Trial Production, Maintain Systems Deliverables: Reconciliation reports, Conversion Plan Execution

ERP SOLUTION SUPPLIERS

SAP is the world's leading provider of e-business software solutions. People in businesses around the globe are improving relationships with customers and partners, streamlining operations, and achieving significant efficiencies throughout their supply chains. Today, more than 17,000 companies in over 120 countries run more than 44,500 installations of SAP software and trust me, that's a pretty huge amount.

With subsidiaries in over 50 countries, the company is listed on several exchanges including the Frankfurt stock exchange and NYSE under the symbol "SAP". SAP Smart Business Solutions Designed to Meet the Needs of Small to Midsize Businesses Today. Small and midsize businesses have unique needs. They require a cost-effective solution that can be up and running quickly—and that will continue to meet their needs as the business grows. That's why SAP created Smart Business Solutions—solutions specifically designed for companies in the small and midsize business (SMB) marketplace. Solutions for Smart Companies Worldwide Nearly half of all SAP installations are in organizations with annual revenues under $200 million. And an increasing number of growing companies around the world are taking advantage of SAP Smart Business Solutions.

1. SAP Business One—This simple yet powerful solution can meet your common business needs, covering accounting, reporting, logistics, sale force automation, and more. It is designed for small companies that require less complex industry-specific functionality from their IT solutions.
2. mySAP All-in-One—These cost-effective, turnkey solutions come prepackaged to meet the needs of your organization, and can be fine-tuned to perform in your industry. They are designed for companies that require a high degree of industry-specific functionality.

SAP Business One

Simple but Powerful: The Solution for Growing Businesses For small and midsize companies eager to emerge as their industries' new leaders, taking that next step in e-business evolution is a critical decision. Their new business management software must be quick to implement, easy to use, and make the best use of their current IT infrastructure. And while it must be sufficiently powerful to manage their business through its future growth, it has to be affordable enough to represent a reasonable investment today. SAP Business One is easy to use.

Featuring intuitive navigation, a familiar Microsoft Windows environment, and multiple customization tools. It's also easy to deploy and maintain. With fast implementation, high performance and scalability, robust security, and the ability to evolve into more sophisticated solutions. Using open standards, SAP Business One easily integrates with other systems. Its "Drag & Relate" feature allows users to drag information from disparate data stores and link them on the desktop.

This close integration opens up new dimensions to other business management systems. It also shortens the learning curve, since users don't have to study new tools to handle analysis and marketing tasks. Most important, SAP Business One is powerful. Its sophisticated analysis tools give management full control of company information and activities.

BAAN

Baan helps industrial enterprises optimize their enterprise performance strategies and compete in the knowledge-driven 'networked economy', with its ever-increasing demands for information, integration, and collaboration. Through its open and powerful iBaan suite of Internet-enabled solutions, Baan is ideally placed to support organizations in the manufacturing, logistics, services, and engineering industries as they move towards tighter integration of their complex processes, closer collaboration throughout their value chain, and greater accessibility of cross-enterprise transactional and analytical information.

Baan has more than 15,000 customer sites worldwide and is part of the Production Management division of Invensys PLC.

Baan ERP solutions gained waves in the early parts of the year 2000s and swept the European nations by great strides. Baan has also achieved top rankings as the number one Enterprise solution kicking ORACLE way to the end of the TOP 10 ERP Solution achievers list.

The BAAN focus

Baan provides ERP solutions to address the needs of several vertical industries. Baan's goal is to build product capabilities based on the best practices in these vertical industries, including: automotive, electronics, process manufacturing (pulp and paper, food and beverage, metals and plastics), project manufacturing (aerospace and defence, heavy engineering), and generic hybrid manufacturing. Baan with BAAN IV; is the current release of the company's Enterprise Resource Planning (ERP) model software. Baan is moving beyond the enterprise to the entire supply chain with its current release of this next generation enterprise business application software. Baan has 1,900 customers worldwide, including global industry leaders such as ABB, the Boeing Company, Mercedes-Benz, GEC Alsthom, Nortel, and Phillips who have all standardized on Baan's systems.

Baan supports multi-site, multi-national operating environments. Baan provides a comprehensive end-to-end solution for supply chain management. It includes capabilities such as sales order management, rules-based configuration, constraint-based intelligent resource planning, production management, engineering data management, integrated product data management, distribution and transportation, project accounting, service, and an advanced finance system.

Baan supports three-tier client/server architecture with inter-enterprise workflow, integrated multidimensional databases (OLAP), and an innovative approach to Internet technologies. These capabilities are allowing Baan's customers to quickly implement a solution based on best practices in their industry, which provides the cornerstone for constant change. Orgware, which is a highly innovative product from Baan, supports quick implementation and continuous change. The overall Baan ERP solution supports various types of manufacturing environments, including engineer to order, make to order, assemble to order, and make to stock. The ease of implementation associated with Baan IV is attributed to Orgware, which allows customers to concentrate on business processes instead of focusing on information technology.

Baan IV Orgware components include: Enterprise Modeler: Which allows users to graphically describe the process? This flow-charting results in the creation of the applications required to implement those modeled parts of the process. This reduces a great part of the code generation. Enterprise Reference Models: This allows implementers to choose from existing models that are used by other companies, and to combine these models in order to make their own system.

Enterprise Performance Manager: This tool allows users to determine performance based on 150 pre-defined indicators. Enterprise Implementer: Analogous to a project management tool or consulting service. Baan IV is more than an application system. It provides capabilities for the corporation to change as needed. Baan has built technology that focuses both on the means and the end, gets you in quickly, and gets the system up and running. Baan IV allows for the configuration and reconfiguration of not only the application, but the IT deployment.

For example, a company can move from a highly decentralized, large number of disparate databases, putting demands on middistribution centers, to a highly centralized large database environment supporting global order entry. In this case, demand would be distributed rather than order processing.

The company would be able to restructure the IT environment without a long, painful process, and without going into the actual application and restructuring parts of the application environment. Baan's ERP solution is highly scalable, supporting as few as eight users to several thousand. Functionally, it provides the ability to support multiple methods of manufacturing that allows a company to adapt its manufacturing operation to changes in the marketplace, providing you with a significant competitive advantage. DEM Orgware provides the means to bring technology to your business problem instead of having you structure your business around the way the software works.

J.D. EDWARDS

A very hot topic in the Middle East and also being used by Shell and Philips, Pakistan for a considerably long period of time, J.D Edwards is getting fast recognition around the world, there are presently no training services in Pakistan for this suite but I would just like to give our readers an overview about J.D technologies: J.D. Edwards & Company (NASDAQ: JDEC) provides the complete spectrum of enterprise and business-to-business software and services to enable companies to engage in collaborative commerce with their suppliers, customers and other business partners.

With a 24-year heritage, J.D. Edwards has built a customer base of more than 6,300 mid-market and large enterprise customers, and generated revenues of nearly $875 million for its 2001 fiscal year. J.D. Edwards' collaborative applications enable customers to share and react in real time to critical information about the design, production and distribution of products and services - both within their own enterprises and throughout the entire supply chain.

J.D. Edwards' c-commerce offering includes comprehensive applications for enterprise resource planning (ERP), supply chain planning and fulfillment, customer relationship management (CRM), and knowledge management, as well as interoperability technologies that connect computing platforms, business processes, and applications within and among enterprises. Through partnerships with best-of-breed technology leaders, J.D. Edwards also provides eprocurement and marketplace management solutions.

Consists of seven product lines:

Tools and Technology

The tools and technology in J.D. Edwards 5 provides the infrastructure for its collaborative enterprise applications, speeding development, deployment and maintenance. The toolset gives a business the ability to understand, implement, use and change J.D. Edwards software to keep their technology infrastructure in step with dynamic business requirements.

Enterprise Resource Planning (ERP)

J.D. Edwards ERP applications are designed to improve a company's internal operations and provide the groundwork for collaborative commerce. The ERP applications assist with managing finance, assets (including inventory, fixed assets and real estate), people, projects, suppliers and the fulfillment and manufacturing processes.

Customer Relationship Management (CRM)

J.D. Edwards CRM focuses on managing customer relationships well beyond automating sales, marketing and customer service agent assistance. J.D. Edwards CRM helps a company manage its entire customer lifecycle, from customer acquisition to post-sales service and support. J.D. Edwards CRM includes Sales Force Automation, Marketing Automation, Partner Relationship Management, Field Service, Customer Self-Service and Advanced Order Configurator.

Supply Chain Management (SCM)

J.D. Edwards SCM comprises fully-integrated planning/ forecasting and fulfillment applications. J.D. Edwards' supply chain products deliver enhanced productivity and efficiency for product driven industries. In addition, the integration between J.D. Edwards Advanced Planning and fulfillment software—such as Order Management, Procurement, Warehouse Management and Transportation Management—enables instantaneous response to events that impact a company's supply chain.

Supplier Relationship Management (SRM)

Buyers have been exchanging information with their suppliers for centuries. Unfortunately, phone, fax, and e-mail will not allow your business to react efficiently to poor forecasts, supply chain interruptions, and rapid demand changes. Therefore, our Supplier Relationship Management offerings go beyond strategic sourcing and e-procurement to optimize the relationship between enterprises and their suppliers— allowing you to compete more effectively.

Business Intelligence

J.D. Edwards Business Intelligence enables companies to extract important information from the data shared among customers, partners and suppliers. Its purpose is to help a company monitor its business activities, identify sources of value and measure the level of value delivered. A Webbased "dashboard" with easy-to-read gauges shows how the organization performs on an ongoing basis. As users tap different categories of information, new and updated information is automatically pushed to their desktop, phone, fax, or wireless device. With J.D. Edwards, users can easily modify their data warehouses and decision-support tools to meet changing information needs.

Collaboration and Integration

J.D. Edwards' collaboration and integration capabilities enable a company to evolve its collaborative commerce strategy over time, as its business needs change. It allows a company to collaborate with multiple suppliers, customers and business partners by linking disparate systems and applications. XPI also readies a business for future Web services technology. J.D. Edwards offers Content Manager, a content creation and change management application that helps users to easily create, manage and distribute text-based, multi-language content across an organization's entire global operation.

ORACLE FINANCIAL SUITE

This is one well-known name in Pakistan. With more than well over 500 installations alone in Pakistan, Oracle has 6,000 installations worldwide. With the launch of Oracle 9i and 11i ebusiness suites, Oracle is once again sweeping the market dominance of small companies. In Pakistan Oracle is being taught at all major business and IT schools and with educational partnerships emerging from Oracle University, the scene seems to be changing rapidly and the best thing about it is the almost all the Pakistani Government departments in one way or the other are running Oracle and the Government is a bright future for Oracle DBAs and Developers, so the certifications are still hot in this sector plus a combination of business and finance related knowledge is an added catalyst for landing a very lucrative job.

ORACLE - E-BUSINESS SUITE

Oracle Corporation (NASDAQ: ORCL) is the world's leading supplier of software for information management, and the world's second largest independent software company. With annual revenues of more than $10.9 billion, the company offers its database, tools and application products, along with related consulting, education, and support services, in more than 145 countries around the world.

Headquartered in Redwood Shores, California, Oracle is the first software company to develop and deploy 100% internet-enabled enterprise software across its entire product line: database, server, enterprise business applications, and application development and decision support tools. Oracle claims to be the only company capable of implementing complete global e- business solutions that extend from front office customer relationship management to back office operational applications to platform infrastructure.

PRODUCT PORTFOLIO SCOPE

On June 26, Oracle unveiled a new suite of online services aimed at capturing the small business market. This new suite, called the Oracle Small Business Suite, is powered by the award winning NetLedger product (which is 55% owned by Oracle's CEO Larry Ellison), and provides small companies, with typically less than 100 employees, an integrated, easy-to-use suite of hosted application services that manage key business processes, including financials, customer relationship management (CRM), purchasing, and e- commerce. Oracle touts that small companies no longer need to use several disparate applications to manage their business, since with the Oracle Small Business Suite, all operations are managed centrally, and are available to users via the Internet.

Further, because the applications are being delivered as an online service, there is no hardware to procure, no large, up-front license fees, and no complex set-ups. Customers can be up and running on the Oracle Small Business Suite in a matter of minutes, according to the company. The Oracle Small Business Suite is available immediately at an introductory price of $99 per month. The new service is available through Oracle, Oracle's online services business, extending Oracle's online service business to all market segments. Currently the Oracle Small Business Suite is available in English, and supports US and Canadian tax requirements. Future versions are planned to support global users. This is yet another of Oracle's attempts in its "war on complexity" that surfaced during its user conference in February.

SIEBEL SYSTEMS

Siebel is a big name in the game for Call Centers and Sales Team Management with a specialized emphasis on Customer Relationship Management. Siebel is once again hardly used anywhere in Pakistan but trust me, a person experienced with Siebel has a very bright future both in the Middle Eastern and European Markets. The market-leading integrated suite of Siebel eBusiness Applications enables organizations to deploy an integrated set of customer-driven best practices across their sales, marketing, and customer service. Derived from experience with more than 3,500+ customer deployments and nearly 10 years of product development and investment, Siebel Systems has documented hundreds of industry-specific best practices for every aspect of CRM and embedded them directly in the functionality of Siebel eBusiness Applications. Siebel Systems redefined the standard for CRM with the delivery of hundreds of business processes embedded in Siebel 7.5, the latest release of Siebel eBusiness Applications.

Siebel Sales

Sales organizations are under increasing pressure to skillfully manage a range of competencies in order to deliver their revenue goals - all in an extremely challenging economic environment. Whether the challenge is revenue forecasting, sales effectiveness, or motivation and focus of sales professionals, companies must find better ways to increase product knowledge among their salespeople and consistently apply best practices across their entire sales organization. Siebel Sales family of products:

- Siebel Sales
- Siebel Sales Forecasting
- Siebel Sales Analytics
- Siebel Incentive Compensation
- Siebel Mobile Sales Companies can drive peak performance by enabling their sales teams to respond more quickly and cogently to customers across a variety of channels.

By offering the right information to customers at the appropriate point in the sales cycle, companies have the opportunity to dramatically increase revenues while achieving increased customer loyalty and satisfaction. The Siebel Sales product family helps selling organizations grow revenues more quickly, predictably and profitably by providing focus on the right deals at the right time. With Siebel Sales, companies respond more effectively to sales opportunities. Comprehensive sales methodologies, like Target Account Selling, can be delivered through Siebel Sales to drive a consistent communications approach throughout the entire sales organization. The Siebel Sales product family is the only solution set that spans the range of implementation environments required by global enterprises today. This includes the critically important support for synchronizing mobile databases and handheld devices, as well as wireless and voice access to Siebel Sales data. In addition, Siebel Sales has achieved measurable ROI for literally hundreds of customers.

Siebel Marketing

What's New in Siebel Marketing 7.5: Superior collaborative marketing capabilities ensure tighter coordination between marketing, sales, partners and vendors. Real-time marketing and decision turn inbound interactions into revenue opportunities. Comprehensive response and lead management capabilities shorten follow-up time and improve lead conversion rates. Enhanced customer and promotion analytics improve visibility into campaign performance and customer preferences. Expanded data quality support for

Western European languages and new universal data quality API connector.

Marketing planning and budgeting capabilities streamline process and improve alignment to corporate goals Siebel Marketing family of applications:

- Siebel Marketing
- Siebel eMarketing
- Siebel eEvents
- Siebel Marketing Analytics

The market for eBusiness solutions has experienced dramatic change, and this is certainly true with respect to marketing solutions. Today's marketing challenge is more than improving the results of direct mail or telesales campaigns, or sending out more emails. Rather, it is about building the quality and value of customer relationships and instilling loyalty for a lifetime. It is about understanding the value of each customer and treating different customers differently. It is about building trust by interacting with the customer in ways that reflect a complete understánding of their needs and preferences. This includes interacting with customers anytime they want through their preferred channels and maintaining a continuous dialogue synchronized across all channels.

And in today's economy, it is about delivering more effective marketing campaigns for less while demonstrating marketing's bottom line contribution. With the Siebel Marketing 7 product family, organizations now have a comprehensive marketing solution to successfully acquire, retain, and grow profitable customer relationships and maximize marketing effectiveness. The Siebel Marketing 7 product family provides a complete closed-loop solution that enables organizations to better understand their customers; flawlessly execute personalized campaigns synchronized across all channels; and optimize strategies through continuous test, measurement and feedback. By utilizing the four fully integrated components of Siebel Marketing 7, organizations can realise better response and retention rates, increase customer lifetime value, operate at a higher velocity, and dramatically improve their marketing return on investment.

SIEBEL CALL CENTRE AND SERVICE

Maximize Service Effectiveness and Reduce Total Cost of Ownership Today's customers expect consistent, professional service and support with every interaction - through any channel, from anywhere in the world. The quality of a company's customer service is often a competitive differentiator and critical to success.

The Siebel Call Centre and Service family of products allows organizations to build customer relationships and deliver consistent, world-class service while driving down the total cost of ownership through greater productivity and reduced costs. This lets organizations improve customer satisfaction by managing, synchronizing, and coordinating all customer touch points whether in the call centre in the field, or over the Internet.

Siebel Call Centre and Service family of products:

- S-Siebel Call Centre
- Siebel Web Service
- Siebel eMail Response
- Siebel eService
- Siebel eCollaboration
- Siebel Field Service
- Siebel Mobile Service
- Siebel Service Analytics
- Siebel Professional Services Automation

SIEBEL INTERACTIVE SELLING

Siebel Interactive Selling is a comprehensive suite of products that enables organizations to engage, and better service customers through a personalized buying experience that complements and extends existing Web, telesales, and partner networks as well as direct and indirect sales channels. Through Siebel Interactive Selling, organizations are able to increase sales effectiveness across all channels via comprehensive needs analysis, product cataloging, fixed and dynamic pricing, and configuration capabilities.

Siebel Advisor Siebel Advisor mimics the needs analysis behaviour of a company's sales, service or consulting staff through a series of interactive questions that allow "what if" scenarios, choices, and instant feedback

Deploy an engaging, personalized Web-based storefront. Customers create and retrieve quotes, search and view placed orders, and get up-to-the-minute order status. Deliver a dynamic buying experience that guides buyers through product selection and customization. Customers complete more orders with fewer errors, and with a higher average order value.

With seamless, consistent pricing, companies can develop, manage and deploy complex pricing rules, providing specialized pricing by product, account, or other pricing criteria. Increase returns on inventory, test product pricing, develop new sales channels, and create better customer experiences through cross-selling and promotion.

SIEBEL PARTNER RELATIONSHIP MANAGEMENT

Siebel Partner Relationship Management (PRM) provides the industry's leading PRM solution to enable organizations to more effectively manage their partner relationships. Siebel PRM (formerly known as Siebel eChannel) delivers an enterprise wide partner management platform that helps organizations work collaboratively with partners to increase revenue, drive customer satisfaction and reduce partner management costs. Siebel PRM consists of six components, including Siebel Partner Manager, Siebel Partner Community, Siebel Partner Portal, Siebel Partner CRM, Siebel Partner Web Services and Siebel Partner Manager and Portal Analytics.

Partner CRM-enables strategic, dedicated partners to use the portal as their primary collaborative CRM application to execute highly coordinated marketing, sales, service and commerce processes. Partner Community-self-service portal enabling brand owners to provide targeted communications and personalized content to partners who use the portal on a more limited, intermittent basis.

Real-Time PRM-enables business-to-business, real-time integration of a brand owner's partnercentric business processes throughout the partner ecosystem. PRM Best

Practices-provides customers with tangible benefits such as partner loyalty and adoption, increased revenue and customer satisfaction, increased partner programme effectiveness and efficiency. Siebel Industry Applications deliver comprehensive, out-of-the-box eBusiness functionality that is uniquely tailored to specific business practices across a broad range of industries.

Developed in close collaboration with customers and partners, Siebel Industry Applications enable organizations to manage, coordinate, and synchronize all customer touch points, including the Web, call centre, field, retail, and distribution channels. Siebel Industry Applications Cover: -Automotive -Communications -Consumer Sector -Energy -Financial Institutions -Healthcare -Homeland Security -Insurance -Life Sciences -Oil, Gas, and Chemical -Public Sector -Travel and Transportation.

SIEBEL EMPLOYEE RELATIONSHIP MANAGEMENT

To achieve success in today's challenging and dynamic macro-economic environment, company executives must rapidly identify market changes, adjust the corporate operating plan, and rapidly realign the organization to execute against the new strategy. Yet, most large, global organizations cannot respond quickly because their disparate systems, business processes, operating plans, and communications do not easily span organizational boundaries creating a "strategy-execution" gap.

Siebel Employee Relationship Management ("ERM") is a breakthrough suite of integrated applications from Siebel Systems helping companies close the strategy-execution gap and drive superior business execution by rapidly aligning organizations around key objectives and generating exceptional business unit and individual employee performance. Siebel ERM includes a range of new capabilities allowing organizations to: Track Key Workforce Performance Metrics - Siebel ERM provides business intelligence and analytic applications that enable organizations to transform data across the enterprise into business and customer insight.

Regularly Monitor and Assess Employee Performance -

Siebel ERM provides an integrated performance management system that enables executives to powerfully translate corporate strategy into actionable business unit and individual objectives.

Communicate Effectively and Retain Corporate Focus - A powerful communication medium between companies and their employees, Siebel ERM enables companies to communicate company news, industry news, and other valuable information to each employee desktop daily. Train to Increase Workforce Skills - Siebel ERM provides a complete Web-based learning system that enables organizations to efficiently and effectively provide employees with the training they need to execute the company's strategy. Leverage Employee Self Service to Increase Productivity - Siebel ERM simplifies and speeds employee's daily activities through a personalized home page that contains directories of key contacts, current company news and events, product and competitor information, unified search tools, and more.

Siebel Analytics

To build business advantage, organizations need to empower all users, not just the few, with rich customer insight, the power to measure the performance of their operations in real-time, and the means to take immediate corrective action if necessary.

Siebel Analytics is an end-to-end nextgeneration analytics solution that provides all users with up-to-the-moment, actionable customer and business insight. Insight based on best practices. Insight that is complete and unlocks the value hidden in data silos by spanning real-time and historical sources across the enterprise. Seamlessly integrated with all Siebel applications, Siebel Analytics drives more intelligent actions and interactions, dramatically improving responsiveness, effectiveness and competitive advantage.

Siebel MidMarket

Siebel MidMarket Edition—a family of multichannel sales, customer service and marketing applications—allows small and mid-size companies to compete more effectively in today's marketplace. It covers: Siebel MidMarket Constitutes: • Siebel eFinance, MidMarket Edition • Siebel eInsurance, MidMarket Edition

Features of Siebel Products

The Siebel Smart Web Architecture sets the industry standard for application performance and sophistication. This unique technology combines a zero-footprint, browser-based Web clientmeaning there is no software to separately install and administer on the desktop-with levels of interactivity traditionally available only in Windows applications. Organizations get the best of both worlds: They get the cost savings associated with administering a zero-install Web client, and they also get the rich, interactive, productive experience available only from a desktop application.

The result is a higher level of user acceptance and increased satisfaction and productivity for both employees and customers. Depth and Breadth of Functionality Industry analysts widely acknowledge that Siebel Systems' products are the most functionally complete on the market. The breadth and depth of functionality of Siebel eBusiness Applications are a result of continued investment in cutting-edge research and development. Siebel eBusiness Applications are finely tuned to support industry-specific business processes, enabling organizations to leverage best practices for sales, marketing, and service that are built into the software.

As a result of this rich functionality and industry expertise, end users rapidly adopt Siebel eBusiness Applications, thus accelerating deployment and the organization's return on investment.

Comprehensive Multichannel Capabilities

Siebel eBusiness Applications are the only true multichannel solution that allows organizations to manage, synchronize, and coordinate customer interactions at all touchpoints across all channels- over the Web, in the call centre, by field sales and service personnel, and through channel partners. This integrated approach allows organizations to establish a common view of the customer, leverage all customer interactions, dramatically increase productivity, maximize revenue and profit, and significantly enhance customer satisfaction.

Industry-Specific Applications

Siebel Industry Applications leverage the breadth and depth of the Siebel platform, providing organizations with comprehensive out-of-the-box functionality that minimizes the need for customization and development resulting in a significantly lower total cost of ownership. Recognizing that each industry has different business processes, competitive challenges, and IT requirements that cannot be addressed with "one size fits all" CRM, all Siebel Industry Applications provide a tailored suite of packaged applications with industry-specific functionality, analytics, business processes, and best practices.

Analytics Everywhere

Siebel 7.5 applications are infused throughout with powerful analytics to provide organizations with real-time customer intelligence. Siebel Analytics 7.5 provides personalized, role-based analytic applications that deliver relevant, actionable, just-in-time intelligence to employees, partners, and customers. With Siebel Analytics 7.5, organizations can access volumes of data from multiple sources including operational systems and deliver fact-based and personalized intelligence to thousands of decision-makers, inside and outside the organization.

ERM Best Practices Drive Superior Business Execution

Siebel 7.5 includes the industry's broadest and most comprehensive suite of packaged employee relationship management (ERM) applications for executives, managers, and employees. Siebel ERM embeds best practice business processes such as performance management; training; employee self-service; and corporate-wide access to resources, news, and other information. With Siebel ERM, companies can adjust the corporate operating plan and quickly realign the organization to execute the plan based on changing market needs.

Universal Application Network and Web Services Support

Recognizing that customer-centric business processes involve data from multiple applications and systems, Siebel Systems has ensured interoperability by supporting Web services and standards- based integration through Universal Application Network.

Universal Application Network takes a standards-based approach to the design and development of cross-application business processes while leveraging the proven integration server technology of leading vendors. Organizations can easily integrate data and business processes across multiple applications with dramatically lower cost and complexity.

Global Deployment Support

Siebel 7.5 expands the global deployment capabilities of previous releases with significant enhancements in the areas of Unicode support, multilingual data, installation, and localization for global deployments.

A Unicode environment supports the uniform storage of and access to data that spans multiple code pages in a single database and can be managed by a single set of application components. Siebel 7.5 provides robust Unicode support, resulting in a dramatic lowering of the deployment and maintenance costs for global organizations.

Automated Upgrades

Incorporating best practices from several thousand previous customer upgrades, the upgrade to the Siebel 7.5 release of Siebel eBusiness Applications is automated, comprehensive, compelling, and proven to work.

The process includes automated upgrades of data and customizations; complete scripting support; complete desktop integration; and a broad array of upgrade services and training, including reviews, workshops, and on-site migration assistance.

Lowest Total Cost of Ownership

Organizations that invest in eBusiness technology must carefully scrutinize not just the initial cost of the software, but also the solution's total cost of ownership over its lifetime. Siebel 7.5 dramatically trims total cost of ownership by reducing costs in several critical areas, including customization, configuration, integration, and maintenance, upgrades, training, and deployment risk.

PEOPLESOFT

Peoplesoft is another leading name in the ERP Scene and has been there for a long time serving clientele from all over the globe. Once again there is no training for this product suite in Pakistan but the future is bright and the most nearest training may be available from the Middle East or Singapore. PeopleSoft has been innovating technology since mid-1980s when company founders Dave Duffield and Ken Morris built the first human resources application on a client-server platform instead of the traditional mainframe, adding needed flexibility and putting more power into the hands of users.

And it's happening again right now, as the generational shift from client-server to Internet architecture brings organizations the opportunity to enhance their interactions with their customers, suppliers, and employees dramatically.

While consumer applications on the Internet have evolved to the mass adoption stage, changing the fabric of everyday life, businesses have just scratched the surface. In 1998, PeopleSoft recognized that Fortune 2000 corporate strategic plans were increasingly looking to the Internet to increase profitability by making customer and vendor transactions faster and better. As a result, Peoplesoft retrenched its internal strategy, halting development of anything that wasn't a pure Internet application. Peoplesoft directed the bulk of their resources—$500 million and 2,000 developers over two years—into their new pure Internet platform for the real-time enterprise. The result is PeopleSoft 8, with more than 150 pure Internet applications. All with no client software to maintain. All designed to build loyal customer relationships, enable better supplier communication, and make employee recruiting and retention more efficient.

Today, more than 1,000 customers in 144 countries are reaping the real-world benefits of our investment. PeopleSoft 8 makes better interactions possible by delivering both the relationship and analytic data one needs to the employee in their organization who needs it, when they need it. Relationship data includes details of past transactions, from the size and status of a vendor's latest shipment to which sport a customer's kids play.

Business analytic data indicates which customers are the most important based on the amount of product they are likely to buy and ones cost of serving them, or which vendors deliver the highest quality products, on time and at the best price. The sales force or customer service teams have that data available from any browser when the customer calls or when the vendor is ready to negotiate a price.

Optimizing interactions, managing real-time business processes, analyzing your business to anticipate opportunities, increasing revenue, and reducing costs. It all adds up to more profitable relationships. It's what an enterprise can expect from PeopleSoft: software and services for the real-time enterprise.

MICROSOFT GRAND PLAINS

Microsoft Business Solutions, a division of Microsoft (NASDAQ: MSFT) provides business management applications that help small and mid-sized companies become more agile in today's interconnected economy. Its products automate financial and operational processes, and allow companies to extend specific information and procedures securely via the Web to employees, customers, suppliers, and partners.

A worldwide network of partner organizations that share the commitment to lasting customer relationships delivers all Microsoft Business Solutions products. These business partners provide personalized service—from planning, to implementation, to ongoing support and education—to ensure that companies receive the precise business solution to meet their needs.

More than 250,000 customers in 132 countries count on Microsoft Business Solutions for financials, inventory and order processing, project management, electronic commerce, human resource management, manufacturing, supply chain management, retail management, business analytics, customer relationship management, and customer service and support solutions.

Released in July 1994, Microsoft Business Solutions-Great Plains is designed for a range of businesses, from smaller companies with less than $5 million in annual revenue to midsize and corporate enterprises with revenues in the hundreds of millions. An enterprise-wide, integrated solution, Microsoft Business Solutions-Great Plains provides functionality for financials, inventory and order processing, human resource management, customer relationship management (CRM), field service, e-commerce, project management, manufacturing, and analytics and reporting. Microsoft Business Solutions address the following business needs:

- *Analytics and Reporting*

A broad range of flexible, customizable reporting options-from advanced consolidation analysis to simple reporting requests-transforms data into valuable information and makes it accessible to decision-makers across your company.

- *Customer Relationship Management*

From the first contact to after-sales service, Web-enabled CRM solutions lets track customer activity, improve sales effectiveness, provide superior customer service, and build profitable customer relationships.

- *E-commerce*

Remove geographical boundaries, strengthen business relationships, and reduce expenses by using these Internet-based solutions to collaborate with and provide self-service to employees, customers, and partners.

- *Field Service*

Automate the essential functions of service organizations to maximize staff's time, let the field service team connect instantly with customer data, increase customer satisfaction and turn fieldservice operations into a profitable centre.

- *Financials*

Whatever business size or industry, these superior financial, reporting and business management applications provide the backbone for business-critical applications.

- *Human Resource Management*

From recruitment to retirement, manages the most valuable assets-people-more effectively. *Inventory and Order Processing* Improve inventory operations with automated sales fulfillment and invoicing, connected distribution systems and integrated inventory tracking. Turn orders around faster, minimize carrying costs and increase inventory accuracy.

- *Manufacturing*

Manage resource planning, production and every aspect of your manufacturing process better to ensure smooth production cycles, and respond quickly to changing customer needs for a competitive advantage.

- *Project Management*

Make projects more profitable with integrated applications that lets forecast costs and budgets accurately, track time and billing, and manage contracts effectively. *Retail Management* From point-of-sale to delivery, increase customer flow and cash-in, speed up lines and tasks, control inventory, and automate purchasing with integrated, scalable, Web-ready applications.

- *Supply Chain Management*

Connects employers, suppliers, distributors and customers to reduce operational costs, improve decision-making and respond faster to customer needs.

FOXBORO

Foxboro has a strong foothold in the Middle East and Japanese ERP markets and has projects worth millions in implementation with companies like Saudi Aramco, Toyota,

Japan. Foxboro covers Plc and Control Room Automation. Invensys Foxboro is part of the Invensys Production Management Division and provides world class Foxboro information technology, automation, and process solutions to a wide range of manufacturing applications for the cement, chemical, metals & mining, oil & gas, pulp & paper, power, pharmaceutical and specialty chemicals.

Besides Foxboro, the division includes APV, Baan, SimSci-Esscor, Triconex and Wonderware. The Invensys Production Management Division of Invensys plc works closely with customers to provide solutions that help them maximize return on investments and optimize performance across their supply chain.

Invensys has performance improvement expertise and technology encompassing the entire value chain—from the production line to executive offices; from customer relationship and procurement management to distribution logistics.

Chapter 11

Media Research

Nielsen Media Research (NMR) is an American firm that measures media audiences, including television, radio, theatre films (via the AMC MAP programme) and newspapers. NMR, headquartered in New York City and operating primarily from Chicago, is best-known for the Nielsen Ratings, a measurement of television viewership.

Nielsen Media Research, the preeminent media research company in the world, began as a division of ACNielsen, a marketing research firm.

In 1996, Nielsen Media Research was split off into an independent company, and in 1999 was purchased by the Dutch conglomerate VNU.

In 2001, VNU also purchased ACNielsen, thereby bringing both companies under the same corporate umbrella. VNU was reorganized and renamed the Nielsen Company in 2007.

The Nielsen TV Ratings have been produced since the 1950s and statistically measure which programs are watched by different segments of the population.

The most well known portion is the "diary". During the 4 sweeps months of February, May, July and November, Nielsen interviewers in Oldsmar, Florida and Radcliff, Kentucky ask homes to participate in filling out a diary of the programs watched in their home for a one week period. Nielsen has ways of measuring American TV viewing other than the diaries. Recently, Nielsen announced the launch of its A2M2 project that would measure television viewing in and out of the home.

Nielsen Media Research is a sister company to Nielsen//

NetRatings, which measures Internet and digital media audiences through a telephone and internet survey, and Nielsen BuzzMetrics, which measures Consumer-Generated Media.

Nielsen also conducts market research for the film industry through National Research Group (NRG). Nielsen recently purchased Telephia - a mobile metrics marketing research firm.

The Media Research Centre (MRC) is a conservative content analysis organization based in Alexandria, Virginia, founded in 1987 by L. Brent Bozell III.

Its stated mission, according to its website, is "to bring balance and responsibility to the news media",and the MRC catalogs and reports on what it asserts to be widespread liberal media bias in the United States press. The MRC has received financial support from several foundations, including the Bradley, Scaife, Olin, Castle Rock, Carthage and JM foundations.

FOUNDATION

Bozell and a group of other young fellow conservatives founded the MRC on October 1, 1987, with only themselves, a black-and-white television set, and rented computer at their headquarters.

Their initial budget was at US$339,000. Prior to founding the MRC, Bozell was the chairman of the National Conservative Political Action Committee; he resigned from that position a month before establishing MRC.

PROJECTS

Reports on the Media

Since 1996, the MRC website has published a daily online newsletter called *CyberAlert* written by editor Brent Baker. Each issue profiles what he perceives to be biased or inaccurate reports about politics in the American news media. Prior to *CyberAlert,* MRC published such reports in a monthly newsletter titled *MediaWatch,* from 1988 to 1999.

Media analysis director Tim Graham and research director Rich Noyes regularly write *Media Reality Check,* another MRC publication documenting alleged liberal bias.

Notable Quotables is its "collection of the most biased quotes from journalists".

In *Notable Quotables,* editors give honors such as the "Linda Ellerbee Awards for Distinguished Reporting" based on the former CNN commentator, who Bozell considered "a liberal blowhard who has nothing to say". Other features on its website include the weekly syndicated news and entertainment columns written by founder Bozell.

MRC staff members have also written editorials and books about their findings of the media.

Bozell has written three books about the news media: *And That's the Way it Isn't: A Reference Guide to Media Bias* (1990, with Brent Baker); *Weapons of Mass Distortion: The Coming Meltdown of the Liberal Media* (2004); and *Whitewash: How The News Media Are Paving Hillary Clinton's Path to the Presidency* (2007, with Tim Graham).

Research director Rich Noyes has also co-authored several published books.

Business and Media Institute

In 1992, the MRC created the Free Market Project to promote the culture of free enterprise and combat what it believes to be media spin on business and economic news.

That division recently changed its name to the Business & Media Institute and is now focused on "Advancing the culture of free enterprise in America." BMI's advisory board includes such well-known individuals as economists Walter Williams and Bruce Bartlett, as well as former CNN anchor David Goodnow.

BMI is led by career journalist Dan Gainor, a former managing editor at CQ, the website for Congressional Quarterly.

It released a research report in June 2006 covering the portrayal of business on prime-time entertainment television during the May and November "sweeps" periods from 2005.

The report concluded that the programs, among them the long-running NBC legal drama *Law & Order*, were biased against business.

Another report of the BMI accused the networks of bias in favour of the Gardasil vaccine, a vaccine intended to prevent cervical cancer.

Parents Television Council

MRC president L. Brent Bozell III branched the Parents Television Council from the Centre in 1995 after he felt that decency on prime-time television was decreasing. The PTC monitors prime-time television for what it believes to be indecent content and publishes content-based reviews of television shows and oversees campaigns to make advertisers withdraw from programs that they believe to be morally offensive. *Extra!*, the magazine published by left-wing group Fairness and Accuracy in Reporting, asserted that the MRC's former newsletter *TV, etc.* inspired the group. *TV, etc.* "tracked the allegedly leftist politics of entertainment industry figures".

In July 2002, MRC and affiliate Parents Television Council (PTC) paid an out-of-court settlement ending a lawsuit which had been launched by World Wrestling Entertainment (WWE) in November 2000.

WWE alleged 13 instances of defamation, copyright infringement and interference with prospective business relations after PTC produced a fundraising video using unauthorized WWE footage, falsely claimed WWE was responsible for the murders of four children, and falsely claimed advertisers had pulled their commercials from the show. MRC paid US$3.5 million. MRC and PTC President Brent Bozell wrote in a lengthy public statement "it was wrong to have stated or implied that WWE or any of its programs caused these tragic deaths." The PTC has been found to have filed the majority of complaints about alleged indecent television content to the Federal Communications Commission.

Cybercast News Service

Bozell founded the Conservative News Service (now

Cybercast News Service) in 1998 to cover stories he believes are ignored by mainstream news organizations. CNSNews provides news articles for Townhall and other websites for a subscription fee.

Its leadership consists of president Brent Bozell and editor Terry Jeffrey. Under editor David Thibault, CNSNews questioned the validity of the circumstances in which Democratic Rep. John Murtha received his purple hearts as a response to Murtha's criticisms of the U.S. War in Iraq. *The Washington Post* and Nancy Pelosi have commented that this approach is similar to the tactics of the Swift Vets and POWs for Truth, which opposed John Kerry's candidacy in the 2004 election.

News Busters

In the summer of 2005, Media Research Centre launched NewsBusters in cooperation with Matthew Sheffield, a conservative blogger involved in the CBS Killian documents story. NewsBusters is styled as a rapid-response blog site that contains posts by MRC editors to selected stories in mass media.

Times Watch

In March 2003, MRC analyst Clay Waters established *Times Watch*, a website monitoring alleged bias in *The New York Times*.

Culture and Media Institute

In October 2006, the MRC created the Culture and Media Institute, the mission of which is "to advance, preserve, and help restore America's culture, character, traditional values, and morals against the assault of the liberal media." Robert H. Knight is the institute's director.

VIEWPOINTS

In its mission to show that there is a "strident liberal bias" in the national news media, the MRC has produced a number of their own analyses and has offered as evidence the claims that news reporters use the "conservative" or "Republican" label to describe conservatives more often than they label liberals or Democrats, that the media is sympathetic to Communism or "dictators", that media coverage of global warming is biased in favour of environmentalism,, and that the media focuses on covering the negative side of the Iraq war.

Beyond the news media, MRC also publishes research about entertainment television. Reports it conducted from 1993 to 1995 found that such programs made more references to religion each later year, most of which became more favorable. In 2003, the MRC urged advertisers to pull sponsorship from *The Reagans,* a miniseries about President Ronald Reagan to be shown on CBS. The network later moved the programme to its co-owned premium cable network Showtime.

MRC released a report in 2007 claiming that the network morning shows devoted more airtime to covering Democratic presidential candidates than Republican ones for next year's election.

Producers for such shows criticized the MRC's methodology as flawed, as did media critic Terry Krepel of the site *ConWebWatch* and organization Media Matters for America. During the 2008 US presidential election, MRC released a report claiming that the vast majority of news stories about Democratic presidential candidate Barack Obama had a positive slant.MRC president Bozell praised MSNBC for having David Gregory replace Chris Matthews and Keith Olbermann as political coverage anchor beginning September 8, 2008, but MSNBC president Phil Griffin disputed the statements by Bozell and others who have accused the network of liberal bias. However, over the network's decision to add Rachel Maddow as primetime host, Tim Graham appeared on the Fox News Channel morning show *Fox and Friends* to criticize the decision, calling Maddow "this lesbian Air America radio host".

CRITICISM

Extra!, the magazine of the progressive media watch

group FAIR, criticized the MRC in 1998 for selective use of evidence. MRC had claimed that there was more coverage of government death squads in right-wing El Salvador than in left-wing Nicaragua in the 1980s, when Amnesty International claimed El Salvador was worse than Nicaragua when it came to extra-judicial killings.

Extra! also characterized a defunct MRC newsletter *TV etc.* tracking the off-screen political comments of actors as bearing "an uncomfortable resemblance to *Red Channels*, the McCarthy Era blacklisting journal."

Progressive media watchdog group Media Matters for America has also repeatedly criticized the MRC, charging they view the media "through a funhouse mirror that renders everything—even the facts themselves—as manifestations of insidious bias".

Chapter 12

Advertising Newspapers

Most newspapers make nearly all their money from advertising. The income from the customer's payment at the news-stand is small in comparison. For that reason newspapers are not expensive to buy, and some (such as AM New York in New York City and Metro in the UK) are free. The portion of the newspaper that is not advertising is called editorial content, or simply editorial, although the last term is also used to refer specifically to those articles in which the newspaper expresses its opinions.

Publishers of commercial newspapers strive for higher circulation so that advertising in their newspaper becomes more effective, allowing the newspaper to attract more advertisers and charge more for the service. But some advertising sales also market demographics: some newspapers might sacrifice higher circulation numbers in favour of an audience with a higher income. Many paid-for newspapers offer a variety of subscription plans. For example, someone might only want a Sunday paper, or perhaps only Sunday and Saturday, or maybe only a workweek subscription, or perhaps a daily subscription.

Some newspapers provide some or all of their content on the Internet, either at no cost or for a fee. In some cases free access is only available for a matter of days or weeks, after which readers must register and provide personal data. In other cases, free archives are provided. Advertising spending online overtook national newspapers' share of the pie for the first time in 2006 as companies continued to chase a growing web audience.

According to data from the Internet Advertising Bureau out today, online spending smashed through the £2bn barrier in 2006 while television revenues fell and press barely budged. A 41% leap put 2006 UK online spending at £2.016bn, representing 11.4% of total advertising revenues. IAB said that helped offset declines in traditional media and meant the overall advertising industry was able to clock up modest growth of 1.1% over the year.

The report highlights Britain's world-leading position, even compared with America. The global average proportion of advertising spending online is 5.8%. The US figure is about 7-7.5%. As advertisers rushed online to target Britain's 31 million web users, their spending countered a 4.7% fall in the TV advertising market. There was a barely discernible 0.2% rise at national newspapers. At £1.9bn - or 10.9% of the total market - press advertising was behind the internet for the first time, in line with IAB's predictions last year.

The online growth also contrasts starkly with commercial radio stations' complaints about a tough market. Magic owner Emap said yesterday that the outlook for radio remained weak and rival GCap, home to Capital and Classic FM, said its like-for-like revenues would probably be down by about 3% for the year to end March. Echoing that, IAB said the internet had overtaken radio as the second most popular medium after TV. The group's chief executive Guy Phillipson is confident the strong growth is sustainable.

"Advertisers are continuing to switch more of their budgets online to build their brands and interact with their customers," he said. "With consumers now enjoying even faster broadband and installing wireless routers in their homes, the growth of online advertising in the UK is set to continue unabated."

The rising popularity of user-generated content such as homemade videos and blogs is also being latched on to by advertisers as a new route to mass audiences, according to the report compiled with PricewaterhouseCoopers and the World Advertising Research Centre. Meanwhile, faster internet connections have improved access to video, which is seen as having a higher impact on consumers than the older "display" forms of online advertising. Advertisers are also increasingly using social networking sites to reach younger consumers in a move demonstrated by the rapid emergence of viral video campaigns, which rely on internet users disseminating content containing a brand message.

Still formats such as banners were themselves "reinvigorated" by adding audio, video and animation, according to IAB. The report suggests that online advertising growth is still fastest in the so-called search area - sponsored listings that advertisers pay for when a consumer clicks through to their site. Spending on search advertising jumped 52% to £1.2bn, giving it a 57.8% share of the online market. Online classified advertising made up 18.8% and experienced growth of 45%, in stark contrast to traditional press where classified advertising fell 7.8%.

But interruptive formats, including pop-ups, have been falling. They are now worth 0.7% of all online spending as advertisers continue to drop formats that mirror the old-fashioned interruptive nature of TV and radio advertising. Mr Phillipson said much of Britain's position is down to the high take-up of broadband in homes and the growing trend among companies to see the internet as their main "battleground", particularly for finance, travel, entertainment and technology.

"If they don't compete in the online space, they will lose market share. They all watch each other," he said. MAGAZINES are not raking in as much ad revenues as newspapers, but they are also less dependent on a few specific sectors. And, while lifestyle products such as readymade apparel and watches have emerged as some of the biggest spenders in magazines, they still spend only a small part of their overall print ad budget on magazines, according to a report by TAM-AdEx.

The top five advertising categories in newspapers last year were two-wheelers, corporate/brand image advertising, cars and jeeps, properties and real estate, and cellular phone services. The top spenders in magazines were readymade apparel, corporate/brand image advertising, cars and jeeps, watches, and insurance. Watches are a big category in lifestyle and general interest magazines, while insurance ads pop up in general interest, business and specialist magazines with a male skew, according to TAM-AdEx.

"While magazines and newspapers are both a part of the same category, print, the forces that lead them and shape them are quite different," said Mr Atul Phadnis, Director - S Group, TAM Media Research, which monitors over 600 media brands.

Overall print ad revenues are estimated at Rs 4,400 crore; magazines currently have a 12.5 per cent share, while newspapers make up for the rest, according to TAM-AdEx. Last year, the average monthly print adspend of two-wheelers was over Rs 20 crore, of which 96 per cent was in newspapers, and just four per cent in magazines. The average monthly print adspend of real estate/property was about Rs 15 crore, of which 98 per cent was in newspapers.

Cell phone service providers spent 98 per cent of their monthly print ad budget of Rs 11 crore in newspapers. In the case of corporate/brand image advertising, 88 per cent of adspend was in newspapers, while cars and jeeps spent 89 per cent of their print ad budget in newspapers, according to TAM-AdEx.

"Interestingly, even the largest product category in magazines — readymade garments — spent only 26 per cent of its press budget on magazines," Mr Phadnis said. "Newspapers simply have a larger influence on overall print ad revenues." Also, while print ad sizes have declined across the board, magazine ad sizes have registered the greatest decline — a whopping 30 per cent over the past eight years, as compared with a 21 per cent decline in newspaper ad sizes.

But, newspapers may be more vulnerable to declines in specific sectors or industries: the top 10 category spenders in newspapers accounted for 35 per cent of overall newspaper ad revenues, while the top 10 categories in magazines only accounted for 29 per cent of overall ad revenues. "While the specialist magazines are dependent on specific categories, magazines overall are much more broad-based, and less dependent on a few top industries or sectors," Mr Phadnis said.

The programme, initially announced in 2006 with 50 newspaper partners and later expanded to 800, was intended to help newspapers to discover more ways to increase their earnings from Internet ad sales at a time when their print ad sales were falling is slated to end Feb. 28, according to a blog posting by Spencer Spinnell, director of Google's print ads.

"While we expected that print ads would produce a new source of income for newspapers and build more relevant advertising for consumers, the product has not created the impact that we and our partners wanted," Spinnell wrote. For Google, which has developed its gigantic reputation as a master of the online advertising business, hence shutting down the print programme is a rare failure. The ad sales will continue until March 31 for customers who already had campaigns booked.

"We were not giving a significant revenue impact to our newspaper partners so we are focusing our efforts on how we can do that quickly and effectively using online tools," Google spokesman Brandon McCormick said.

The programme, which had pulled in more than 800 U.S. newspapers since it was rolled out, seems like both Google and newspapers are wrestling with a poor advertising market worsened by the world financial crisis. Google said last week it would lay off 100 full-time recruiters and close three engineering offices.

"Some advertisers have seen good results," Spinnell wrote on the company blog. "But as we grow, it is important that we focus on products that can benefit the most people and solve the most important problems."

Google's plan was to be an ad broker for newspapers to help them fill their remainder ad space, and then share the revenue. The concept was that Google could get some of its hundreds of thousands of online advertisers to consider newspaper advertising, many of whom had never marketed their products in print.

At that time it was a golden opportunity for Google to diversify its business, which depends almost entirely on online advertising revenue. But in the end, however, the idea faded away and only few advertisers wanted to shift to newspapers. Spinnell said that a team at Google will continue to look at how they can help newspaper companies, which are undergoing a major retrenchment because of declining advertising.

The decision to close print does not impact other offline advertising initiatives in radio and television advertising, according to a company spokesman.

Google's print ad partners included many of the biggest U.S. newspaper publishers, such as New York Times Co., Washington Post Co., Gannett Co. and Tribune Co. The programme took bids from advertisers for newspaper space, with Google getting a cut of the sale. The company's goal was to make print ad prices more fluid, letting publishers charge rates that better reflect demand. A Google spokesman declined to state how much money the search engine company and its newspaper partners expected to make from Print Ads.

"It is a very little part of our revenue stream," said New York Times spokeswoman Catherine Mathis.

Under the provisions of the Print Ads programme, Google AdWords customers could place newspaper ads in the same way they buy Web page, radio or TV ad space. Google remains "dedicated to working with publishers to develop new ways for them to earn money, distribute and aggregate content and attract new readers online," its blog post said. It is still not apparent what effect this would have on an advertising consortium that Yahoo has with hundreds of newspapers. Many papers are members of both Google's and Yahoo's groups.

The company said last week it would relocate 70 engineering employees from its offices in Austin, Texas; Trondheim, Norway; and Lulea, Sweden, in a cost-cutting move. Google, based in Mountain View, California, already dragged down its shares with the broader market, fell 5.65 percent to close at $282.75 on the Nasdaq stock market.

Chapter 13

Broadcast Television and Radio

Broadcast journalism is the field of news and journals which are "broadcast", that is, published by electrical methods, instead of the older methods, such as printed newspapers and posters. Broadcast methods include radio (via air, cable, and Internet), television (via air, cable, and Internet), and, especially recently, the Internet generally. Such media disperse pictures (static and moving), visual text, and/or sounds. Scripts for speaking to be broadcast tend to be written differently than text to be read by the public. For instance, the former is generally less complex and more conversational. Radio and television are designed to be seen and heard sooner and more often than is a daily or weekly newspaper.

Broadcast "stories" (articles) can be written in "packages", "readers", "voice overs", and "sound on tape". A "package" is an edited set of video clips for a news story and is common on television. It is narrated typically by a reporter. It is a story with audio, video, graphics and video effects. The anchor usually reads a "lead in" (introduction) before the package is aired and may conclude the story with additional information, called a tag. A "reader" is an article read without accompanying video or sound. Sometimes an "over the shoulder graphic" is added. A voice over, or VO, is a video article narrated by the anchor. Sound on tape, or SOT, is sound and/or video, usually recorded in the field. It is usually an interview or "soundbite".

RADIO

Radio was the first medium for broadcast journalism.

Many of the first radio stations were co-operative community ventures not making a profit. Later, advertising to pay for programs was pioneered in radio. Later, television displaced radio and newspapers as the main news sources for most of the public in industrialized countries. Some of the programming on radio is locally produced; some is broadcast by a network, by syndication, etc. The "talent" (professional voices) talk to the audience, including reading the news. People tune in to hear engaging personalities, music, and information that they want. In radio news, stories include speech "sound bites", the recorded sounds of events themselves, and the anchor or host.

The radio industry has undergone a radical consolidation of ownership, with fewer companies owning the thousands of stations. Large media conglomerates such as Clear Channel Communications own most of the stations in the United States. That has resulted in more "niche" formats and the sharing of resources within clusters of stations, de-emphasizing local news and information. There has been concern over whether that concentration of power serves the public. The opposition says that the range of political views expressed and supported is greatly narrowed and that local concerns are neglected, including local emergencies, for which communication is critical. Automation has resulted in many stations broadcasting for many hours a day with no one on the station premises.

Radio broadcasting is an audio (sound) broadcasting service, traditionally broadcast through the air as radio waves (a form of electromagnetic radiation) from a transmitter to an antenna and a thus to a receiving device. Stations can be linked in radio networks to broadcast common programming, either in syndication or simulcast or both. Audio broadcasting also can be done via cable FM, local wire networks, satellite and the Internet. The earliest radio stations were simply radiotelegraphy systems and did not carry audio. The first claimed audio transmission that could be termed a *broadcast* occurred on Christmas Eve in 1906, and was made by Reginald Fessenden.

While many early experimenters attempted to create

systems similar to radiotelephone devices where only two parties were meant to communicate, there were others who intended to transmit to larger audiences. Charles Herrold started broadcasting in California in 1909 and was carrying audio by the next year. For the next decade, radio tinkerers had to build their own radio receivers. Dr. Frank Conrad began broadcasting from his Wilkinsburg, Pennsylvania garage with the call letters KDKA. Later, the equipment was moved to the top of an office building in Pittsburgh, Pennsylvania and purchased by Westinghouse. KDKA of Pittsburgh, under Westinghouse's ownership, started broadcasting as the first licensed "commercial" radio station on November 2, 1920.

In The Hague, the Netherlands, PCGG started broadcasting almost a year earlier, on November 6, 1919. The commercial designation came from the type of license; advertisements did not air until years later. The first broadcast was the results of the U.S. presidential election, 1920. The Montreal station that became CFCF began programme broadcasts on May 20, 1920, and the Detroit station that became WWJ began programme broadcasts beginning on August 20, 1920, although neither held a license at the time.

Radio Argentina began regularly scheduled transmissions from the Teatro Coliseo in Buenos Aires on August 27, 1920, making its own priority claim. The station got its license on November 19, 1923. The delay was due to the lack of official Argentine licensing procedures before that date. This station continued regular broadcasting of entertainment and cultural fare for several decades.

INTERNET RADIO

When Internet-based radio became feasible in the mid-1990s, the new medium required no licensing and stations could broadcast from anywhere in the world without the need for over the air transmitters. This greatly reduced the overhead for establishing a station, and in 1996, George Maat started 'A' Net Station (A.N.E.T.) under the now defunct domain Advice-Net, and began broadcasting commercial-free from Antarctica.

MIT developed the "Radio Locator" List of Radio Stations. After stations started streaming audio on the Internet, Radio-Locator added this to their search engine so anyone could locate a station's website and listen to a station offering a worldwide stream. This list also tracks "terrestrial" radio stations who may not have live audio on the net, or even a website, but are able to find station information by various other search queries.

TYPES

The best known type of radiostation are the ones that broadcast via radiowaves. These include foremost AM and FM stations. There are several subtypes, namely commercial, public and nonprofit varieties as well as student-run campus radio stations and hospital radio stations can be found throughout the developed world. Although now being eclipsed by internet-distributed radio, there are many stations that broadcast on shortwave bands using AM technology that can be received over thousands of miles (especially at night). For example, the BBC has a full schedule transmitted via shortwave. These broadcasts are very sensitive to atmospheric conditions and solar activity.

Also, many other non-broadcast types of radio stations exist. These include base stations for police, fire and ambulance networks, military base stations, dispatch base stations for taxis, trucks, and couriers, emergency broadcast systems, and amateur radio stations. Arbitron, the United States based company which reports on radio audiences defines a "radio station" as one of: government-licensed AM or FM station an HD Radio (primary or multicast) station, an internet stream of an existing government-licensed station or one of the satellite radio channels from XM Satellite Radio or Sirius Satellite Radio.

OVER RADIOWAVES

SHORTWAVE

See Shortwave for the differences between shortwave,

medium wave and long wave spectra. Used largely for international broadcasts by organs of state propaganda, religious organizations, militaries and others.

AM

AM stations were the earliest broadcasting stations to be developed. AM refers to amplitude modulation, a mode of broadcasting radio waves by varying the amplitude of the carrier signal in response to the amplitude of the signal to be transmitted.

Many countries outside of the U.S. use a similar frequency band for AM transmissions. Europe also uses the long wave band. In response to the growing popularity of FM radio stereo radio stations in the late 1980s and early 1990s, some North American stations began broadcasting in AM stereo, though this never gained popularity, and very few receivers were ever sold.

Advantages

One of the advantages of AM is that its unsophisticated signal can be detected (turned into sound) with simple equipment. If a signal is strong enough, not even a power source is needed; building an unpowered crystal radio receiver was a common childhood project in the early years of radio. Another advantage to AM is that it uses a narrower bandwidth than FM.

AM broadcasts occur on North American airwaves in the medium wave frequency range of 530 to 1700 kHz (known as the "standard broadcast band"). The band was expanded in the 1990s by adding nine channels from 1620 to 1700 kHz. Channels are spaced every 10 kHz in the Americas, and generally every 9 kHz everywhere else.

Disadvantages

The signal is subject to interference from electrical storms (lightning) and other EMI. AM transmissions cannot be ionospherically propagated during the day due to strong absorption in the D-layer of the ionosphere. In a crowded channel environment this means that the power of regional channels which share a frequency must be reduced at night or directionally beamed in order to avoid interference, which reduces the potential nighttime audience. Some stations have frequencies unshared with other stations in North America; these are called clear-channel stations.

Many of them can be heard across much of the country at night. *(This is not to be confused with Clear Channel Communications, merely a brand name, which currently owns many U.S. radio stations.)* During the night, this absorption largely disappears and permits signals to travel to much more distant locations via ionospheric reflections. However, fading of the signal can be severe at night.

AM radio transmitters can transmit audio frequencies up to 15 kHz (now limited to 10 kHz in the US due to FCC rules designed to reduce interference), but most receivers are only capable of reproducing frequencies up to 5 kHz or less. At the time that AM broadcasting began in the 1920s, this provided adequate fidelity for existing microphones, 78 rpm recordings, and loudspeakers. The fidelity of sound equipment subsequently improved considerably, but the receivers did not. Reducing the bandwidth of the receivers reduces the cost of manufacturing and makes them less prone to interference.

AM stations are never assigned adjacent channels in the same service area. This prevents the sideband power generated by two stations from interfering with each other. Bob Carver created an AM stereo tuner employing notch filtering that demonstrated that an AM broadcast can meet or exceed the 15 kHz baseband bandwidth allocted to FM stations without objectionable interference. After several years, the tuner was discontinued. Bob Carver had left the company and the Carver Corporation later cut the number of models produced before discontinuing production completely. AM stereo broadcasts declined with the advent of HD Radio.

FM

FM refers to frequency modulation, and occurs on VHF airwaves in the frequency range of 88 to 108 MHz everywhere (except Japan and Russia). Japan uses the 76 to 90 MHz band. FM stations are much more popular in economically developed regions, such as Europe and the United States, especially since higher sound fidelity and stereo broadcasting became common in this format. FM radio was invented by Edwin H. Armstrong in the 1930s for the specific purpose of overcoming the interference (static) problem of AM radio, to which it is relatively immune.

At the same time, greater fidelity was made possible by spacing stations further apart. Instead of 10 kHz apart, they are 200 kHz apart. For example, the difference between the lowest current FM frequency in the U.S., 88.1 MHz, and the next lowest, 88.3 MHz. This was far in advance of the audio equipment of the 1940s, but wide interchannel spacing was chosen to take advantage of the noise-suppressing feature of wideband FM.

In fact, 200 kHz is not needed to accommodate an audio signal — 20 kHz to 30 kHz is all that is necessary for a narrowband FM signal. The 200 kHz bandwidth allowed room for ±75 kHz signal deviation from the assigned frequency plus a 20 kHz guardband to eliminate adjacent channel interference. The larger bandwidth allows for broadcasting a 15 kHz bandwidth audio signal plus a 38 kHz stereo "subcarrier" — a piggyback signal that rides on the main signal. Additional unused capacity is used by some broadcasters to transmit utility functions such as background music for public areas, GPS auxiliary signals, or financial market data.

The AM radio problem of interference at night was addressed in a different way. At the time FM was set up, the available frequencies were far higher in the spectrum than those used for AM radio - by a factor of approximately 100. Using these frequencies meant that even at far higher power, the range of a given FM signal was much lower, thus its market was more local than for AM radio. The reception range at night is the same as at daytime.

The original FM radio service in the U.S. was the Yankee Network, located in New England. Regular FM broadcasting began in 1939, but did not pose a significant threat to the AM broadcasting industry. It required purchase of a special receiver. The frequencies used, 42 to 50 MHz, were not those used today. The change to the current frequencies, 88 to 108 MHz, began after the end of World War II, and it was to some extent imposed by AM radio owners so as to attempt to cripple what was by now realized to be a potentially serious threat.

FM radio on the new band had to begin from the ground floor. As a commercial venture it remained a little-used audio enthusiasts' medium until the 1960s. The more prosperous AM stations, or their owners, acquired FM licenses and often broadcast the same programming on the FM station as on the AM station ("simulcasting"). The FCC limited this practice in the 1970s. By the 1980s, since almost all new radios included both AM and FM tuners, FM became the dominant medium, especially in cities. Because of its greater range, AM remained more common in rural environments.

Amateur Radio

Independent "ham" radio operators, largely hobbyists, licensed by respective national bodies and assigned callsigns.

Citizens Band Radio

Citizens' band radio or CB is usually unlicensed broadcasting over frequencies set aside for that purpose.

Other Types of Radio Communication Over Radiowaves

Radio communications have been and are used for all variety of data transmissions. The earliest radio application, Morse code, can still be heard today. Experiments in sending pictures and text date back to the early days of radio.

A variety of clock signals are also broadcast. Another early use of radio was coded transmission of information by national governments in peace and war. During the Cold War the USSR and allied governments had national programs to block shortwave and other frequency transmissions by using jamming techniques.

One signal known as Russian woodpecker suddenly appeared on July 4, 1976 and just as suddenly disappeared at the end of 1989, and is still something of a mystery. More and more radio frequencies are being used to send digital packets of information of varying degrees of complexity.

An early form of digital radio broadcasting was packet radio, which combines digital information with traditional radio broadcasting over the air. Digital radio broadcasting has emerged, first in Europe (the UK in 1995 and Germany in 1999), and later in the United States, France, the Netherlands, South Africa and many other countries worldwide. The most simple system is named DAB Digital Radio, for Digital Audio Broadcasting, and uses the public domain EUREKA 147 (Band III) system. DAB is used mainly in the UK and South Africa. Germany and Holland use the DAB and DAB+ systems, and France use the L-Band system of DAB Digital Radio.

In the United States digital radio isn't used in the same way as Europe and South Africa - instead the IBOC system is named HD Radio and owned by a consortium of private companies called iBiquity. An international non-profit consortium Digital Radio Mondiale (DRM), has introduced the public domain DRM system.

Satellite

Satellite radiobroadcasters are slowly emerging, but the enormous entry costs of space-based satellite transmitters, and restrictions on available radio spectrum licenses has restricted growth of this market. In the USA and Canada, just two services, XM Satellite Radio and Sirius Satellite Radio exist.

PROGRAMME FORMATS

Radio programme formats differ by country, regulation and markets. For instance, the U.S. Federal Communications Commission designates the 88–92 megahertz band in the U.S. for non-profit or educational programming, with advertising prohibited. In addition, formats change in popularity as time passes and technology improves. Early radio equipment only allowed programme material to be broadcast in real time, known as *live* broadcasting. As technology for sound recording improved, an increasing proportion of broadcast programming used pre-recorded material. A current trend is the automation of radio stations. Some stations now operate without direct human intervention by using entirely pre-recorded material sequenced by computer control.

TELEVISION

Television (TV) news is considered by many to be the most influential medium for journalism. For most of the American public, local and national TV newscasts are the primary news sources.

Not only the numbers of viewers, but the effect on each viewer is considered more persuasive, as described by Marshall McLuhan ("the medium is the message" in his book *Understanding Media*). Television is dominated by attractive visuals (including beauty, action, and shock), with short sound bites and fast "cuts" (changes of camera view).

Television journalism viewership has become fragmented, with all-news cable channels such as CNN starting in 1980 and Fox News Channel and MSNBC in the 1990s. There are several broadcast television systems in use in the world today. An analogue television system includes several components: a set of technical parameters for the broadcast signal, a system for encoding colour, and possibly a system for encoding multi-channel audio. In digital television, all of these elements are combined in a single digital transmission system.

LOCAL TELEVISION

The industry divides television into local markets. Such markets are defined by viewing area and are ranked by the number of viewers. New broadcast journalists generally start in the smaller markets (fewer viewers) and move up to larger stations after gaining experience. The larger stations usually have more resources and better pay.

United States stations typically broadcast local news 3 or 4 times a day: around 5 or 6 am, noon, 5 or 6 pm, and 10 or 11 at night. Most of their nightly local newscasts are 30 minutes and include sports and weather. Anchors are shown sitting at a desk in a studio. They read teleprompters. Reporters frequently tell their stories in live shots outside the studio where the news is occurring. Morning shows include more "soft" news and feature pieces, while the evening news emphasizes "hard" news.

NEWS JOBS

Anchors (formerly "anchormen") serve as masters of ceremonies and are usually shown facing the camera in a studio while reading unseen teleprompters. They are often in pairs (co-anchors) side by side, often alternating their reading. Meteorologists describe and forecast weather and show "graphics" (maps, charts, and pictures). Any of those people can become the most recognizable faces of a station. Reporters research and write the stories and sometimes edit them into a package.

Reporters are usually accompanied by a videographer at the scenes of the news. The latter holds the camera. That person or assistants manage the audio and lighting. They are in charge of setting up live shots and might edit, too. The producer might choose, research, and write stories, as well as deciding the timing and arrangement of the newscast. An associate producer, if any, might specialize in elements of the show such as graphics.

PRODUCTION JOBS

A newscast director is in charge of show preparation, including assigning camera and talent (cast) positions on the set, as well as selecting the camera shots and other elements (recorded and live). The technical director operates the video switcher which controls and mixes all the elements of the show.

At smaller stations, the director and technical director are the same person. A graphics person operates a character generator that produces the name keys (on-screen titles) and full-page graphics. The audio technician operates the audio board. The technician is in charge of the microphones, music, and audio tape. Often, production assistants operate the teleprompters and cameras, and serve as lighting and rigging technicians ("grips").

ON-LINE CONVERGENCE

Convergence is the sharing and cross-promoting of content from a variety of media, which in theory might all converge and become one medium eventually. In broadcast news, the Internet is key part of convergence. Frequently, broadcast journalists also write text stories for the Web, usually accompanied by the graphics and sound of the original story.

Web sites offer the audience an interactive form where they can learn more about a story, can be referred to related articles, can offer comments for publication, and can print stories at home, etc. Convergence also lets newsrooms collaborate with other media. Broadcast outlets sometimes have partnerships with their print counterparts.

ANALOGUE TELEVISION SYSTEMS

All but one analogue television system began life in monochrome. Each country, faced with local political, technical, and economic issues, adopted a colour system which was effectively grafted onto an existing monochrome system, using gaps in the video spectrum (explained below) to allow the colour information to fit in the channels allotted.

In theory, any colour system could be used with any monochrome video system, but in practice some of the original monochrome systems proved impractical to adapt to colour and were abandoned when the switch to colour broadcasting was made. All countries use one of three colour systems: NTSC, PAL, or SECAM.

FRAMES

Ignoring colour, all television systems work in essentially the same manner. The monochrome image seen by a camera (now, the luminance component of a colour image) is divided into horizontal *scan lines*, some number of which make up a single image or *frame*. A monochrome image is theoretically continuous, and thus unlimited in horizontal resolution, but to make television practical a limit had to be placed on the bandwidth of the television signal, which puts an ultimate limit on the horizontal resolution possible. When colour was introduced, this limit of necessity became fixed. All current analogue television systems are *interlaced*; alternate rows of the frame are transmitted in sequence, followed by the remaining rows in their sequence.

Each half of the frame is called a *field*, and the rate at which fields are transmitted is one of the fundamental parameters of a video system. It is related to the frequency at which the electric power grid operates, to avoid flicker resulting from the beat between the television screen deflection system and nearby mains generated magnetic fields.

All digital, or "fixed pixel", displays have progressive scanning and must deinterlace an interlaced source. Use of inexpensive deinterlacing hardware is a typical difference between lower- vs. higher-priced flat panel displays (PDP, LCD, etc.).

All movies and other filmed material shot at 24 frames per second must be transferred to video frame rates in order to prevent severe motion jitter effects. Typically, for 25 frame/s formats (countries with 50 Hz mains supply), the content is sped up, while a techniques known as "3:2 pulldown" is used for 30 frame/s formats (countries with 60 Hz mains supply) to match the film frames to the video frames without speeding up the play back.

VIEWING TECHNOLOGY

Analog television signal standards are designed to be displayed on a cathode ray tube (CRT), and so the physics of these devices necessarily controls the format of the video signal. The image on a CRT is painted by a moving beam of electrons which hits a phosphor coating on the front of the tube. This electron beam is steered by a magnetic field generated by powerful electromagnets close to the source of the electron beam.

In order to reorient this magnetic steering mechanism, a certain amount of time is required due to the inductance of the magnets; the greater the change, the greater the time it takes for the electron beam to settle in the new spot. For this reason, it is necessary to shut off the electron beam (corresponding to a video signal of zero luminance) during the time it takes to reorient the beam from the end of one line to the beginning of the next (*horizontal retrace*) and from the bottom of the screen to the top (*vertical retrace* or *vertical blanking interval*). The horizontal retrace is accounted for in the time allotted to each scan line, but the vertical retrace is accounted for as *phantom lines* which are never displayed but which are included in the number of lines per frame defined for each video system. Since the electron beam must be turned off in any case, the result is gaps in the television signal, which can be used to transmit other information, such as test signals or colour identification signals.

The temporal gaps translate into a comb-like frequency spectrum for the signal, where the teeth are spaced at line frequency and concentrate most of the energy; the space between the teeth can be used to insert a colour subcarrier.

HIDDEN SIGNALING

Broadcasters later developed mechanisms to transmit digital information on the phantom lines, used mostly for teletext and closed captioning:

- PAL-Plus uses a hidden signalling scheme to indicate if it exists, and if so what operational mode it is in.
- NTSC has been modified by the Advanced Television Standards Committee to support an anti-ghosting signal that is inserted on a non-visible scan line.
- Teletext uses hidden signalling to transmit information pages.
- NTSC Closed Captioning signalling uses signalling that is nearly identical to teletext signalling.
- Widescreen All 625 line systems incorporate pulses on line 23 that flag to the display that a 16:9 widescreen image is being broadcast, though this option is not currently used on analogue transmissions.

Overscan

Television images are unique in that they must

incorporate regions of the picture with reasonable-quality content, that will never be seen by some viewers.

Interlacing

In a purely analogue system, frame order is merely a matter of convention. For digitally recorded material it becomes necessary to rearrange the sub frame order when conversion takes place from one standard to another.

Image Polarity

Another parameter of analogue television systems, minor by comparison, is the choice of whether vision modulation is positive or negative. In positive modulation, the maximum luminance value is represented by the maximum carrier power; in negative modulation, the maximum luminance value is represented by a zero carrier power. Most current video systems were defined to use negative modulation since this system has a far greater immunity to noise. The original 405 line system (System A) used positive modulation and suffered consideably from even modest amounts of interference as it was interpreted as synchronising information.

The French (older) system C and the current system L transmissions continue to be so plagued. Positive modulation was chosen for no reason other than the render French TV sets incapable of receiving 'unsuitable' broadcasts from neighboring countries. Another advantage of negative modulation is, that since the synchronising pulses represent maximum carrier power, it is relatively easy to arrange the receiver Automatic Gain Control to only operate during sync pulses and thus get a constant amplitude video signal to drive the rest of the TV set. This was not possible for many years with positive modulation as the peak carrier power varied depending on picture content. Modern digital processing circuits have achieved a similar effect but using the front porch of the video signal.

Modulation

Given all of these parameters, the result is a mostly-continuous analogue signal which can be modulated onto a radio-frequency carrier and transmitted through an antenna. All analogue television systems use vestigial sideband modulation, a form of amplitude modulation in which one sideband is partially removed. This reduces the bandwidth of the transmitted signal, enabling narrower channels to be used.

AUDIO

In analogue television, the sound portion of a broadcast is invariably modulated separately from the video. Most commonly, the audio and video are combined at the transmitter before being presented to the antenna, but in some cases separate aural and visual antennas can be used.

In almost all cases, standard wideband frequency modulation is used for the standard monaural audio; the exception is systems used by France, which are AM. Stereo, or more generally multi-channel, audio is encoded using a number of schemes which (except in the French systems) are independent of the video system.

The principal systems are NICAM, which uses a digital audio encoding; double-FM (known under a variety of names, notably Zweikanalton, A2 Stereo, West German Stereo, German Stereo or IGR Stereo), in which case each audio channel is separately modulated in FM and added to the broadcast signal; and BTSC (also known as MTS), which multiplexes additional audio channels on the video carrier. All three systems are compatible with monaural FM audio, but only NICAM may be used with the French AM audio systems.

EVOLUTION

For historical reasons, some countries use a different video system on UHF than they do on the VHF bands. In a few countries, most notably the United Kingdom, television broadcasting on VHF has been entirely shut down. Note that the British System A, unlike all the other systems, suppressed the upper sideband rather than the lower—befitting its status as the oldest operating television system to survive into the colour era (although was never officially broadcast with colour encoding). System A was tested with all three colour systems, and production equipment was designed and ready to be built; System A might have survived, as NTSC-A, had the British government not decided to harmonize with the rest of Europe on a 625-line video standard, implemented in Britain as PAL-I on UHF only.

The French System E was a post-war effort to advance France's standing in television technology. Its 819 scan lines were almost high definition even by today's standards. Like the British system A, it was VHF only and remained black & white until its shutdown in the 1980s. It was tested with SECAM in the early stages, but later the decision was made to adopt colour in 625 lines. Thus France adopted system L on UHF only and abandoned system E.

In some urban areas of Germany, notably in and around Berlin and some other major cities, all analogue TV broadcasting has been shut down in 2003–2005 in favour of reallocating the frequencies to digital broadcasting in the DVB-T standard. Analogue signals are still on air in the non-colored areas of the map. The rest of the country is scheduled to follow suit by 2010. Many other countries are planning a shutdown of analogue broadcasting, and as of 2007 a few smaller countries have already done so.

LIST OF ANALOGUE TELEVISION SYSTEMS

PRE–WORLD WAR II SYSTEMS

A number of experimental and broadcast pre WW2 systems were tested. The first ones were mechanically based and of very low resolution, sometimes with no sound. Later TV systems were electronic.

- The UK 405 line system was the first to have an allocated ITU System Letter Designation.

ITU IDENTIFICATION SCHEME

On an international conference in Stockholm in 1961, the International Telecommunications Union has defined an identification scheme for broadcast television systems. Each monochrome system is assigned a letter designation (A-M); in combination with a colour system (NTSC, PAL, SECAM), this completely specifies all of the monaural analogue television systems in the world (for example, PAL-B, NTSC-M, etc).

The following table gives the principal characteristics of each system. Defunct TV systems are shown in grey text, previous ones never designated by ITU are not yet shown. Except for lines and frame rates, other units are megahertz (MHz).

Notes by system:

A: Old United Kingdom and Ireland VHF system (B&W only). First electronic TV system, introduced in 1936. Vestigal sideband filtering introduced in 1949. Discontinued on 23 November 1982 in Ireland and on 2 January 1985 in the UK.

B: VHF only in most countries (combined with system G and H on UHF); VHF and UHF in Australia.

C: Old VHF system; used only in Belgium, Italy, the Netherlands and Luxembourg, as a compromise between Systems B and L. Disçontinued in 1977.

D: Used on VHF only in most countries (combined with system K on UHF). Used in the People's Republic of China on both VHF and UHF.

E: Old French VHF system (B&W only); very good (near HDTV) picture quality but uneconomical use of bandwidth. Sound carrier separation +11.15 MHz on odd numbered channels, -11.15 MHz on even numbered channels. Discontinued in 1984 (France) and 1985 (Monaco).

F: Old VHF system used only in Belgium, Italy, the Netherlands and Luxembourg; allowed French 819-line programming to be broadcast on the 7 MHz VHF channels used in those countries, at a substantial cost in horizontal resolution. Discontinued in 1969.

G: UHF only; used in countries with system B on VHF, except Australia.

H: UHF only; used only in Belgium, Luxembourg and the

Netherlands. Similar to System G with an 1.25 MHz vestigal sideband.

I: Used in the UK, Ireland, Southern Africa, Macau, Hong Kong and Falkland Islands.

J: Used in Japan. Identical to system M except that a different black level of 0 IRE is used instead of 7.5 IRE. Although the ITU specified a frame rate of 30 fields, 29.97 was adopted with the introduction of NTSC colour to minimize visual artifacts.

K: UHF only; used in countries with system D on VHF, and identical to it in most respects.

L: Used only in French overseas departments and territories.

M: Used only in France. On VHF Band 1 only, the audio is at "6.5 MHz. It is the last system using positive video modulation and AM sound that is still running.

N: Used in most of the Americas and Caribbean, Philippines, South Korea, Taiwan (all NTSC-M), Brazil (PAL-M) and Laos (SECAM-M). Although the ITU specified a frame rate of 30 fields, 29.97 was adopted with the introduction of NTSC colour to minimize visual artifacts. PAL-M continues to use a frame rate of 30 because not so affected.

O: Used in Argentina, Paraguay and Uruguay (all PAL-N). Allows 625-line, 50-frame/s video to be broadcast in a 6-MHz channel, at some cost in horizontal resolution.

Because an interlaced system requires accurate positioning of scanning lines it is important to make sure that the horizontal and vertical timebase are in a precise ratio. This is accomplished by passing the one through a series of electronic divider circuits to produce the other.

Each division is by a prime number. Therefore there has to be a straightforward mathematical relationship between the line and field frequencies, the latter being derived by dividing down from the former.

Technology constraints of the 1930s meant that this division process could only be done using small integers, preferably no greater than 7, for good stability. The number of lines was odd because of 2:1 interlace. The 405 line system used a vertical frequency of 50 Hz (Standard AC mains supply frequency in Britain) and a horizontal one of 10,125 Hz (50 × 405 ÷ 2)

- 2 × 3 × 3 × 5 Gives 90 (Non Interlaced)
- 2 × 2 × 2 × 2 × 2 × 3 Gives 96 (Non Interlaced)
- 2 × 2 × 3 × 3 × 5 Gives 180 (Non Interlaced)
- 2 × 2 × 2 × 2 × 3 × 5 Gives 240 (Used for the experimental Baird transmissions in Britain
- 3 × 3 × 3 × 3 × 3 Gives 243
- 7 × 7 × 7 Gives 343 (Early North American system also used in Poland before WW2)
- 3 × 5 × 5 × 5 Gives 375
- 3 × 3 × 3 × 3 × 5 Gives 405 (Used in Britain, Ireland and Hong Kong before 1985)
- 2 × 2 × 2 × 5 × 11 Gives 440 (Non Interlaced)
- 3 × 3 × 7 × 7 Gives 441 (Used by RCA in North America before the 525 NTSC standard was adopted and widely used before WW2 in Continental Europe with different frame rates)
- 2 × 3 × 3 × 5 × 5 Gives 450 (Non Interlaced)
- 5 × 7 × 13 Gives 455 (Used in France before WW2)
- 3 × 5 × 5 × 7 Gives 525 (A compromise between the RCA and Philco systems. Still used today in most of the Americas and parts of Asia)
- 3 × 3 × 3 × 3 × 7 produces 567 (used for a while after WW2 in the Netherlands)
- 5 × 11 × 11 Gives 605 (Proposed by Philco in North America before the 525 standard was adopted)
- 5 × 5 × 5 × 5 Gives 625 (Still used today in most parts of the world)
- 2 × 3 × 5 × 5 × 5 Gives 750 @ 50 fields (Used for 720p/50)
- 2 x 2 x 2 x 2 x 3 x 3 x 5 Gives 750 @ 60 fields (Used for 720p/60)
- 3 × 3 × 7 × 13 Gives 819 (Used in France in the 1950's)
- 3 × 7 × 7 × 7 Gives 1029 (Proposed but never adopted around 1948 in France)

- 3 × 3 × 5 × 5 x 5 Gives 1125 @ 25 fields (Used for 1080i/25 and 1080p/25)
- 2 × 3 × 3 × 3 × 5 × 5 Gives 1125 @ 30 fields (Used for 1080i/30 and 1080p/30)

CONVERTING FROM ONE TV SYSTEM TO ANOTHER

Converting between different numbers of lines and different frequencies of fields/frames in video pictures is not an easy task. Perhaps the most technically challenging conversion to make is from any of the 625-line, 25-frame/s systems to system M, which has 525 lines at 29.97 frames per second. Historically this required a frame store to hold those parts of the picture not actually being output (since the scanning of any point was not time coincident). In more recent times, conversion of standards is relatively easy task for a computer.

Aside from the line count being different, it's easy to see that generating 60 fields every second from a format that has only 50 fields might pose some interesting problems. Every second, an additional 10 fields must be generated seemingly from nothing. The conversion has to create new frames (from the existing input) in real time. There are several methods used to do this, depending on the desired cost and conversion quality. The simplest possible converters simply drop every 5th line from every frame (when converting from 625 to 525) or duplicate every 4th line (when converting from 525 to 625), and then duplicate or drop some of those frames to make up the difference in frame rate. More complex systems include inter-field interpolation, adaptive interpolation, and phase correlation.

DIGITAL TELEVISION SYSTEMS

The situation with worldwide digital television is much simpler by comparison. Most current digital television systems are based on the MPEG-2 multiplexed data stream standard, and use the MPEG-2 video codec. They differ significantly in the details of how the MPEG stream is converted into a broadcast signal, in the video format prior to encoding (or alternately, after decoding), and in the audio format. This has not prevented the creation of an international standard that includes both major systems, even though they are incompatible in almost every respect.

The two principal digital broadcasting systems are ATSC, developed by the Advanced Television Systems Committee and adopted as a standard in the United States and Canada, and DVB-T, the Digital Video Broadcast — Terrestrial system used in most of the rest of the world. DVB-T was designed for format compatibility with existing direct broadcast satellite services in Europe (which use the DVB-S standard, and also sees some use in direct-to-home satellite dish providers in North America), and there is also a DVB-C version for cable television. While the ATSC standard also includes support for satellite and cable television systems, operators of those systems have chosen other technologies (principally DVB-S for satellite and OpenCable for cable). Japan uses a third system, closely related to DVB-T, called ISDB-T, which is compatible with Brazil's SBTVD. The People's Republic of China has developed a fourth system, named DMB-T/H.

ATSC

The terrestrial ATSC system (unofficially ATSC-T) uses a proprietary Zenith-developed modulation called 8-VSB; as the name implies, it is a vestigial sideband technique. Essentially, analogue VSB is to regular amplitude modulation as 8VSB is to eight-way quadrature amplitude modulation. This system was chosen specifically to provide for maximum spectral compatibility between existing analogue TV and new digital stations in the United States' already-crowded television allocations system, although it is inferior to the other digital systems in dealing with multipath interference; however, it is better at dealing with impulse noise which is especially present on the VHF bands that other countries have discontinued from TV use, but are still used in the U.S. There is also no hierarchical modulation.

After demodulation and error-correction, the 8-VSB

modulation supports a digital data stream of about 19.2 Mbit/s, enough for one high-definition video stream or several standard-definition services. On cable, ATSC usually uses 256QAM, although some use 16VSB. Both of these double the throughput to 38.4Mb/s within the same 6MHz bandwidth. ATSC is also used over satellite. While these are logically called ATSC-C and ATSC-S, these terms were never officially defined. ATSC was never designed for mobile use, but the ATSC group is currently (as of 2008) considering how this can be done through its ATSC-M/H.

DMB-T/H

DMB-T/H is the digital television broadcasting standard of the People's Republic of China (including Hong Kong). This is a hybrid system, part of which is ATDB, in turn very similar to ATSC-T.

DVB

DVB-T uses coded orthogonal frequency division multiplexing (COFDM), which uses as many as 8000 independent carriers, each transmitting data at a comparatively low rate. This system was designed to provide superior immunity from multipath interference, and has a choice of system variants which allow data rates from 4 MBit/s up to 24 MBit/s. One U.S. broadcaster, Sinclair Broadcasting, petitioned the Federal Communications Commission to permit the use of COFDM instead of 8-VSB, on the theory that this would improve prospects for digital TV reception by households without outside antennas (a majority in the U.S.), but this request was denied. (However, one U.S. digital station, WNYE-DT in New York, was temporarily converted to COFDM modulation on an emergency basis for datacasting information to emergency services personnel in lower Manhattan in the aftermath of the September 11 terrorist attacks.) In Spain is also known as TDT (Television Digital Terreste).

DVB-S is the original Digital Video Broadcasting forward error coding and modulation standard for satellite television and dates from 1995. It is used via satellites serving every continent of the world, this is even true in North America. DVB-S is used in both MCPC and SCPC modes for broadcast network feeds, as well as for direct broadcast satellite services like Sky Digital (UK & Ireland) via Astra in Europe, Dish Network in the U.S., and Bell TV in Canada. The transport stream delivered by DVB-S is mandated as MPEG-2.

DVB-C stands for Digital Video Broadcasting - Cable and it is the DVB European consortium standard for the broadcast transmission of digital television over cable. This system transmits an MPEG-2 family digital audio/video stream, using a QAM modulation with channel coding.

ISDB

ISDB is very similar to DVB, however it is broken into 13 subchannels. Twelve are used for TV, while the last serves either as a guard band, or for the 1seg (ISDB-H) service. Like the other DTV systems, the ISDB types differ mainly in the modulations used, due to the requirements of different frequency bands.

The 12 GHz band ISDB-S uses PSK modulation, 2.6 GHz band digital sound broadcasting uses CDM and ISDB-T (in VHF and/or UHF band) uses COFDM with PSK/QAM. It was developed in Japan with MPEG-2, and is now used in Brazil with MPEG-4. Unlike other digital broadcast systems, ISDB includes digital rights management to restrict recording of programming.

Chapter 14

Cable Television

Cable television is a system of providing television to consumers via radio frequency signals transmitted to televisions through fixed optical fibers or coaxial cables as opposed to the over-the-air method used in traditional television broadcasting (via radio waves) in which a television antenna is required.

FM radio programming, high-speed Internet, telephony, and similar non-television services may also be provided. The abbreviation CATV is often used to mean "Cable TV". It originally stood for Community Antenna Television, from cable television's origins in 1948: in areas where over-the-air reception was limited by mountainous terrain, large "community antennas" were constructed, and cable was run from them to individual homes.

It is most commonplace in North America, Europe, Australia and East Asia, though it is present in many other countries, mainly in South America and the Middle East. Cable TV has had little success in Africa, as it is not cost-effective to lay cables in sparsely populated areas. So-called "wireless cable" or microwave-based systems are used instead.

CABLE TELEVISION DEPLOYMENTS

ASIA

Mongolia

There are several cable tv providers in Mongolia. The main three are "SuperVision", "Hiimori" and "Sansar CATV".

All three cover approximately 10 national channels and 40 foreign channels, such as CNN, BBC, NHK. Among them "SuperVision" is known for its superior quality and gives much more interesting channels, such as National Geographic and Discovery. "Sansar" and "Hiimori" and other smaller companies fill their channel list with Chinese and Indian channels.

Maldives

There over 100 cable TV operators across the country. As the population of the Maldives is separated across around 200 inhabited islands, there is a cable TV operator for nearly every island. Media Net Pvt. Ltd. is the country's largest cable TV operator.

Media Net is a Male-based cable TV operator that provides cable and MMDS service to five islands near Male. Media Net holds the license of distribution for 41 channels and distributes channels to nearly all the operators of the country. In Maldives, cable TV subscribers can get most premium channels available in Asia.

CENTRAL AMERICA

Panamá

From 2000, Cable TV adoption has been impulsed with the fusion of Cable Onda and Corporación Medcom. Several companies compete for the Panamanian market, such as CTV, Cable Onda, Cablevision, and others. Cable Onda is the largest. The penetration of CableTV in Panamá is at 40%.

EUROPE

United Kingdom

When the infant BBC Television service was started in 1932, Rediffusion, which had supplied cable radio services since 1928, started providing "Pipe TV" to its customers who had difficulties tuning into the weak TV broadcast signal. The service was suspended during World War II, and when it was re-established in June 1946, it had only one transmitter, at Alexandra Palace, which served the London area.

From the end of 1949, new transmitters were steadily opened to serve other major conurbations, and then smaller areas of population. The areas on the fringes of the transmitter coverage provided an opportunity for Rediffusion and other commercial companies to expand cable systems to enlarge the viewing audience for the one BBC television channel which then existed.

The first was in Gloucester in 1950 and the process gathered pace over the next few years, especially after a second television channel, ITV, was launched in 1955 to compete with the BBC. By the late 1970s, two and a half million British homes received their television service via cable.

By law, these cable systems were restricted to the relay of the public broadcast channels, which meant that as the transmitter network became more comprehensive the incentive to subscribe to cable was reduced and they began to lose customers. In 1982, a radical liberalisation of the law on cable was proposed by the Information Technology Advisory Panel, for the sake of promoting a new generation of broadband cable systems leading to the wired society.

After setting up and receiving the conclusions of the Hunt Inquiry into Cable Expansion and Broadcasting Policy, the Government decided to proceed with liberalisation and two pieces of legislation: the Cable and Broadcasting Act and the Telecommunications Act, were enacted in 1984.

The result was that cable systems were permitted to carry as many new television channels as they liked, as well as providing a telephone service and interactive services of many kinds (as since made familiar by the Internet). To maintain the momentum of the perceived commercial interest in this new investment opportunity, in 1983 the Government itself granted eleven interim franchises for new broadband systems each covering a community of up to around 100,000 homes, but the competitive franchising process was otherwise left to the new regulatory body, the Cable Authority, which took on its powers from 1 January 1985.

The franchising process proceeded steadily, but the actual construction of new systems was slow, as doubts about an adequate payback from the substantial investment persisted. By the end of 1990 almost 15 million homes had been included in franchised areas, but only 828,000 of these had been passed by broadband cable and only 149,000 were actually subscribing. Thereafter, however, construction accelerated and take-up steadily improved.

The first new television channels launched for carriage on cable systems (going live in March 1984) were Sky Channel, Screensport, Music Box and TEN - the Movie Channel. Others followed, some were merged or closed down, but the range expanded. A similar flux was seen among the operators of cable systems: franchises were granted to a host of different companies, but a process of consolidation saw the growth of large multiple system operators, until by early in the 2000s virtually the whole industry was in the hands of two companies, NTL and Telewest.

In 2005 it was announced that NTL and Telewest would merge, after a period of co-operation in the preceding few years. This merger was completed on 3 March 2006 with the company being named ntl Incorporated. For the time being the two brand names and services were marketed separately. However, following NTL's acquisition of Virgin Mobile, the NTL and Telewest services were rebranded *Virgin Media* on 2007-02-08 creating a single cable operator covering more than 95% of the UK cable market.

There are a small number of other surviving cable television companies in the UK outside of NTL including WightCable (Isle of Wight) and Smallworld (Ayrshire, Carlisle and Lancashire). Cable TV faces intense competition from British Sky Broadcasting's Sky Digital satellite television service. Most channels are carried on both platforms. However, cable often lacks "interactive" features (e.g. text services, and extra video-screens), especially on BSkyB owned channels, and the satellite platform lacks services requiring high degrees of two-way communication, such as true video on demand.

However, subscription-funded digital terrestrial television

proved less of a competitive threat. The first system, ITV Digital, went into liquidation in 2002. Top Up TV later replaced it, however this service is shrinking as the DVB-T multiplex owners are finding FTA broadcasting more profitable. Another potential source of competition in the future will be TV over broadband internet connections; this is known as IPTV. Some IPTV services are currently available in London, while services operated in Hull ceased in April 2006.

As the speed and availability of broadband connections increase, more TV content can be delivered using protocols such as IPTV. However, its impact on the market is yet to be measured, as is consumer attitude toward watching TV programmes on computers instead of television sets. At the end of 2006, BT (the UK's former state owned monopoly phone company) started offering BT Vision, which combines the digital free-to-air standard Freeview through an aerial, and on-demand IPTV, delivered over a BT Broadband connection through the Vision set-top box (BT have chosen to deploy Microsoft's Mediaroom platform for this.)

NORTH AMERICA

USA

Consumers may be concerned by how businesses and government get on. The US cable industry spends millions of dollars annually on government relationships. Regularly this industry employs the spouses, sons and daughters of influential mayors, councilmen, commissioners, and other officials to assure its continued local monopoly and preferred market allocations, many of which have been questioned as unethical.

The monopoly on cable television has historically been enforced by local governments. Cable maintains thousands of such de facto monopolies. In order to provide service to individual homes, a cable provider must place its cable wiring along and across local streets or other rights-of-way. To do so, the provider must get permission from the local government(s) that own those streets via rights-of-way permits. Operational permission comes in the form of a document called a local franchise agreement.

Most of local government(s) chose to grant permission to only one company, however, recently states have developed broader franchising laws to drive more investment and competition.

Changes in the federal law in 1992 had forced local governments to grant permission to other companies to provide service, however the U.S. Government found in 2006 that only 2% of U.S. households had a competitive choice. In some cases Comcast, with municipal government approval, had entered into market allocation schemes. By agreeing to not compete head to head, consumers thus are perpetually locked into a single monopoly cable provider with annual price escalations reaching 93% in the past decade.

CUSTOMER SURVEYS

A recent third party survey of citizens found approximately 62% of the respondents were very dissatisfied (along with another 25% who were dissatisfied) with the cost of cable television service. A majority of the respondents were satisfied with the friendliness and courtesy of customer service personnel, however, approximately 30% of the respondents rated the cable company's performance as poor.

With regard to open-ended comments, respondents felt that the cost of the cable service was too high, a need for cable competition existed and the desire for a basic cable package offering was desired. Although respondents cited these critical issues, the local monopoly structure could be considered to preserve the status quo of poor customer service, limited product choices, no direct competition and uncontrollable annual cable TV price increases.

Relief for consumers is being created by state level a multi jurisdictional franchise and service process that will spur investment and competition; thus driving economic development sought by state and local government leaders.

The industry strongly lobbies against federal "family tier" and "a la carte cable television" bills that would give consumers the option to purchase individual channels rather than a broad tier of programming. These anti-consumer issues continue to garner attention from state governments, Congress and FCC Chairman Martin.

When the infant BBC Television service was started in 1932, Rediffusion, which had supplied cable radio services since 1928, started providing "Pipe TV" to its customers who had difficulties tuning into the weak TV broadcast signal.

OTHER CABLE-BASED SERVICES

Coaxial cables are capable of bi-directional carriage of signals as well as the transmission of large amounts of data. Cable television signals use only a portion of the bandwidth available over coaxial lines. This leaves plenty of space available for other digital services such as broadband internet and cable telephony.

Broadband internet is achieved over coaxial cable by using cable modems to convert the network data into a type of digital signal that can be transferred over coaxial cable. One problem with some cable systems is the older amplifiers placed along the cable routes are unidirectional thus in order to allow for uploading of data the customer would need to use an analog telephone modem to provide for the upstream connection.

This limited the upstream speed to 31.2k and prevented the always-on convenience broadband internet typically provides. Many large cable systems have upgraded or are upgrading their equipment to allow for bi-directional signals, thus allowing for greater upload speed and always-on convenience, though these upgrades are expensive.

In North America, Australia and Europe many cable operators have already introduced cable telephone service, which operates just like existing fixed line operators. This service involves installing a special telephone interface at the customer's premises that converts the analog signals from the customer's in-home wiring into a digital signal, which is then sent on the local loop (replacing the analog last mile, or POTS) to the company's switching centre, where it is connected to the PSTN. The biggest obstacle to cable telephone service is the need for nearly 100% reliable service for emergency calls. One of the standards available for digital cable telephony, PacketCable, seems to be the most promising and able to work with the Quality of Service demands of traditional analog POTS service.

The biggest advantage to digital cable telephone service is similar to the advantage of digital cable TV, namely that data can be compressed, resulting in much less bandwidth used than a dedicated analog circuit-switched service.

Other advantages include better voice quality and integration to a VoIP network providing cheap or unlimited nationwide and international calling. Note that in many cases, digital cable telephone service is separate from cable modem service being offered by many cable companies and does not rely on IP traffic or the Internet.

Beginning in 2004 in the United States, the traditional cable television providers and traditional telecommunication companies increasingly compete in providing voice, video and data services to residences. The combination of TV, telephone and Internet access is commonly called triple play regardless of whether CATV or telcos offer it.

CONSUMER ISSUES

Using a cable service naturally requires that access to a cable network be installed at the customer location, laying/maintaining this cable has costs. From the consumers viewpoint, having a choice of who provides this service may be deemed desirable, however from a business viewpoint may be undesirable; as this would require multiple companies investing in laying many generally identical cables to the same location. Altogether that could mean greater costs, since there is more physical cable in existence.

Therefore the idea of a natural monopoly may apply, whereby in most places only one cable provider is preferable (seemingly for all concerned). Competition in one place may therefore come in the form of terrestrial or satellite providers. As with all situations where competition is in some way limited, there is a potential for consumers to feel they are unfairly treated by the market. Market regulators therefore may tend to limit such consumer concerns by broadening the consumers choice from a single provider, for instance in expecting them to offer different priced channel selections, improving service other times (for instance, by making use of technological progress) and measures such as providing free-for-all (public) TV.

In the 1950s, there were four television networks in the United States. Because of the frequencies allotted to television, the signals could only be received in a "line of sight" from the transmitting antenna. People living in remote areas, especially remote mountainous areas, couldn't see the programs that were already becoming an important part of U.S. culture.

In 1948, people living in remote valleys in Pennsylvania solved their reception problems by putting antennas on hills and running cables to their houses. These days, the same technology once used by remote hamlets and select cities allows viewers all over the country to access a wide variety of programs and channels that meet their individual needs and desires. By the early 1990s, cable television had reached nearly half the homes in the United States.

Today, U.S. cable systems deliver hundreds of channels to some 60 million homes, while also providing a growing number of people with high-speed Internet access. Some cable systems even let you make telephone calls and receive new programming technologies! In this article, we'll show you how cable television brings you so much information and such a wide range of programs, from educational to inspirational to just plain odd.

The earliest cable systems were, in effect, strategically placed antennas with very long cables connecting them to subscribers' television sets. Because the signal from the antenna became weaker as it traveled through the length of cable, cable providers had to insert amplifiers at regular intervals to boost the strength of the signal and make it acceptable for viewing. According to Bill Wall, technical director for subscriber networks at Scientific-Atlanta, a leading maker of equipment for cable television systems, limitations in these amplifiers were a significant issue for cable system designers in the next three decades.

"In a cable system, the signal might have gone through 30 or 40 amplifiers before reaching your house, one every 1,000 feet or so," Wall says. "With each amplifier, you would get noise and distortion. Plus, if one of the amplifiers failed, you lost the picture.

Cable got a reputation for not having the best quality picture and for not being reliable." In the late 1970s, cable television would find a solution to the amplifier problem. By then, they had also developed technology that allowed them to add more programming to cable service.

Chapter 15

Yellow Page

The term *Yellow Pages* refers to a telephone directory of businesses, categorized according to the product or service provided. As the name suggests, such directories were originally printed on yellow paper, as opposed to white pages for non-commercial listings. The traditional term *Yellow Pages* is now also applied to online directories of businesses. To avoid the increasing cost of yellow paper, the yellow background of the pages is currently printed on white paper using ink. Yellow paper is no longer used.

The name and concept of "Yellow Pages" came about in 1883, when a printer in Cheyenne, Wyoming working on a regular telephone directory ran out of white paper and used yellow paper instead.

In 1886 Reuben H. Donnelley created the first official yellow pages directory, inventing an industry. Today, the expression *Yellow Pages* is used globally, in both English-speaking and non-English speaking countries. In the United States, it refers to the category, while in some other countries it is a registered name and therefore a proper noun.

IN GENERAL

Yellow Pages (YP) are a print directory which provides an alphabetical listing of businesses within a specific geographical area (e.g., Greater Chicago), which are segregated under headings for similar types of businesses (e.g., Plumbers). Traditionally these directories have been published by the local phone company, but due to the highly profitable nature of the business there are numerous independent directory publishers.

Some YP publishers focus on a particular demographic (e.g., Christian Yellow Pages or Business Pages).

Yellow Pages directories are usually published annually, and distributed for free to all residences and businesses within a given coverage area. The majority of listings are plain and in small black text, usually in the Bell Gothic or Bell Centennial typefaces.

The YP publishers generate profit by selling advertising space or listings under each heading. Advertising may be sold by a direct sales force or by approved agencies (CMR's). Available advertising space varies among publishers and ranges from bold names up to four colour twin page ads ("double trucks"). Advertising rates typically increase every year regardless of distribution or usage fluctuations.

In the United States, the predominant yellow pages are the RH Donnelley's DEX, Yellowbook, the AT&T Real Yellow Pages, and the Verizon Superpages.

In some countries, the familiar "walking fingers" logo is not protected as a trademark and may be used by anyone. This logo is used in varying forms by almost every YP publisher; however, there are companies that use it to imitate mainstream publishers. In Israel and the Republic of Ireland, the directory, although using the Yellow Pages logo, is called "Golden Pages".

Business listings used for publication are obtained by several methods. Local phone companies that publish YP directories rely on their own customer lists and include business listings that are provided by phone service providers (CLEC's). Business owners that utilize phone services other than the local phone company (typically a Bell Company) should make certain that their information has been sent to the publisher for printing in upcoming directories.

Advertising in YP directories requires payment in full prior to printing or may be billed monthly over the life of the contract, which is usually 12 months. Typically, a sales representative will assist the customer in creating their ad design and provides a Proof Copy for review and approval. Advertisers should be aware that many contracts have automatic renewal clauses and require action on the part of the advertiser to end future billing.

Yellow Pages print usage is reported to be declining with both advertisers and shoppers increasingly turning to Internet search engines and online directories. According to a study by Knowledge Networks/SRI, in 2007, print Yellow Pages were referenced 13.4 billion times, while Internet Yellow Pages references increased to 3.8 billion, up from 2006's 3.3 billion online searches.

As a result most YP publishers have attempted to create online versions of their print directories. These online versions are referred to as IYP or Internet Yellow Pages. Independent ad agencies or Internet marketing consultants can assist business owners in determining sound opportunities for YP advertising and provide objective information on usage, possession and preferences.

INTERNET YELLOW PAGES

Online Yellow Pages are known as IYP or Internet Yellow Pages. On a broader scale they are known as vertical directories. There are consumer oriented and business oriented varieties. All providers of IYP offer online advertising. IYP's have largely formed as a result of yellow pages publishers needing to replace rapidly declining print revenue by chasing the migration of shoppers toward web-based information.

IYP offers listings differently than standard search engines. Where search engines return results based on relevancy to the true search term, IYP returns results based on a geographic area. Studies by independent companies such as Nielson and comScore have shown that Internet Yellow Pages have a very slim percentage of total Internet searches. The majority, over 85% of all Internet searches, occur on the major search engines Google, Yahoo and MSN.

Advertising on IYP is typically available with numerous a la carte choices. These choices become small "individual sales presentations" which makes it easier for sales reps to sell large advertising packages. Advertisers should closely monitor any IYP ad programs to measure their ROI.

A newer version of IYPs are classified as local search directories which provide similar content with the added ability for customer reviews and comments for a listed business.

The user advantage is that local search is not dominated by high paying corporate advertising. All services offer paid advertising options which typically offer preferred placement on search results pages.

MOBILE MEDIA (LOCAL SEARCH)

The Yellow Pages are also available on mobile devices (such as mobile phones and GPS navigators) with static (embedded) and real-time (online) databases. The usage method varies (such as SMS, a WAP session, voice, or a dedicated application on the device), but usually relies on the input of the search keywords, and a return from the application with the points of interest.

This kind of yellow page query is more and more being referred to as a local search. Local searches are a growing area where marketing dollars are being invested due to the targeted and focused customer base it develops to the Yellow Pages advertisers.

Voice recognition is also being used in the interfacing; the Canadian Yellow Pages Group has commercially been using a voice local search "Hello Yellow" (in 2007 renamed "YellowPages411") since 2005, enabling one to find local businesses using only one's voice. In 2008 a multi-million pound stand alone advertisement was launched by Mother Agency.

The campaign tells the story of the spoilt schoolboy Marcus, played by actor Max Gill, and his demands of Fresno (Normski) and Carrie (Catherine Bailey), Yell party organisers, which become increasingly bizarre. In 2009, Yellow Pages asked Weebl to produce an ad for their online and mobile services, dubbed "118 24 7"

Chapter 16

Magazine

Magazines, periodicals, glossies or serials are publications, generally published on a regular schedule, containing a variety of articles, generally financed by advertising, by a purchase price, by pre-paid magazine subscriptions, or all three. Magazines can be distributed through the mail; through sales by newsstands, bookstores or other vendors; or through free distribution at selected pick up locations.

PUBLICATION

The various elements that contribute to the production of magazines vary wildly. Core elements such as publishing schedules, formats and target audiences are seemingly infinitely variable. Typically, magazines which focus primarily on current events, such as *Newsweek* or *Entertainment Weekly*, are published weekly or biweekly. Magazines with a focus on specific interests, such as *Cat Fancy*, may be published less frequently, such as monthly, bimonthly or quarterly.

A magazine will usually have a date on the cover which often is later than the date it is actually published. Current magazines are generally available at bookstores and newsstands, while subscribers can receive them in the mail. Many magazines also offer a 'back issue' service for previously published editions.

Most magazines produced on a commercial scale are printed using a web offset process. The magazine is printed in sections, typically of 16 pages, which may be black-and-white, be in full colour, or use spot colour. These sections are then bound, either by stapling them within a soft cover in a process sometimes referred to as 'saddle-stitching', or by gluing them together to form a spine, a process often called 'perfect-binding'.

Some magazines are also published on the internet. Many magazines are available both on the internet and in hard copy, usually in different versions, though some are only available in hard copy or only via the internet: the latter are known as online magazines.

Most magazines are available in the whole of the country in which they are published, although some are distributed only in specific regions or cities. Others are available internationally, often in different editions for each country or area of the world, varying to some degree in editorial and advertising content but not entirely dissimilar.

OTHER PUBLICATIONS

Although similar to a magazine in some respects, an academic periodical featuring scholarly articles written in a more specialist register is usually called an "academic journal". Such publications typically carry little or no advertising. Articles are vetted by referees or a board of esteemed academics in the subject area.

The Gentleman's Magazine, first published in 1731, in London, is considered to have been the first general-interest magazine. Edward Cave, who edited *The Gentleman's Magazine* under the pen name "Sylvanus Urban", was the first to use the term "magazine", on the analogy of a military storehouse of varied *materiel,* originally derived from the Arabic *makazin* "storehouses".

The oldest consumer magazine still in print is *The Scots Magazine,* which was first published in 1739, though multiple changes in ownership and gaps in publication totaling over 90 years weaken that claim. Lloyd's List was founded in Edward Lloyd's England coffee shop in 1734; it is still published as a daily business newspaper.

ENVIRONMENTAL IMPACT

A life cycle study shows that the CO2 emissions caused

by the production and distribution of one copy of an average sized .39 pound magazine in the USA total about .95 kilograms (2.1 pounds) — including paper from trees, materials, production, shipping and customer use. The loss of natural habitat potential from the .39 pound magazine is estimated to be .73 square meters (7.9 square feet).

Publishing your own genre magazine can be very similar to publishing a book.

Plan your method and think everything through long and hard, so your magazine best suits your original vision, and you can avoid easy pitfalls. Deciding on a focused idea, and knowing what unique feel you want, will help to set your 'zine apart from the pack.

Successful publishing often depends on your brand and the following that it generates. Despite the numerous failed publications that come and go, a unique, well thought out concept, can be turned into a winner. For example, *Cemetery Dance* was a hobby for editor Richard Chizmar, but has been one of the premier horror magazines since the early 90s.

This magazine's success is due in part to its unique feel, and catering to a niche audience, but it has also invested money in featuring excellent authors. Other successful genre magazines, such as *The Magazine of Fantasy and Science Fiction* and *Alfred Hitchcock's Mystery Magazine* also invest in excellent authors to create an excellent product.

HOW TO CHOOSE STORIES FOR YOUR GENRE MAGAZINE

The selection process for your genre magazine can be a very long and painstaking one, but you do have several options. One option is to post market guidelines on websites like Ralan. When you post your guidelines, remember to note your response times, and whether or not you accept simultaneous submissions. One caveat of an open submission period is that you might become flooded with off-target submissions and inferior writing.

Chapter 17

Interactive

Interactive media, a type of Collaborative media, refers to media that allows for active participation by the recipient, hence interactivity. Traditional information theory would describe interactive media as those media that establish two-way communication. In media theory, interactive media are discussed along their cultural implications. The field of Human Computer Interaction deals with aspects of interactivity and design in digital media. Other areas that deal with interactive media are new media art, interactive advertising and video game production.

While much traditional analog electronic media and print media qualifies as interactive media, the term is sometimes misunderstood as exclusive to digital media. The significant increase in possibilities for interactivity (especially over vast distances) brought by the internet boosted the availability of digital interactive media. Still, e.g. language in face-to-face communication would formally belong to the category of interactive media.

Interactive media are often designed by information designers. As all media they rely on communication. In the case of e.g. computer games this is visual, acoustic, and haptic communication between the user (player) and the game. In Mobile telephony, the communication happens between two people and is purely acoustic at the first glance. Yet, according to media theory the cultural implications of the medium have to be taken into account. Thus, aspects like constant availability, customization of the mobile phone and Short Message Service are also part of the interactive medium called

Mobile telephony. Media restrain from being translated to technological entities.

TERMINOLOGY

Any form of interface between the end user/audience and the medium may be considered interactive. Interactive media is not limited to electronic media or digital media. Board games, pop-up books, gamebooks, flip books and constellation wheels are all examples of printed interactive media. Books with a simple table of contents or index may be considered interactive due to the non-linear control mechanism in the medium, but are usually considered non-interactive since the majority of the user experience is non-interactive sequential reading.

Interactive art is a form of installation-based art that involves the spectator in some way. Some installations achieve this by letting the observer walk in, on, and around them. Works frequently feature computers and sensors to respond to motion, heat, meteorological changes or other types of input their makers programme them to respond to. Most examples of virtual Internet art and electronic art are highly interactive. Sometimes visitors are able to navigate through a hypertext environment; some works accept textual or visual input from outside; sometimes an audience can influence the course of a performance or can even participate in it.

Interactive art can be distinguished from Generative art, Electronic art, or Immersive virtual reality in that it constitutes a dialogue between the art work and the participant; specifically, the participant has agency, or the ability to act upon the art work and is furthermore invited to do so within the context of the piece, i.e. the work affords the interaction. In an increasing number of cases an installation can be defined as a responsive environment, especially those created by architects and designers. By contrast, Generative Art, which is interactive, but not responsive per se, tends to be a monologue - the artwork may change or evolve in the presence of the viewer, but the viewer may not be invited to engage in the reaction but merely enjoy it.

A hybrid emerging discipline drawing on the combined interests of specific artists and architects has been created in the last 10–15 years. Disciplinary boundaries have blurred, and significant number of architects and interactive designers have joining electronic artists in the creation of new, custom-designed interfaces and evolutions in techniques for obtaining user input (such as dog vision, alternative sensors, voice analysis, etc.); forms and tools for information display (such as video projection, lasers, robotic and mechatronic actuators, led lighting etc.); modes for human-human and human-machine communication (through the Internet and other telecommunications networks); and to the development of social contexts for interactive systems (such as utilitarian tools, formal experiments, games and entertainment, social critique, and political liberation).

Interactive architecture has now been installed on and as part of building facades, in foyers, museums and large scale public spaces, including at airports, in a number of global cities. A number of leading museums, for example, the National Gallery, Tate, Victoria & Albert Museum and Science Museum in London (to cite the leading UK museums active in this field) were early adoptors in the field of interactive technologies, investing in educational resources, and more latterly, in the creative use of MP3 players for visitors. In 2004 the Victoria & Albert Museum commissioned curator and author Lucy Bullivant to write Responsive Environments (2006), the first such publication of its kind. Interactive designers are frequently commissioned for museum displays; a number specialise in wearable computing.

There are number of globally significant festivals and exhibitions of interactive and media arts Prix Ars Electronica is a major yearly competition and exhibition that gives awards to outstanding examples of (technology-driven) interactive art. Association of Computing Machinery's Special Interest Group in Graphics (SIGGRAPH), DEAF Dutch Electronic Arts Festival, Transmediale Germany, FILE - Electronic Language International Festival Brazil, and AV Festival England, are among the others. CAiiA, Centre for Advanced Inquiry in the

Interactive Arts, first established in 1994 at the University of Wales, Newport, and later in 2003 as the Planetary Collegium, was the first doctoral and post doc research centre to be established specifically for research in the interactive art field.

INTERACTIVE ART

Interactive art is a genre of art in which the viewers participate in some way. Unlike traditional art forms wherein the interaction of the spectator is merely a mental event, interactivity allows for various types of navigation, assembly, and/or contribution to an artwork, which goes far beyond purely psychological activity. Interactive art installations are generally computer-based and frequently rely on sensors, which gauge things such as temperature, motion, proximity, and other meteorological phenomena that the maker has programmed in order to elicit responses. In interactive artworks, both the audience and the machine work together in dialogue in order to produce a completely unique artwork for each audience to observe.

Though some of the earliest examples of interactive art have been dated back to the 1920s, most digital art didn't make its official entry into the world of art until the late 1990s. Since this debut, countless museums and venues have been increasingly accommodating digital and interactive art into their productions. This budding genre of art is continuing to grow and evolve in a somewhat rapid manner.

Some of the earliest examples of interactive art were created as early as the 1920s. An example is Marcel Duchamp's piece named *Rotary Glass Plates*. It required the viewer to turn on the machine and stand at a distance of one metre. The idea of interactive art began to flourish more in the 1960s for partly political reasons. At the time, many people found it inappropriate for artists to carry the only creative power within their works. Those artists who held this view wanted to give the audience their own part of this creative process.

Aside from this "political" view, it was also current wisdom that interaction and engagement had a positive part to play within the creative process. In the 1970s artists began to use new technology such as video and satellites to experiment with live performances and interactions through the direct broadcast of video and audio. Interactive art became a large phenomenon due to the advent of computer based interactivity in the 1990s . Along with this came a new kind of art-experience. Audience and machine were now able to more easily work together in dialogue in order to produce a unique artwork for each audience. In the late 1990s, museums and galleries began increasingly incorporating the art form in their shows, some even dedicating entire exhibitions to it. This continues today and is only expanding.

FEATURES

Interactive art involves the viewers in some way in order to determine the outcome. Interactivity as a medium produces meaning. There are many different forms of interactive art. Such forms range from interactive dance, music, and even drama. New technology, primarily computer systems and computer technology, have enabled a new class of interactive art. Examples of such interactive art are installation art and interactive architecture.

Interactive advertising uses online or offline interactive media to communicate with consumers and to promote products, brands, services, and public service announcements, corporate or political groups.

In the inaugural issue of the Journal of Interactive Advertising, editors Li and Leckenby (2000) defined Interactive Advertising as the "paid and unpaid presentation and promotion of products, services and ideas by an identified sponsor through mediated means involving mutual action between consumers and producers." This is most commonly performed through the Internet as a medium.

INTERACTIVE ADVERTISING OBJECTIVES

It is these mutual actions or interactions that enhance what Interactive Advertising is trying to achieve. But to understand how these help we must study the objectives of Interactive Advertising. The goals of interactive advertising are usually akin to the traditional objectives of advertising. This in turn means that many of the traditional elements of advertising impact and effectiveness remain relevant, even within the scope of interactive media. However, according to the *Journal of Interactive Advertising* 2001, interactive advertising also has some properties that expand the range of potential objectives and that facilitate the acquisition of traditional measures of advertising effectiveness. Interactive advertising also has the potential to lessen the consequential losses associated with poorly coordinated advertising, to reduce the difficulties commonly encountered in clearly communicating an advertising message and to help overcome new product hurdles, such as a consumer rejection.

ELEMENTS OF INTERACTIVE ADVERTISING

There are many different facets to Interactive Advertising, including varying methods and types. Using many different types of cognitive tools and advert presentations, organizations can enhance the impact of their campaigns with this type of advertising. According to Thorson (1996), all advertisements can be classified into one of five basic categories, including: product/service, public service announcement, issue, corporate and political. Advert types also interact with the user's motives to influence outcomes, or consumer responses, reinforcing the need for Interactive Advertising as a means of persuading potential consumers and target audiences.

Using the Internet as the main medium for Interactive Advertising to study the methods, types and outcomes, we can then sound out the different user or advertiser controlled aspects.

USER GENERATED/CONTROLLED ASPECTS

Functions, Internet motives and mode are the main factors of user controlled aspects. In fact, a number of researchers and practitioners argue that consumers have more control on the Internet than do advertisers. Some have gone so far as to argue that interactive marketing and advertising techniques will not work unless practitioners "step into the shoes" of and approach the Internet from the consumer's vantage point.

Advertiser controlled aspects

Internet aspects that are under the control of the advertiser. Most of these variables include structural elements, such as ad types, formats and features. This does not mean that consumers never control the structure of the interactive ads. Banner Ads, pop-up ads, sponsorship, hyperlinks and non-carrier websites are examples of Advertiser controlled Interactive Advertising.

Chapter 18

Media Comparisons: Advantages and Disadvantages

NEWSPAPERS

ADVANTAGES

- Your ad has size and share, and can be as large as necessary to communicate as much of a story as you care to tell.
- The distribution of your message can be limited to your geographic area.
- Split-run tests are available to test your copy and your offer.
- Free help is usually available to create and produce your ad.
- Fast closings. The ad you decide to run today can be in your customer's hands two days from now.

DISADVANTAGES

- Clutter. Your ad has to compete for attention against large ads run by supermarkets and department stores.
- Poor photo reproduction limits creativity.
- A price-oriented medium. Most ads are for sales.
- Short shelf life. The day after a newspaper appears, it's history.
- Waste circulation. You're paying to send your

message to a lot of people who will probably never be in the market to buy from you.

- A highly visible medium. Your competitors can quickly react to your prices.

MAGAZINES

ADVANTAGES

- High reader involvement means more attention will be paid to your advertisement.
- Less waste circulation. You can place your ads in magazines read primarily by buyers of your product or service.
- The smaller the page (generally eight and half by eleven inches) permits even small ads to stand out.

DISADVANTAGES

- Long lead times (generally 90 days) mean you have to make plans a long time in advance.
- The cost for space is higher in addition to higher creative costs.

YELLOW PAGES

ADVANTAGES

- Everyone uses the yellow pages.
- Ads are reasonably inexpensive.
- You can easily track your responses.

DISADVANTAGES

- All of your competitors are listed so you run the ad as a defensive measure.
- Ads are not very creative since they follow certain formats.

RADIO

ADVANTAGES

- A universal medium. Can be enjoyed at home, at

work, and while driving. Most people listen to the radio at one time or another during the day.

- Permits you to target your advertising dollars to the market most likely to respond to your offer.
- Permits you to create a personality for your business using only sounds and voices.
- Free creative help is usually available.
- Rates can generally be negotiated.
- Least inflated medium. During the past ten years, radio rates have gone up less than other media.

DISADVANTAGES

- Because radio listeners are spread over many stations, to totally saturate your market you have to advertise simultaneously on many stations.
- Listeners cannot refer back to your ads to go over important points.
- Ads are an interruption to the entertainment. Because of this, radio ads must be repeated to break through the listener's "tune out" factor.
- Radio is a background medium. Most listeners are doing something else while listening, which means your ad has to work hard to be listened to and understood.
- Advertising costs are based on ratings which are approximations based on diaries kept in a relatively small fraction of a region's homes.

TELEVISION

ADVANTAGES

- Permits you to reach great numbers of people on a national or regional level.
- Independent stations and cable offer new opportunities to pinpoint local audiences.
- Very much an image-building medium.

DISADVANTAGES

- Ads on network affiliates are concentrated in local news broadcasts and on station breaks.
- Creative and production costs can quickly mount up.
- Lead time can result in items being sold out before ad runs.
- Most ads are ten or thirty seconds long, which limits the amount of information you can communicate.

DIRECT MAIL

ADVANTAGES

- Your advertising message is targeted to those most likely to buy your product or service.
- Your message can be as long as necessary to fully tell your story.
- You have total control over all elements of creation and production.
- A "silent" medium. Your message is hidden from your competitors until it's too late for them to react.

DISADVANTAGES

- Long lead times required for creative printing and mailing.
- Requires coordinating the services of many people: artists, photographers, printers, etc.
- Each year over 20% of the population moves, meaning you must work hard to keep your mail list up to date.
- Likewise, a certain percentage of the names on a purchased mailing list is likely to be no longer useful.

TELEMARKETING

ADVANTAGES

- You can easily answer questions about your product/ service.

- It's easy to prospect and find the right person to talk to.
- Cost effective compared to direct sales.
- Highly measurable results.
- You can get a lot of information if your script is properly structured.

DISADVANTAGES

- Many business use telemarketing.
- Professionals should draft the script and perform the telemarketing in order for it to be effective.
- Can be extremely expensive.
- Most appropriate for high-ticket retail items or professional services.

SPECIALTY ADVERTISING (BALLOONS, SANDWICH BOARDS, KEY CHARMS, ETC.)

ADVANTAGES

- Can be attention grabbers if they are done well.
- Can give top-of-mind awareness.
- Gets your name in front of people.

DISADVANTAGES

- Difficult to target your market.
- Can be an inappropriate medium for some businesses.
- Difficult to find items that are appropriate for certain businesses.

MASS MEDIA ADVANTAGE

This study, conducted in 1997, aimed to explore in depth the views and experiences of women with breast cancer concerning diseaserelated mass media information. Three age-stratified, unstructured focus group discussions were convened with thirty women with breast cancer (n = 11, 12 and 7). The discussions were audiotaped and transcribed in full and the transcripts were analysed using theme analysis.

A number of themes concerning mass media breast cancer information were identified. Women sought and paid attention to information from a variety of mass media sources, including medical books and journals, leaflets, videotapes, women's magazines, newspapers and television programmes. Mass media information was thought to possess a number of advantages. In particular, participants viewed mass media sources such as magazines and television as helpful in raising breast cancer awareness in the general population.

Mass media information, however, was also viewed as having a number of disadvantages. For example, once diagnosed, participants thought that mass media sources such as magazines were frightening and depressing owing to their often negative and sensationalised nature. This finding was particularly worrying as women with breast cancer looked for and were often 'drawn' to such communication vehicles. To conclude, mass media information has advantages and disadvantages and its impact upon individuals may depend on their disease status. It is important that editors of mass media sources such as women's magazines are aware of this dichotomy and are prepared to provide accurate, factual and le

advantages. In particular, participants viewed mass media sources such as magazines and television as helpful in raising breast cancer awareness in the general population. Mass media information, however, was also viewed as having a number of disadvantages.

Mass media has both positive and negative affects, but I believe that it has far more advantages to offer to the world than disadvantages. From taking us to a far off land to teaching us about the intricacies of the life inside a colony of ants we learn and experience things and events that no humans ever before in history have experienced through this miracle we call mass media. Mass media is a powerful way of spreading the knowledge and information. Kudos to those who first invented this concept, if not for the advances in the mass media the world wouldn't have been as it is today. It virtually brings the whole world to our door. There are many who has never had the chance to be at an ocean or desert, but still they are able to describe how it is. A great example would be the fantastic execution of the Olympics 2008 in china.

Not everyone in the world can get into the Olympics stadium to cheer their countries. But no one can take away your luxury of sitting back on the couch and enjoying the stunning performance of the participants. We human beings are social animals living in groups and societies. What can be a more effective way to communicate with larger groups than mass media? It is the easiest way to keep oneself updated with the current affairs and to know the contemporary world. It increases the general awareness in the masses. It is the means through which the government can communicate with its citizens, and vice verse. On this front mass media is also called by many as people's voice. Mass media acted as a very effective way of communication when government wanted to make its people aware of the family planning methods.

Its share point portal where people have the chance to share their experiences. Individuals have the opportunity of learning from these experiences. An example of this would be articles like "How to present yourself in an interview", "how to deal with your adolescent kids". If you are ready to get the word out about your business, one of the steps that you need to do is to select the right media where you will advertise and promote your business. For a small business, every dollar is precious. Small businesses do not advertise for the sake of advertising. Instead, they want to get the most return for their investment. Your advertising campaign should translate to greater sales, more profits and healthier bottom line.

While there are a number of venues where you can promote your business, you need to ask three important questions:

- Where are my target buyers?
- What is the best medium to reach them?
- Can I afford to launch an effective campaign using this medium?

An important step to developing your sales and marketing plan is to select the right media to send out your message.

There are no hard-and-fast rules as to which media is better. The right media for one business may be wrong for another. Based on an excellent small business reference book "How to Start and Operate a Successful Small Business: Winning the Entrepreneurial Game" by David E. Rye, as well as contributions from our staffers, below are the relative advantages and disadvantages of the advertising media most frequently used by small businesses:

Newspapers are one of the traditional mediums used by businesses, both big and small alike, to advertise their businesses.

Advantages:

- Allows you to reach a huge number of people in a given geographic area
- You have the flexibility in deciding the ad size and placement within the newspaper
- Your ad can be as large as necessary to communicate as much of a story as you care to tell
- Exposure to your ad is not limited; readers can go back to your message again and again if so desired.
- Free help in creating and producing ad copy is usually available
- Quick turn-around helps your ad reflect the changing market conditions. The ad you decide to run today can be in your customers' hands in one to two days.

Disadvantages:

- Ad space can be expensive
- Your ad has to compete against the clutter of other advertisers, including the giants ads run by supermarkets and department stores as well as the ads of your competitors
- Poor photo reproduction limits creativity
- Newspapers are a price-oriented medium; most ads are for sales
- Expect your ad to have a short shelf life, as newspapers are usually read once and then discarded.
- You may be paying to send your message to a lot of

people who will probably never be in the market to buy from you.
- Newspapers are a highly visible medium, so your competitors can quickly react to your prices
- With the increasing popularity of the Internet, newspapers face declining readership and market penetration. A growing number of readers now skip the print version of the newspaper (and hence the print ads) and instead read the online version of the publication.

Magazines are a more focused, albeit more expensive, alternative to newspaper advertising. This medium allows you to reach highly targeted audiences.

Advantages:
- Allows for better targeting of audience, as you can choose magazine publications that cater to your specific audience or whose editorial content specializes in topics of interest to your audience.
- High reader involvement means that more attention will be paid to your advertisement
- Better quality paper permits better colour reproduction and full-colour ads
- The smaller page (generally 8 ½ by 11 inches) permits even small ads to stand out

Disadvantages:
- Long lead times mean that you have to make plans weeks or months in advance
- The slower lead time heightens the risk of your ad getting overtaken by events
- There is limited flexibility in terms of ad placement and format.
- Space and ad layout costs are higher

There are several forms of Yellow Pages that you can use to promote and advertise your business. Aside from the traditional Yellow Pages supplied by phone companies, you can also check out specialized directories targeted to specific markets (e.g. Hispanic Yellow Pages, Blacks, etc.); interactive or consumer search databases; Audiotex or talking yellow pages; Internet directories containing national, local and regional listings; and other services classified as Yellow Pages.

Advantages:

- Wide availability, as mostly everyone uses the Yellow Pages
- Non-intrusive
- Action-oriented, as the audience is actually looking for the ads
- Ads are reasonably inexpensive
- Responses are easily tracked and measured
- Frequency

Disadvantages:

- Pages can look cluttered, and your ad can easily get lost in the clutter
- Your ad is placed together with all your competitors
- Limited creativity in the ads, given the need to follow a pre-determined format
- Ads slow to reflect market changes

Advantages:

- Radio is a universal medium enjoyed by people at one time or another during the day, at home, at work, and even in the car.
- The vast array of radio programme formats offers to efficiently target your advertising dollars to narrowly defined segments of consumers most likely to respond to your offer.
- Gives your business personality through the creation of campaigns using sounds and voices
- Free creative help is often available
- Rates can generally be negotiated
- During the past ten years, radio rates have seen less inflation than those for other media

Disadvantages:

- Because radio listeners are spread over many stations, you may have to advertise simultaneously on several stations to reach your target audience
- Listeners cannot go back to your ads to go over important points

- Ads are an interruption in the entertainment. Because of this, a radio ad may require multiple exposure to break through the listener's "tune-out" factor and ensure message retention
- Radio is a background medium. Most listeners are doing something else while listening, which means that your ad has to work hard to get their attention

Advantages:

- Television permits you to reach large numbers of people on a national or regional level in a short period of time
- Independent stations and cable offer new opportunities to pinpoint local audiences
- Television being an image-building and visual medium, it offers the ability to convey your message with sight, sound and motion

Disadvantages:

- Message is temporary, and may require multiple exposure for the ad to rise above the clutter
- Ads on network affiliates are concentrated in local news broadcasts and station breaks
- Preferred ad times are often sold out far in advance
- Limited length of exposure, as most ads are only thirty seconds long or less, which limits the amount of information you can communicate
- Relatively expensive in terms of creative, production and airtime costs

Direct mail, often called direct marketing or direct response marketing, is a marketing technique in which the seller sends marketing messages directly to the buyer. Direct mail include catalogs or other product literature with ordering opportunities; sales letters; and sales letters with brochures.

Advantages:

- Your advertising message is targeted to those most likely to buy your product or service.
- Marketing message can be personalized, thus helping increase positive response.

- Your message can be as long as is necessary to fully tell your story.
- Effectiveness of response to the campaign can be easily measured.
- You have total control over the presentation of your advertising message.
- Your ad campaign is hidden from your competitors until it's too late for them to react
- Active involvement - the act of opening the mail and reading it — can be elicited from the target market.

Disadvantages:

- Some people do not like receiving offers in their mail, and throw them immediately without even opening the mail.
- Resources need to be allocated in the maintenance of lists, as the success of this kind of promotional campaign depends on the quality of your mailing list.
- Long lead times are required for creative printing and mailing
- Producing direct mail materials entail the expense of using various professionals - copywriter, artists, photographers, printers, etc.
- Can be expensive, depending on your target market, quality of your list and size of the campaign.

Telephone sales, or telemarketing, is an effective system for introducing a company to a prospect and setting up appointments.

Advantages:

- Provides a venue where you can easily interact with the prospect, answering any questions or concerns they may have about your product or service.
- It's easy to prospect and find the right person to talk to.
- It's cost-effective compared to direct sales.
- Results are highly measurable.
- You can get a lot of information across if your script is properly structured.

- If outsourcing, set-up cost is minimal
- Increased efficiency since you can reach many more prospects by phone than you can with in-person sales calls.
- Great tool to improve relationship and maintain contact with existing customers, as well as to introduce new products to them
- Makes it easy to expand sales territory as the phone allows you to call local, national and even global prospects.

Disadvantages:

- An increasing number of people have become averse to telemarketing.
- More people are using technology to screen out unwanted callers, particularly telemarketers
- Government is implementing tougher measures to curb unscrupulous telemarketers
- Lots of businesses use telemarketing.
- If hiring an outside firm to do telemarketing, there is lesser control in the process given that the people doing the calls are not your employees
- May need to hire a professional to prepare a well-crafted and effective script
- It can be extremely expensive, particularly if the telemarketing is outsourced to an outside firm
- It is most appropriate for high-ticket retail items or professional services.

This kind of advertising entails the use of imprinted, useful, or decorative products called advertising specialties, such as key chains, computer mouse, mugs, etc. These articles are distributed for free; recipients need not purchase or make a contribution to receive these items.

Advantages:

- Flexibility of use
- High selectivity factor as these items can be distributed only to the target market.
- If done well, target audience may decide to keep the

items, hence promoting long retention and constant exposure

- Availability of wide range of inexpensive items that can be purchased at a low price.
- They can create instant awareness.
- They can generate goodwill in receiver
- The items can be used to supplement other promotional efforts and media (e.g. distributed during trade shows).

Disadvantages:

- Targeting your market is difficult.
- This can be an inappropriate medium for some businesses.
- It is difficult to find items that are appropriate for certain businesses
- Longer lead time in developing the message and promotional product
- Possibility of saturation in some items and audiences
- Wrong choice of product or poor creative may cheapen the image of advertiser

The print media is considered to be one of the most flourishing industries today. This medium is also particularly very popular to reach the target audience for advertisers. The different types of print media give a plethora of options for people to reach a varied bracket of users. So, be it newspapers or magazines, every medium has its particular advantages, a thing which should be considered to be of utmost importance by all advertisers and clients. However, print media also has its own disadvantages. Here, we shall take a quick look at the advantages and disadvantages of print media.

Advantages of Print Media:

- Different types of print media (newspapers and magazines) have a loyal readership. This can be very useful for advertisers as compared to advertising on the Internet.
- If you are targeting a particular geographical area, you can do so with ease through print media. For example, a local newspaper would be a best medium to advertise about a new shopping complex.

- You can choose the size of the advertisement space. This will help you to plan the budget of the expenses to be incurred while advertising.
- Certain forms of print media have a very loyal fans following in terms of readers. This would guarantee you added readership.
- Magazines and newspapers are always in the eye amongst public. Magazines are read for a period of a month, which brings more attention to an advertisement.
- You can even advertise through brochures or leaflets depending upon your target audience. If the information is in detail, a brochure can prove to be an apt option. A leaflet in that case, would be useful for a brief message.

Disadvantages of Print Media:

- The cost incurred can sometimes be expensive considering the medium you choose.
- The shelf life of any particular print medium is limited. Newspapers for example, are amongst the public eye only for a day.
- This medium may not always give you a wide reach. Internet, on the other hand, can target a global audience.
- There is a limitation in terms of the kind of people who may actually read your message. The particular newspaper may not actually be accessible every time to your target group, which means, your message may be missed! The Internet on the other hand, can be accessed from anywhere.
- You may have to plan months in advance to advertise in print media. It does not offer you flexibility when you are faced with a tight deadline.
- Advertisements may get lost in all the clutter of editorial and ads by competitors.

Thus, we can see, there are certain pros and cons of print media. With proper planning, you can opt for the right form to gain maximum coverage and make the best of this medium! Read more about mass media.

Chapter 19

The Future of Media Selling

ACCOUNTING SYSTEMS

Once a deal for the sale of advertising time is struck and the contract signed, data from that sale is input into a medium's operations, production, or traffic system, depending on the medium. Data flows from these systems into the organization's accounting system. The importance of the proper handling of insertion orders, or sales orders, scheduling of advertising, and monitoring the pace of sales and unsold inventory or space cannot be overstated, for a medium's financial health is at stake. All media organizations must comply with legal requirements such as reporting for tax purposes, in publicly traded companies for annual reports, and last, but not least, for the career health of sales managers and salespeople.

I know of a sales manager of a television station who was dismissed after the station the sales manager worked for ran three Public Service Announcements (PSAs) during local commercial availabilities in a Super Bowl telecast. Unsurprisingly, the station's general manager was watching and was less than amused. Computers have revolutionized operations, production, and traffic systems. I remember working at radio stations during the 1970s at which traffic was done manually using long, thin cardboard-like strips that had advertisers' names and commercial lengths typed on them that were then inserted in chronological order into metal holders. Once the metal holder was filled, it was photocopied and the result was a programme log listing the programme to be aired and the commercials to be aired in those programs. Today's systems and the reports they generate make that system look barbaric.

Not only do current computerized systems manage data, they analyse it to help management maximize revenue. Revenue management, which is the application of mathematical and analytical techniques to set prices so as to maximize revenue on every order, began to applied in the late 1970s. Revenue management was first applied in industries with wasting inventories that expired with the passage of time, such as airline seats or hotel rooms, much like radio and television inventory. Yield management is considered a branch of revenue management and has been used in the airline industry since the 1970s but is now used in many industries, including broadcasting and cable.

A number of companies offer integrated operations, traffic, production and financial reporting systems, which include revenue management or yield management software. However, it is my observation and belief that, while revenue management software is now being used more, commercial inventory and pricing analyses are still mostly being done manually by sales management at media companies. Standard these days are comprehensive data systems that interconnect traffic and operations, and the accounting or business office. An accounting system supports all of the other departments of an organization, including sales, as accounts receivable supports billing of advertising and the collection of receivables due.

The importance of accounting should be obvious. While many people get involved in the media industries for reasons other than the bottom line, media companies, like any other business enterprise, must earn profits in order to survive. The reason for sales is to bring in the revenue that makes profitability possible. But, without accounting, one wouldn't know if the quest for profitability were successful.

FINANCIAL REPORTS

While some small media companies may report their

historical financial performance using cash basis accounting, the vast majority of companies, including all that have to report their financial results to government agencies, such as public traded companies, or financial institutions to which these companies are indebted, use Generally Accepted Accounting Principles (or GAAP). While cash basis accounting is acceptable, but not mandatory, for tax reporting purposes, it is unacceptable for financial reporting purposes. GAAP are set by the Financial Accounting Standards Board (FASB), a private organization based in Norwalk, Connecticut. GAAP change over time, as several new accounting principles are issued each year, on average.

GAAP mandates use of accrual accounting, which means that revenues must be recognized when actually earned—in the case of the media, when advertising runs—not when cash is collected. Expenses are recorded when services or goods are used, not when they are paid for. The General Ledger, which lists all accounts in an accounting system, feeds into the financial statements.

A complete set of financial statements will include a balance sheet, sometimes referred to as a Statement of Financial Position, an income statement, a statement of cash flows, and a statement of stockholders'—or partners' or members'—equity. Because of its relative unimportance to having a basic understanding of how businesses operate on the financial side, I will not address the statement of stockholders' equity.

BALANCE SHEET

Open the file "Balance Sheet" in the Library link, which shows an example of a balance sheet, and print it out. This is the balance sheet for Regent Communications, Inc., a publicly traded radio company, for their 2000 and 2001 fiscal years. A balance sheet is always a financial snapshot at a single point in time. On a balance sheet, assets always equal the sum of liabilities and owners', or shareholders', equity. If that doesn't make sense offhand, think of it this way. If you have something—an asset—either someone else owns it, and thus, it is a liability, or you own it, and, thus, it becomes equity.

Assets are listed on the left side of the balance sheet and liabilities and owners' equity are on the right side. Assets start with Current Assets, which include Cash and Cash Equivalents, which are stable value instruments with a maturity date less than 90 days into the future. Accounts Receivable are a current asset, as are Prepaid Expenses, assuming the service that was prepaid will be used within one year. Assets are also not supposed to be stated at more than their Net Realizable Value. Therefore, a reserve needs to be estimated for Accounts Receivable that are not likely to be collected.

While inventory is certainly a term used in media selling, it is not inventory in the usual sense of the term (i.e., merchandise currently owned by a retailer that is for sale) in the current assets section of a balance sheet. When inventory is accounted for on a balance sheet, it is usually accounted for using the FIFO (First In, First Out) or the LIFO (Last In, First Out) method in terms of recognizing which items to expense and which to retain in inventory. Inventory accounting is usually not an issue for businesses in non-inflationary times. Long-term assets are those that are expected to be used over a period longer than one year, and they usually start with Property, Plant and Equipment (PP&E), also known as tangible assets. PP&E is stated at cost less depreciation and amortization over the course of its life.

Over the lives of tangible assets, the depreciation and amortization systematically reduce the assets' net values. Land is not depreciated for either financial reporting or tax purposes because it is not a depreciating asset like printing presses are, for example, which wear out. Land doesn't wear out and need to be replaced. Sometimes companies list intangible assets as long-term, non-current, assets. In the media industries, the most valuable intangible assets include FCC licenses, cable franchises, network affiliation agreements, and customer mailing and subscriber lists.

Programme rights are a major intangible asset category for television companies. As with PP&E, programme rights are booked when they are purchased and amortized as they are used, when the programs are aired. Intangible assets are recognized, or booked, only if they are acquired alone or as part of a going concern business. Self-created intangible assets are not booked if they are developed internally. That is, if a salesperson develops a relationship with a particular advertiser or advertising agency that leads to revenue, that is not recognized as an asset on the books of the station. There can be many valuable self-created intangible assets with a company, but they are never explicitly recognized on the balance sheet. This is part of the tenet of conservatism of financial statements, to be addressed later in this chapter.

After intangible assets are acquired, they are amortized, almost without exception, in a straight line over 15 years for tax purposes. For financial reporting purposes, intangible assets that have a finite life are amortized (decreased in value), with that amount recognized as an expense on the income statement, year by year, over the useful life of the assets.

Intangible assets that have an indefinite life are not amortized but are reviewed each year to make sure that their value on the financial statements, also known as book value or carrying value, is not greater than their fair value. If the asset's fair value is less than its book value, its book value must be reduced to be equal to its fair value, with the difference recognized as an expense on the income statement in that year.

Other Assets are other long-term assets that may have significant value, sometimes well above their book value. I once heard a business appraiser at a valuation conference state that he just about signed a valuation report valuing the equity of a closely-held corporation when it dawned on him to inquire as to what was included in the Other Assets of that corporation.

The book value of Other Assets was quite low and the assets, therefore, appeared minor in nature at first glance. What he learned was that it was Wal-Mart Stores stock that had been acquired many years earlier. In the interim, the stock had appreciated many times over, so his valuation would have been wrong if he had just assumed that the book value of Other Assets was the fair market value of Other Assets.

Historical cost and Net Realizable Value are used in

financial statements because of the concept of conservatism in historical financial statements.

With the exception of certain marketable securities, assets are booked at cost and never increased in book value, even if they increase in fair market value.

Conservatism is supposed to be an essential tenet of financial statements, even though one might not know it from recent financial scandals involving major corporations. Conservatism brings greater credibility to financial statements so that people using financial statements can know that claims made on financial statements are reliable and not overstated.

Looking at the right side of the balance sheet, Current Liabilities are liabilities such as Accounts Payable or Accrued Expenses, goods or services used that haven't been paid for yet and that are to be paid for in less than one year.

That also includes the portion of long-term debt that is payable in less than one year, if any. Current Assets minus Current Liabilities equals Working Capital. Long-term debt consists of loans, notes, and bonds that have maturity dates more than one year into the future. Programme payments to be paid in the future are also listed as liabilities, with payments to be made within the next year listed as a current liability. Magazines' and newspapers' subscriptions are also considered as a liability because subscribers are owed magazines or newspapers in the future.

The shareholders' equity section of the balance sheet, and it lists the various types of equity of involved, preferred stock, if any, and various classes of common stock, for example. The book values of some of these items may not be even close to the fair market value of those securities.

The book value of shareholders' equity can be negative, but, of course, the market value of an equity security cannot go below zero. In terms of order of interests to be paid off upon liquidation of a corporation, debt has priority over preferred stock, which has priority over common stock. That is why preferred stock is called preferred, even though returns for holders of common stock have been higher over time. Common stock is the residual, or last, claimant on a liquidated corporation and is, therefore, considered riskier than other securities of a corporation.

INCOME STATEMENT

Open "Income Statement" file in the Library and print it out. An income statement covers a period of time such as one month or one year. In internal financial statements, the income statement style I prefer shows revenue and expense categories down the middle, with the past month's actual results, past month's budget, with plus or minus variance percentage, and past month for the previous year, with plus or minus variance percentage, on the left.

On the right, there should be year-to-date actual results, a year-to-date budget, with plus or minus variance percentage, and year-to-date for the previous year with plus or minus variance percentage. This style is seen by going and in the Library section, clicking on "Internal Income Statement," although the numbers are not from any particular media company.

With an income statement, revenues are, of course, listed at the top. Revenues are usually listed by category such Local, Regional, National, Network Compensation, Political, Trade, Production, Equipment Leasing. Subtracted from gross revenues in media industry financial statements are advertising agency commissions and commissions paid to national sales representative firms.

This reporting is somewhat incongruous, in my opinion, because advertising agencies are agents of advertisers, while national sales representative firms work for the media companies. Local salespeople also work for local media companies, but their commissions are included in sales department expense, which is an expense that is listed below net revenues. Nevertheless, this has been the standard industry accounting treatment of national sales representative expenses for a long time and there is no known prospect of that changing.

Be careful when looking at reported or estimated market revenues in the media, and in radio and television in particular.

You need to know if they include trade revenues or not; generally, they don't but sometimes they do. It is particularly important to know when you are estimating the revenue share of a radio or television station within its market.

As with anything else, you don't want to compare apples with oranges. Expenses are best listed by functional departments in income statements, with a more detailed of expenses by category within functional departments below. It is important to know exactly what someone means when they use the term Operating Income. In the media industries, that term is frequently used to mean either Operating Cash Flow (OCF), which is the case most of the time, or Earnings Before Interest Taxes, Depreciation, and Amortization (EBITDA).

However, in financial statements among most non-media businesses, the term Operating Income is synonymous with Earnings Before Interest and Taxes (EBIT). Therefore, depreciation and amortization is treated as an operating expense in the financial statements. If depreciation and amortization expense is not given its own line in the income statement, it will have a separate line in the Statement of Cash Flows.

It is a reconciling item between Net Income and Cash from Operating Activities, because it is a non-cash expense. Adding depreciation and amortization expense back to EBIT will give you EBITDA. To get from EBITDA to OCF, corporate overhead expenses, sometimes called management fees, which are charged, for example, by a corporate headquarters office to each of its owned media properties, must be added back. The only expenses that should be deducted from revenues in arriving at OCF are operating expenses of a station, excluding corporate management expense and depreciation and amortization expense.

Historically, the most recognized profitability measure in the media industry has been Operating Cash Flow (OCF). OCF is all revenues minus all station operating expenses (including advertising agency commissions and sales commissions). OCF is also defined as EBITDA (Earnings Before Interest, Taxes,

Depreciation, and Amortization) with corporate expense added back.

It is very important to know what OCF is not, however. It is not a measure of true cash flow in the literal sense of the term. OCF is not a profit measure that is recognized in Generally Accepted Accounting Principles (GAAP) and it is not equivalent to Cash Flow from Operations that is seen in the Statement of Cash Flows, which is part of a complete set of financial statements.

Operating Cash Flow may be defined differently by different people. I know someone whom I greatly respect who defines OCF without including trade revenues or trade expenses. Including them in calculating OCF may change OCF in a given year due to timing differences of revenue and expense recognition, but inclusion of trade revenues and trade expenses is part of GAAP.

There are other problems associated with OCF and EBITDA, so it should definitely not be used as the only measure of earnings of business. Among the problems is that EBITDA and OCF never take into account either depreciation or amortization of a business' assets, capital expenditures for new equipment, or expenditures for purchases of other businesses. EBITDA and OCF also ignore additions to working capital and overstate cash flow in periods when growth of working capital is necessary to sustain a business and nurture its growth.

In analyzing media company financial statements, besides knowing whether they are cash or accrual basis financial statements, one should know how trade revenue is treated. In the media industries, advertising time is frequently traded not for cash, but for goods or services. In television, sometimes programs are purchased for a station with no cash outlay, but the programme supplier gets to keep a certain number of commercial availabilities to sell to local advertisers within the programme. Other radio or television stations may trade the use of a new car for the general manager in return for commercials on the station, without any cash actually changing hands.

Financial Accounting Standard (FAS) 63 states that all trade and barter revenue should be recorded at the estimated value of the goods or services received. FAS 63 also states that, as with cash transactions, trade revenue is recognized when earned and trade expense is recognized when a good or service is used.

If goods or services are received before commercials are aired, a liability for the advertising must be recognized until the commercial is aired. If the commercial is broadcast before the goods or services are received, an asset must be recognized until the goods or services are used by the station.

Frequently in these financial statements, trade revenues and expenses are listed separately, below the line, that is below the determination of OCF and EBITDA on the income statement. Some income statements will list trade revenues among the gross revenues and list trade expenses among the regular operating expenses.

Still other income statements, although a small minority, will make no distinction between cash and trade revenues on the income statement, simply including trade revenues with cash revenues in the appropriate category of gross revenues. Some financial statements (although not GAAP compliant) don't recognize trade revenues and trade expenses at all. Because trade revenues and expenses can be much higher in the media industry than in any other kids of businesses, it is important to know how they are accounted for.

Even though its seems obvious that trade involves no exchange of cash, it is important that the terms of trade deals struck by stations with various advertisers are understood by station executives. I know of a programme director of a television station that did not use all of a trade with a local department store.

The trade was advertising time in exchange for clothing for news anchors and other on-air personnel. There was a time expiration on the clothing side of the trade. When asked why some of the trade credit went unused, the programme director said, "I thought I was saving the station money." Instead, the station was shortchanged some clothing. If you're in charge of effecting either side of a trade deal, be sure you know all the parameters of the deal, as well as how the accounting for the trade is to be handled.

Because trade deals can be easily abused (e.g., merchandise received in a trade can be stolen, or services can be diverted to personal, rather than business, use), internal management controls must be in place in the approval process, and to make sure the trade deals are implemented and executed properly.

There is a lot of chatter and slang used about margins, profit margins, or cash flow margins, especially in the media industry. A margin is a percentage, or a ratio, with a numerator and denominator. If you don't know for sure what the numerator and denominator are, and I mean not what the numbers are specifically but what they represent, ask. Is the ratio Operating Cash Flow divided by gross revenues or something else? What you may find is that the person dispensing the margin information does not know what constitutes the ratio.

STATEMENT OF CASH FLOWS

Open the file "Statement of Cash Flows" in the Library link and print it out. The Statement of Cash Flows, is a very important financial statement, because this shows the actual cash flows of a business entity. Remember, the term Operating Cash Flow is a misnomer and should not be relied upon for flows of actual cash.

The Statement of Cash Flows is divided into three sections: Cash Flows from Operating Activities, Cash Flows from Investing Activities, and Cash Flows from Financing Activities. Operating activities are the operation of the business; investing activities include things such as capital expenditures; financing activities include the raising of cash through the sale of debt and equity securities, or the buyback of those securities, interest payments and dividend payments.

It is in the Statement of Cash Flows that one really sees the true cash flows in a business or an entity that owns a business. Cash, after all, is the true lifeblood of a business.

Regardless of other assets, revenues, or profitability, if a business doesn't have cash, or cannot raise cash, it cannot function.

One of the most important parts of a full set of financial statements are the footnotes. You should be able to read and understand footnotes because they amplify and elucidate other portions of the financial statements. If you don't understand what you read in financial footnotes, ask the entity's management or their investor relations department. Don't be satisfied with vague explanations that don't make complete sense.

Any questions about the financial statements, including the footnotes, should be answered clearly and forthrightly for you, assuming you have a right to know or a need to know, for example, if you are a debt or equity holder. If you are a salesperson looking at financial statements to see if a company is creditworthy or has enough money to be a good prospect, you can ask someone in your own business or accounting department, or ask your company's accounting or auditing firm to help you.

FINANCIAL INFORMATION

Many radio and television stations voluntarily participate in market revenue compilations. In many, but not all, radio and television markets, an accounting firm or some other entity is hired to survey all the radio or television stations in that market regarding the amounts of their respective revenues. The survey taker keeps each station's submission confidential, but adds the data for all stations together and then sends the market totals to every station, along with the overall rank number for that station, and its rank in various revenue categories. This information illuminates the market revenue situation for everyone and allows management to see objectively how their station(s) stack up versus intramarket competition. The National Association of Broadcasters (NAB) publishes an annual book on television market revenues for many surveyed television markets, and it can be purchased from the NAB.

Other historical broadcasting data, including radio and television market revenues, is estimated and published by several firms. BIA Financial Network, Inc. publishes several reference books on the radio and television industries, including a unique software reference source called *Media Access Pro*.

BIA plans to published reference books and software on other media and telecommunications industries in the future. *Advertising Age* magazine every year publishes magazine revenue, number of advertising pages sold, and circulation for the top 300 magazines and the information can be found.

Types of Financial Statements

Financial statements are always the product of management, but are compiled, reviewed or opined on by outside accountants. There are essentially four types of financial statements:

- Internal financial statements. These are statements that are produced by management. These are usually done on an accrual basis but are sometimes done on a cash basis, particularly in smaller companies.
- Compiled financial statements. These financial statements are developed by an outside accountant or accounting firm based on information supplied by a client. The data is accepted essentially without review or questioning by the outside accountant.
- Reviewed financial statements. These are financial statements for which an accountant performs some analytical and review procedures trying to identify major problems that need correction, if any. These procedures are far less than those employed in a full audit.
- Audited financial statements. This is a full set of financial statements, including footnotes, that include an audit opinion from an outside, independent accounting firm as to whether the financial statements are stated in accordance with GAAP. Audits are performed in accordance with Generally

Accepted Auditing Standards (GAAS). Audited financial statements are mandated by the SEC for any annual financial statements that are filed with it. Companies that have any publicly traded debt or equity must file with the SEC, except for certain very small companies. Also, it is a standard covenant in loan agreements that the debtor give annual audited financial statements to the creditor as long as the loan is outstanding. Business partners or shareholders in closely-held companies sometimes demand audited financial statements as a condition of their investment.

Accounting may not be the most exciting aspect of media sales, but it is of unquestioned importance to the success of media businesses. Without a proper accounting of assets and liabilities, and an accurate income statement, it would not be possible to gauge the resources that are available to operate a media business or assess whether the business is creating more value for society than it is consuming in creating that value.

The feedback that accounting provides is invaluable in helping salespeople and management make value-maximizing decisions for a business' owners and other stakeholders. Without accounting, media company operations would soon degenerate into anarchy. With proper accounting, great success and value creation can be achieved.

EMOTIONAL INTELLIGENCE

OLD-FASHIONED MODELS OF SELLING

In 1957, books on selling, such as Sizzlemanship!, Frank Bettger's How I Raised Myself from Failure to Success in Selling, and Og Mandino's ode of humility, The Greatest Salesman in the World, preached a model of selling that was developed in 1920s, 1930s, and 1940s. Books on selling urged the use of techniques and tricks that were relatively successful for products that could be sold in one encounter, that were often low-cost, and for which people could be badgered into buying, often just to get rid of the salesperson.

These outmoded selling models used a simple mnemonic to guide salespeople, AIDA, which stood for Attention, Interest, Desire, and Action. The old-time practitioners urged outrageous, often silly, techniques for getting a prospect's attention. They advocated manipulative techniques such as "sizzlemanship" to get interest and create desire (usually by overselling and over-promising).

And they advocated a number of techniques that pressured prospects to act immediately, allowing the salesperson to slam down a one-time sale. While there is nothing wrong with the AIDA mnemonic, these old-fashioned, manipulative, hard-sell techniques, which include the "tell and sell" model, are largely responsible for the bad reputations that salespeople are often saddled with today.

OLD MODELS DON'T WORK TODAY

Carl Zaiss and Thomas Gordon point out in their excellent book, Sales Effectiveness Training, that old selling models do not work in today's highly competitive, interactive, and sophisticated business environment. This is due to increased competition, the increased need for stronger customer loyalty and long-term relationships, the increased cost of developing new business, and the current trend in business toward solutions selling.

Rather than being seen as the manipulators and hard closers of the past, salespeople want to be perceived as trusted and respected partners who get results for their customers. Unhappy with the pressure and grind of one-shot sales, today's media salespeople prefer long-term relationships.

While many experts on selling have helped shift the focus from the old-fashioned, hard-sell approach to a gentler needs-based and consultative approach, four men stand out in the field. They are Larry Wilson with his Counselor Selling Programme and training seminars and books, Mack Hanna with his Consultative Selling Programme, Tony Allesandro with his book Non-Manipulative Selling, and Neil Rackham with his book, SPIN Selling.

While the consultative selling approach has now evolved

into a solutions-selling approach, I still recommend reading the Allesandra and Rackham books.

SOLUTION SELLING AS THE CURRENT MODEL

Buyers and customers of the media are hypersensitive to the tricks and manipulations of the past. With complex alternatives and problems, buyers need established and ongoing relationships based on mutual trust. This is the first step for successful solutions selling and requires emotional intelligence.

Emotional Intelligence

The term, emotional intelligence, was popularized by Daniel Goleman, a Harvard-educated PhD in psychology, in his best seller, Emotional Intelligence: Why it can matter more than IQ, which expanded on the work of the world-renowned educational psychologist, Howard Gardner, Robert Sternberg and others.

Gardner, Sternberg and others questioned accepted definitions of intelligence and began to look beyond a number or IQ (intelligence quotient). After exploring the topic thoroughly, they realized that what IQ tests measured was only a person's ability to take an IQ test and was not the enormously complex construct that had been referred to in the past as "intelligence." While Howard Gardner broadly defined intelligence as "the ability to solve problems or to create products that are valued within one or more cultural settings," in his influential book, Frames of Mind: The Theory of Multiple Intelligences, he identified seven facets of intelligence.

These are linguistic, logical-mathematical, musical, bodily-kinesthetic, spatial, interpersonal, and intrapersonal. In his book, Intelligence Reframed: Multiple Intelligences for the 21 st Century, he added three more facets of intelligence: naturalist, spiritual, and existential. Daniel Goleman concentrated his research on the importance of the personal intelligences, which he labeled emotional intelligence. Beginning in Emotional Intelligence, published in 1995, and in three subsequent books, Working With Emotional

Intelligence, Primal Leadership: Realizing the Power of Emotional Intelligence, and Social Intelligence Goleman has continued to refine and simplify his construct of emotional intelligence (EI) and social intelligence.

In Working With Emotional Intelligence, Goleman defined emotional intelligence as the "capacity for recognizing our own feelings and those of others, for motivating ourselves, and for managing emotions well in ourselves and in our relationships.

Goleman makes the case that, contrary to previously held theories, intelligence or IQ might not be an accurate predictor of life success. "At best IQ contributes about 20 percent to the factors that determine life success, which leaves 80 percent to other forces.

As one observer notes, 'The vast majority of one's ultimate niche in society is determined by non- IQ factors, ranging from social class to luck.'" A study of Harvard graduates in the fields of law, medicine, teaching, and business found that scores on entrance exams, a surrogate for IQ, had zero or negative correlation with eventual career success.

A study initiated in 1968 by the Stanford Graduate School of Business reinforced the importance of EI for success in business. It conducted in-depth interviews with the members of its graduating class, which examined the students' academic records and grades, their extra-curricular and social activities, and their reputation among their fellow students. The school kept track of the graduates' careers and levels of success with re- interviews in 1978 and in 1988.

When the school published the findings of its 20-year study in 1988, it concluded that the only two things that the most successful graduates (top five percent in title, position, money, for example) had in common was that all of the most successful graduates were in the bottom half of their class in grades and all of them were popular. In other words, relationship skills were more important for success than grades.

A major element of EI and success is optimism. A study of salesmen at Met Life by Martin Seligman revealed that "Being able to take a rejection with grace is essential in sales of all kinds, especially with a product like insurance, where the ratio of nos to yeses can be so discouragingly high. For this reason, about three quarters of insurance salesmen quit in their first three years. Seligman found that new salesmen who were by nature optimists sold 37 percent more insurance in their first two years on the job than did pessimists. And during the first year the pessimists quit at twice the rate of the optimists."

Media salespeople sell an intangible product similar to what insurance salespeople sell, but media salespeople do not have quite the same rejection rate, which makes media selling more desirable and satisfying. However, the above research reinforces the importance of optimism in selling. Optimism is defined in terms of how people explain to themselves their own successes and failures. People who are optimistic believe failures are the result of something that can be changed so that they can be successful the next time around. Pessimists take personal blame for failures, blaming them on some inherent characteristic they are helpless to change.

Pessimists also often blame their parents or their bosses or even the weather for their failures. Their attitude is that they expect failure; therefore, they create failures and a disastrous future. On the other hand, optimists expect success, and therefore create a successful future Hopefully your answers to the above questions placed you more than half-way toward the side of possessing EI, which means that you know you have an opportunity for improvement.

This is a positive frame for the concept of deficiency and your first lesson in the use of framing. People are sometimes tempted to use personality tests to determine their EI, but most of these tests, developed in the 1960s and 1970s, do not have much value in predicting success, uncovering motivation, and understanding yourself and others. Instead, they attempt to pigeonhole people into types such as "feeling" or "thinking" or expressive." Most psychological tests are not designed to find EI.

Psychological tests are often used by companies to screen job applicants, are designed to diagnose psychological disorders, and are poor predictors of motivation and how people will manage relationships.

Goleman feels that emotional intelligence can be learned. In Working With Emotional Intelligence he writes: "Unlike IQ, which changes little after our teens years, emotional intelligence seems to be largely learned, and it continues to develop as we go through life and learn from our experiences – our competence in it can keep growing. In fact, studies that have tracked people's level of emotional intelligence through the years show that people get better and better in these capabilities as they grow more adept at handling their own emotions and impulses, at motivating themselves, and at honing their empathy and social adroitness.

There is an old-fashioned word for this growth in emotional intelligence: maturity." Some of the things you can do to improve your EI are: 1. Work on controlling your impulses – "there is no psychological skill more fundamental than resisting impulses." 2. Work on developing a positive, optimistic, hopeful outlook and a belief that you are the master over the events in your life and can meet the challenges as they come up. Work on improving your communication and listening skills.

Now that you have learned about emotional intelligence is and how EI can help you improve your relationships, the next step is to relate EI to selling. Using the three Golden Rules of Selling is the optimum way to apply EI to selling.

Rule 1: Do unto others as they would have others do unto them. Unlike the Bible's Golden Rule, this does not make the assumption others like the same things that you like. Modern psychology and EI indicate that it is better to recognize people's diversity and differences and to value their needs, wants, desires, or preferences. Empathy requires that you find out how others feel, what they like, what they want and then base your response to them according to how they want to be treated.

Rule 2: People like and trust people exactly like themselves. This rule reinforces the notion that people are most comfortable with other people who are similar, a fact we observe everyday as people gather in groups and cliques.

Rule 3: People don't care how much you know until they know how much you care. This rule reminds us that feeling and communicating a sense of caring for another person comes first in any relationship. In other words, you put another's concerns before your own. These rules should be applied in the following steps:

Step 1: Just before sales conversations or meetings, ask yourself how you feel at that moment and then pause, exhale, and proceed. It is important to exhale because when we are nervous or tense, we tend to hold our breath, which tightens us up and makes fluid movement difficult. Exhaling is a sports training technique in which athletes release tension and improve performance. Taking time to recognize your feelings, to relax, and to exhale will allow you to manage your emotions consciously, and to control and use your emotions and your tensions to help you.

Step 2: Sense the mood and the emotional climate of the person or group you are meeting with. Beginning salespeople are usually nervous and anxious when they meet with customers, particularly the first time, and are unaware that customers are probably as nervous, anxious, and uncomfortable as they are. Effective leaders, politicians, and entertainers develop a knack for sensing the mood of a crowd or audience and playing to it. Salespeople must develop similar radar.

Step 3: Set the mood, the emotional tone and climate, for the meeting. Emotion is contagious, so by taking charge and energetically exuding a sense of confidence and enthusiasm (yes, "enthusiasm!" like my first sales manager often repeated) you infect the others with your contagious enthusiasm and positive vibes. Enthusiasm does not have to be the loud, excited, highly demonstrated type we often associate with back-slapping, broad-grinning used-car salesmen, but honest enthusiasm can come through in a restrained, calm, confident way that is in harmony with the emotional state of the other person or people in a meeting.

As Goleman points out in Emotional Intelligence, "We

transmit and catch moods from each other in what amounts to a subterranean economy of the psyche in which encounters are toxic, some nourishing. This emotional exchange is typically at a subtle, almost imperceptible level; the way a salesperson says "thank you" can leave us feeling ignored, resented, or genuinely welcomed and appreciated. We catch feelings from one another as though they were some kind of social virus." Make sure the viruses you transmit are positive, caring ones.

Step 4: Let the person or people you are meeting with know that you care. The best way to accomplish this step in a first meeting with a person is to begin by being very open about yourself. The goal is to reach out with personal details about yourself to enable the other person to get to know you. At that point you can ask the question, "How about you?" to learn more about the other person. People will normally reciprocate with openness and talk about themselves, their families, their hobbies, and interests. As they are talking, you must search for common interests and associations, such as being married, having children, or loving sports.

This is an application of Golden Rule of Selling, people like and trust people exactly like themselves, and your job is to talk about and emphasize those things in each of your personal lives that are similar. By showing a genuine sense of caring about their personal interests, they will know that you care. After the meeting, write down all the personal details for future reference. Be prepared to encounter different responses from men and women, for as Goleman writes, men generally "... take pride in a lone, tough-minded independence and autonomy..."and women generally "... see themselves as part of a web of connectedness." These gender differences are pointed out to encourage you to be aware of your own tendencies and to know what you might expect in an initial encounter with someone to be more like them and to build rapport. You can and probably should change these gender generalizations and initial stereotypes once you have had the opportunity to get to know someone better. Also, when meeting with a group of people for the first time, it pays large dividends to research their personal backgrounds and interests prior to your meeting.

Step 5: Listen with "emotional synchrony," as Goleman calls it. "The degree of emotional rapport people feel in an encounter is mirrored by how tightly concentrated their physical movements are as they talk... One person nods just as the other makes a point, both shift chairs at the same moment, or one leans forward as the other leans back."

This type of synchrony is a major way to transmit a "social virus" or emotional state or mood. It is also makes you more similar to the other person in the conversation, gets you closer, and makes them feel that you care. Having learned about the importance of emotional intelligence in building relationships in this chapter, you will learn how to put your EI knowledge to work in communicating with, listening carefully to, and understanding what makes people tick.

Bibliography

Curran, J. and Gurevitch, M. (eds) (2001) Mass Media and Society. London: Edward Arnold.

Curran, J. and Seaton, J. (2004) Power without Responsibility: The Press and Broadcasting in Britain, 5th edn. London: Routledge.

Deacon, D. and Golding, P. (2004) Taxation and Representation: The Media, Political Communication and the Poll Tax. London: John Libbey.

Demac, D.A. and Sung, L. (2003) New communication technologies and deregulation. In J. Downing, A. Mohammadi and A. Sreberny-Mohammadi (eds) Questioning the Media: A Critical Introduction, 2nd edn. London: Sage.

Glasser, T. (2002) Press responsibility and First Amendment values. In D. Eliott (ed.), Responsible Journalism. London and Newbury Park, CA: Sage.

Hall, S. (2003) Thatcherism amongst the theorists: toad in the garden. In C. Nelson and L. Grossberg (eds) Marxism and the Interpretation of Culture. London: Macmillan.

Hill, P., Young, M. and Sargant, T. (2002) More Rough Justice. London: Penguin.

Houghton, W.E. (2000) The Victorian Frame of Mind. New Haven: Yale University Press.

Ingham, B. (2004) Kill the Messenger. London: Harper Collins.

Kedourie, E. and Mango, A. (2003) Talking about the BBC. Encounter, 71 Sep/Oct: 60-4.

McQuail, D. (2001) Mass Communication Theory, 3rd edn. London: Sage.

Index

F

G

I

J

L

M

O

P